Serious Creativity

USING THE POWER OF LATERAL THINKING TO CREATE NEW IDEAS

Edward de Bono

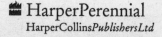
HarperPerennial
HarperCollins*Publishers*Ltd

First published in hardcover by HarperCollins Publishers Ltd: 1992

First HarperPerennial edition: 1993

Canadian Cataloguing in Publication Data

De Bono, Edward, 1933-
    Serious creativity : using the power of lateral thinking to create new ideas

1st HarperPerennial ed.
Includes index.
ISBN 0-00-637896-X

1. Creative thinking. 2. Lateral thinking. 3. Creative ability in business. I. Title.

BF408.D42 1993   153.3′5   C93-093018-5

---

93 94 95 96 97 RRD 10 9 8 7 6 5 4 3 2 1

Designed by Joan Greenfield

Contents

Note on the Author

Dr. Edward de Bono is regarded by many as the leading international authority on the direct teaching of creative thinking. He has 25 years' experience in this field and has worked in 45 countries.

In an interview in the *Washington Post* on September 30, 1984, Peter Ueberroth, the organizer of the very successful 1984 Los Angeles Olympic Games, told how he had used lateral thinking to change the Games from an event that no city in the world wanted to an event for which cities competed. At an opera reception in Melbourne, Australia, John Bertrand, the skipper of the successful 1983 Australian bid for the America's Cup, told Dr. de Bono how he and his crew had used lateral thinking at every point. Ron Barbaro, president of Prudential Insurance, attributed his invention of "living benefits" to his use of lateral thinking. This is regarded as the most significant invention in the life insurance business for 120 years.

Dr. Edward de Bono is the originator of the concept of "lateral thinking," which now has an official place in the English language, with an entry in the Oxford English Dictionary and an attribution to Dr. de Bono. He is also the inventor of the new word *po* to signal provocations.

Lateral thinking is a systematic approach to creative thinking with formal techniques that can be used deliberately. These tools are based directly on the behavior of the human brain. The self-organizing behavior of neural networks was put forward by Dr. de Bono in 1969 in *The Mechanism of Mind*. Today these ideas are mainstream thinking about the brain, and there are three introductions to his recent book, *I Am Right You Are Wrong*, by Nobel physicists.

Dr. de Bono was a Rhodes Scholar at Oxford and has held appointments at the universities of Oxford, Cambridge, London, and Harvard. He has written 40 books, and his work has been translated into 25 languages, including Japanese, Korean, Russian, Chinese, Arabic, Hebrew, Bahasa, Urdu, and all the major European languages. He has made two television series, which have been shown widely around the world.

Dr. de Bono is the author of the CoRT Thinking program, which is widely used internationally as the major program for the direct teaching of thinking as a school subject. The use of this program is spreading in the United States and in some countries it is already mandatory in all schools.

Dr. de Bono's client list includes the top five corporations in the world and such other well-known names as Citicorp, NTT (Japan), Ericsson (Sweden), Ciba-Geigy (Switzerland), BHP (Australia), Total (France), Heineken (Netherlands), Montedison (Italy), Kuwait Oil Company (Kuwait), Petronas (Malaysia), and Vitro Fama (Mexico). He is the founder of the International Creative Forum, which brings together the leading corporations in the world in each field to focus on serious creativity. At the time of this writing, members of this forum include IBM, Du Pont, Prudential, Merck, British Airways, Guinness, and BAA.

The essence of Dr. de Bono's work has been to produce thinking techniques that are simple, practical, usable, and powerful. A perfect example of this is the Six Thinking Hats method, which is now being widely used by major corporations because of its simplicity and its power to change thinking behavior.

In this major book Dr. de Bono brings his 25 years of experience in the direct teaching of creative thinking up to date. The book also includes material that has never before appeared in print.

Introduction

If I were to sit down and say to myself, "I need a new idea here [insert actual need area]," what should I do?

I could do research and try to work out a new idea logically.

I could borrow or steal an idea used by someone else.

I could sit and twiddle my thumbs and hope for inspiration.

I could ask a creative person to produce an idea for me.

I could hastily convene a brainstorming group.

Or I could quietly and systematically apply a deliberate technique of lateral thinking (such as the random word technique), and in 10 to 20 seconds I should have some new ideas.

It is now 25 years since I started working in the field of creative thinking. It is now time to tidy up and to bring things up to date. It is time to clarify and restate various techniques that have been borrowed and weakened in the process. It is time to apply the huge wealth of experience that has accumulated in that time, during which I have taught creative thinking in many countries and across different cultures to business, education, government, and other parts of society.

What has happened over these last 25 years in this important field? In some ways a lot has happened and in other ways very little.

In 1969 I wrote a book with the title *The Mechanism of Mind,*[*] in which I described how the nerve networks in the human brain might act as a self-organizing information system. At that time those ideas were somewhat strange. Today such ideas are mainstream thinking about the brain and a whole academic discipline has grown up to consider the behavior of self-organizing systems. One of my more recent books (*I Am Right You Are Wrong*) has introductions by three Nobel prize physicists.[†] Neural network computers are based on the same principles. So science has caught up with what was a conceptual model.

---

[*]Simon & Schuster, New York, 1969, and Jonathan Cape, London, 1969; now available from Penguin Books, London.

[†]Viking/Penguin, New York, 1991, and London, 1990.

A few people, a very few people, now know that there is an absolute mathematical necessity for human creativity because of the way human perception works as a self-organizing information system. Such systems demand creativity and also provocation.

There is now a great deal more interest in creative thinking than there was 25 years ago. Almost every major business advertises itself as "the creative corporation." There is a huge amount of lip service given to the central importance of creativity, but my experience has shown that this lip-service is not accompanied by any serious effort to use creativity.

Over the last ten years business has been involved in three major games. There was the restructuring game, which included acquisitions, mergers, leveraged buy-outs (LBOs), de-mergers, and so on. Growth and profitability was going to come from buying growth. Bankers prospered, as did a few of the new structures.

Then there was cost-cutting, a game that is still running. If you could cut costs, then your balance sheet looked much better. Cutting costs is something into which you can get your teeth. You can see targets and measure achievement. Profits improve. But there comes a time when all the fat is gone and further cuts remove the muscle.

The latest game has been quality (and customer service). This is a highly commendable game that should have a great need for creative thinking.

But what happens when you have a lean and competent organization? What is this lean and competent organization going to do? What happens when your competitors are just as lean and competent as you and your cost-effectiveness is no longer a unique advantage? The more able senior executives know that creativity is now the main hope. Even the economies of Japan and Germany, which have rightly placed so much emphasis on quality and excellence, are now beginning to show great interest in creativity.

Sadly, very few governments around the world have yet come to realize that creative change is just as important to them as it is to business. There is a huge need for better ways of doing things and for new concepts in government services. The governments of Singapore, Malaysia, Australia, and Canada are waking up to this need. Others still feel that cost-cutting is sufficient. The public should expect more than cost-cutting.

Although it is now beginning to do a little bit about the direct teaching of thinking as a skill, education does very little indeed

about teaching creative thinking. There is the assumption that
creativity belongs in the "art" world and is a matter for talent,
anyway. This view is so old-fashioned as to be medieval.

The rest of society is not often called upon actually to make
things happen and is satisfied with description and argument.

Nevertheless, there is a growing group of individuals in all areas who have come to realize that the future needs better thinking
and that part of this better thinking is going to demand creativity.

There are some very good reasons why we have not yet paid
serious enough attention to creativity.

The first and most powerful reason is that every valuable
creative idea must always be logical in hindsight. If an idea were
not logical in hindsight then we would have no way of seeing
the value of that idea and it would simply be a "crazy" idea. If
every valuable creative idea is indeed logical in hindsight, then
it is only natural to suppose, and to claim, that such ideas could
have been reached by logic in the first place and that creativity
is unnecessary. This is the main reason why, culturally, we have
never paid serious attention to creativity. I would say that over
95 percent of academics worldwide still hold this view. Sadly,
this view is totally wrong.

In a passive information system (externally organized system),
it is perfectly correct to claim that any idea that is logical in
hindsight must be accessible to logic in the first place. But it is
not so in an active information system (self-organizing system)
in which the asymmetry of patterns means that an idea may
be logical and even obvious in hindsight but invisible to logic
in the first place. Unfortunately, this point can be visible only
to those who are able to move from the paradigm of externally
organized systems to the paradigm of self-organizing systems.
I shall come to this point later in the book. Most people are
unwilling or unable to make that paradigm change and so must,
forever, believe in the sufficiency of logic.

Then there are those who believe in the importance and reality of creativity but hold that nothing can be done about it.
Such people believe that creativity is a matter of semi-mystical
talent that some people have and others do not have. Here there
is a considerable confusion between artistic creativity (which is
often not creative) and the ability to change concepts and perceptions. There is a parallel belief that new ideas depend on a
fortuitous combination of events and circumstance and that such
confluences cannot be planned. The general notion here is that
ideas have always happened and will always continue to happen
and there is nothing that can be done or need be done, about it.

INTRO-
DUCTION

The only thing to do is to find creative people and to encourage them.

There is a growing number of people who do believe that creative thinking skills can be improved through direct effort and attention. Here we run into two difficulties.

Because inhibition—the fear of being wrong and the fear of making mistakes—prevents the risk-taking of creativity, there is the belief that removal of inhibitions is enough to make a person creative. This has become a dominant theme, particularly in North America, and it has held back the development of serious creative thinking methods. Efforts are made to free a person up so that natural creativity can assert itself. This does bring about a mild level of creativity but not much. The brain is not designed to be creative, so liberating the brain from inhibitions does not make it creative. Releasing the brake on a car does not automatically make you a skilled driver. I shall return to this point later.

We come now to the considerable damage done by the concept of "brainstorming." This was a genuine and useful attempt to provide a more relaxed setting in which to generate ideas without immediate fear of rejection. The intention was admirable and some of the underlying principles are sound. Unfortunately, brainstorming has become synonymous with deliberate creative effort and has blocked the development of serious creative thinking skills.

Those who want to use deliberate creativity believe that the (weak) processes of brainstorming are enough. Others who might be motivated to develop creative thinking skills are turned off by the "scatter-gun" approach of brainstorming. The idea that from a ferment of consideration an idea might emerge which might be useful has a value in the advertizing world (where brainstorming originated) but much less value where novelty is not, by itself, a sufficient value.

It is difficult to condemn brainstorming because it has some value and does sometimes produce results; but, in my experience, it is old-fashioned and inefficient. We can do much better with deliberate systematic techniques. Nor is there any need for creativity to be a group process as in brainstorming. An individual can be even more creative on his or her own—with the proper skills.

Instead of brainstorming, I might suggest the concept of "brain-sailing" to suggest a deliberate controlled process in which we change tack as we wish instead of being tossed about in a "storm."

Associated with brainstorming has been the notion that deliberate creative thinking has to be "crazy" or "off-the-wall" in order to be effective. This notion of craziness is a complete misunderstanding of the nature of creativity and is fostered by those who do not really understand the true nature of provocation. Because provocation is different from normal experience and because anything "crazy" is also different from normal experience, it is assumed the two are the same.

It has to be said that much of the difficulty is caused by the poor quality of teaching of many who set up to teach creative thinking. Because creative thinking does not seem to require either logic or experience, anyone can enter the field. Techniques and processes are borrowed from here and there without a full understanding of their proper use. The result is an instant "expert" on creative thinking. Many clients are persuaded that this is the correct approach to creative thinking and many others are put off. The general result is that creative thinking is devalued and not treated seriously. It is regarded as something of a peripheral gimmick that might have an occasional success.

For all the sound reasons given here, creativity does not yet have the central place that it should occupy. In summary, there are those who believe that logic is enough. There are those who believe that creativity is a matter of talent or chance and that nothing deliberate can be done about it. There are those who are put off by the "crazy" approaches to deliberate creativity that are available.

I have deliberately included the word "serious" in the title of this book in order to move forward from the "crazy" notions of creativity. In this book I intend to put forward deliberate and systematic techniques that can be used in a formal manner by both individuals and groups. These techniques are directly and logically based on the behavior of human perception as a self-organizing pattern-making system. There is no mystique at all about them. It was precisely to get away from the vague and mystical notion of creativity that I invented the term "lateral thinking" 25 years ago. Lateral thinking is specifically concerned with changing concepts and perceptions.

There are those who will be horrified by the notion of "serious" creativity and will see it almost as a contradiction in terms. To such people creativity means being free to mess around in the hope that somehow a new idea will emerge. It is true that in order to be creative we must be free of constraints, free of tradition, and free of history. But that freedom is more effectively obtained by using certain deliberate techniques than just by hoping to be free. A solid file is a better way of getting out of prison than exhortations to be free.

There are those who believe that systematic and deliberate tools cannot lead to creativity because any structures will immediately limit freedom. This is nonsense. There are indeed restricting structures such as railway lines and locked rooms. But many structures are liberating. A ladder is a liberating structure that allows you to get to places you would not otherwise have reached. Yet you are free to choose where to go with your ladder. A cup or glass is a liberating structure that allows us to drink much more conveniently. But the cup does not force our choice of drink. Mathematical notation is a liberating structure that allows us to do many things we would never be able to do otherwise. So there is nothing contradictory about systematic techniques that free us to develop new concepts and perceptions.

I regard creative thinking (lateral thinking) as a special type of information handling. It should take its place alongside our other methods of handling information: mathematics, logical analysis, computer simulation, and so on. There need be no mystique about it. A person sitting down with the deliberate intention of generating an idea in a certain area and then proceeding to use a lateral thinking technique systematically should represent a normal state of affairs.

In the book I shall be covering the three broad approaches to lateral thinking:

1. Challenge
2. Alternatives
3. Provocation

In each area there are methods and techniques that can be learned, practiced, and applied. The story of Peter Ueberroth and the Los Angeles Olympic Games illustrates how these techniques can be learned and applied. Peter Ueberroth had first learned about lateral thinking when he was my faculty host when I gave a 90-minute talk to the Young Presidents' Organization in Boca Raton, Florida, in 1975. Nine years later, according to his interview in the *Washington Post*, he used lateral thinking to generate the new concepts that made such a success of the Los Angeles Olympic Games.

I want to make it clear that while this book may become a reference book on creative thinking, it has not been my purpose to lay out the principles of "teaching" creative thinking. That is not something that can be properly done in a book as it requires interactive experience and guidance. I shall, however, be setting up formal training sessions for those who do want to learn how to teach creative thinking.* This book is a user's book to help those who want to use creative thinking themselves.

This book is written for three categories of reader.

1. Those who sense that creativity is going to become more and more important and want to know what can be done about it
2. Those who have always considered themselves to be creative and want to enhance their creative skill
3. Those who see no necessity at all for creativity

I am aware that those in the third category are somewhat unlikely to buy the book in the first place. So their only hope of getting a better understanding of creative thinking is if someone makes them a present of the book in order to indicate what creative thinking is about and why it is important.

At this point I would like to distinguish between two types of creative output. We usually suppose that creative thinking will turn up a new idea that represents some sort of risk. Because the idea is new we are not sure if it will work. There may have to be an investment of time, money, energy, and hassle before the idea pays off. Many people and most organizations are somewhat reluctant to make this investment in time, money, energy, and hassle, even though they know that such investments are essential in the long run. But this is only one type of creative output. There is also a completely different types of idea.

The other type of creative output is an idea that immediately makes sense. You can see at once that the new idea is going to work and is going to save money or time or offer some other benefit. Let me illustrate this with a very simple example.

Add up the numbers from 1 to 10. The task is not difficult and you should get the answer 55. Now add up the numbers from 1 to 100. Again the task is not difficult, but it is very tedious and you might well make mistakes. Now imagine the numbers from 1 to 100 written down in a row as suggested below:

$$1 \quad 2 \quad 3 \quad \ldots \quad 98 \quad 99 \quad 100$$

Now repeat the numbers from 1 to 100 but write them backwards under the first set of numbers as shown:

$$1 \quad 2 \quad 3 \quad \ldots \quad 98 \quad 99 \quad 100$$
$$100 \quad 99 \quad 98 \qquad 3 \quad 2 \quad 1$$

*Send enquiries to Kathy Myers, APT/T Fax (515) 278-2245.

If you add up each pair, you will always get 101. This must be so because as you go along the top number increases by 1 and the bottom number decreases by 1 so the total must stay the same. So the total is 100×101. This is, of course, twice the total we needed because we have used two sets of numbers from 1 to 100. So we divide by 2 and get 50×101, or 5050. This method is not only very quick but there is little chance of making an error. In short, it is a much faster and much better way of adding the numbers 1 to 100.

In hindsight the method is perfectly logical. In practice very few people work out this method for themselves.

Another approach might be to "fold" the numbers over on themselves to give:

| 50 | 49 | 48 | ... | 3 | 2 | 1 |
| 51 | 52 | 53 | | 98 | 99 | 100 |

This gives 50×101, or 5050.

I am making no claims for creativity here because this sort of approach might be obtained by creative thinking or by visualization. The point I am making is that the new approach is immediately seen to be valuable. There is no risk involved.

There are times when creative thinking can produce this type of output: an idea that immediately makes sense. That it is logical in hindsight does not mean that it could have been reached by logic in foresight (as I have mentioned and as we shall again see later).

This is an important point because one of the main purposes for the use of creative thinking is to find better ways of doing things. It would be quite wrong to assume that creative thinking means only risk. Creativity also means insight and new perceptions that at once make sense.

The book is divided into three parts:

Part I: The need for creativity

Part II: Techniques and methods

Part III: Application of creative thinking

There is nothing more marvelous than thinking of a new idea.

There is nothing more magnificent than seeing a new idea working.

There is nothing more useful than a new idea that serves your purpose.

PART 1

The Need for Creative Thinking

Take-Away Value

What sort of benefits do I hope readers might derive from reading this book? What are the "take-away" values? With any book there might be the enjoyment of the time spent reading the book. There might be some new insights. There might be welcome confirmation of views you already hold.

In writing this book there are three intended levels of take-away value. Whether the book actually achieves these objectives is another matter.

The three levels are:

1. Understanding the nature and logic of creativity
2. The will and intention to make a creative effort
3. Specific tools, techniques, and methods

UNDERSTANDING THE NATURE AND LOGIC OF CREATIVITY

Creativity is a messy and confusing subject and seems to range from devising a new toothpaste cap to Beethoven's writing his Fifth Symphony. Much of the difficulty arises directly from the words "creative" and "creativity."

At the simplest level "creative" means bringing into being something that was not there before. In a sense, "creating a mess" is an example of creativity. The mess was not here before and has been brought into being. Then we ascribe some value to the result, so the "new" thing must have a value. At this point we can begin to have artistic creativity because what the artist produces is new and has value.

We now have the notion that the creative output should not be "obvious" or "easy." There has to be something unique or rare about it. Exceptional craftsmanship would fit here.

When we start to introduce concepts of "unexpectedness" and "change," we begin to get a different view of creativity.

There are some artists who are "productive stylists." Such artists have a style of perception and a style of expression, both

3

of which may be of high value. They work within this style. Since what is done today is not a repetition of what was done yesterday, there is something new and something of high value. So we rightly call such artists creative. But the element of change is missing.

I believe that the crude word "creativity" covers a wide range of different skills. In this book I do not set out to talk about artistic creativity. I have been told by playwrights, composers, poets, and rock musicians that they sometimes use my techniques of lateral thinking. That is always nice to hear, but I am not setting out to improve the skills of artistic creativity as such. I am very specifically concerned with the creative skills needed to change concepts and perceptions.

We can look at creativity as a mystery. Brilliant new ideas are produced and we do not know how they came about. We can study and analyze the behavior of creative people, but this will not tell us very much, because often such people are themselves unaware of what triggered the brilliant idea.

My preference is to look directly at the behavior of self-organizing information systems. These systems are patterning systems. They make and use patterns. From an analysis of the behavior and potential behavior in such systems we can get a very clear idea of the nature of creativity. All at once the mystique of creativity falls away. We can see how creativity works. We can also see how we might devise techniques to increase the possibility of new ideas. In a sense we come to look at the "logic" of creativity. The logic of creativity is the logic of patterning systems, as we shall see in a later chapter. No leap of faith or mystical acceptance is required. There is no mysterious black box labeled "in here it all happens." The essence of creativity (or more properly, lateral thinking) is laid bare.

Many years ago I gave a talk to 1200 Ph.D.s working for the 3M company in Minneapolis. I believe it was the bulk of their research department. About eight years later a senior research executive told a friend of mine that that talk had had more effect on their research thinking than anything else they had ever done. The audience had consisted of technical people: electronic engineers, physicists, materials scientists, chemists, and so on. Such people tend to believe that creativity is fine for advertisers, packagers, marketers, and designers, but is not needed where there are physical laws and measurements to guide behavior. Once, however, they could see the "logic" of creativity as the behavior of patterning systems, their attitude was changed permanently.

This is an important point, because there are many people who do see the value of creative new ideas but are not prepared to accept the need of creativity if this need remains at an exhortation level. But once such people see the actual logical necessity for creativity—explained in a logical way—then the whole attitude changes.

Understanding the logic of creativity does not itself make you more creative. But it does make you aware of the necessity for creativity. It also explains the design of certain creative techniques and shows why apparently illogical techniques are actually quite logical within the logic of patterning systems. Above all, understanding the logic of creativity motivates a person to do something about creativity.

Some people claim not to be interested in the logic of creativity and are impatient to get on with the practical techniques. This is a mistake, because you will not use the tools effectively unless you know what lies behind the design of the tool. Those trainers who treat creative techniques as a bag of assorted tools should not be surprised if their students come to regard the techniques as mere gimmicks.

FOCUS AND INTENTION

This second level of take-away is concerned with motivation. It is the willingness of a person to pause and to focus on some point and then to set out to do some lateral thinking. At this moment no specific techniques might be involved. What is required is the investment of time, effort, and focus. There is the will to find a new idea.

At a reception in Melbourne, Australia, a young man came up to me and introduced himself as John Bertrand. He told me how he had been the skipper of the 1983 Australian challenge for the America's Cup yacht race. This cup had never in all its 130-year history been taken away from the United States. John Bertrand told me how he and his crew had focused on point after point and set out to find new ideas. The most obvious was in the design of the winged keel. For the first time in history, the America's Cup was taken away from the United States. This is a classical example of the will to find new ideas, the will to use lateral thinking.

Another story also comes from Australia. It was told to a friend of mine by the founder of the Red Telephone Company.

5

Red Telephones were pay phones maintained at a high standard and owned by a private company that has since been bought by Australian Telecom. The difficulty was that in Australia local calls were not timed; for the same initial cost, a user could talk for a long time. Long calls would reduce the revenue to the Red Telephone Company, since the phones would be occupied and others wanting to make several short calls could not do so. The company got only revenue per call, irrespective of the time of the call. I believe the founder came across my first book on lateral thinking and set himself the task of getting shorter telephone calls. Any obvious way of limiting the call or asking for further payment was ruled out because such approaches would put the Red Telephones at a disadvantage compared with other phones.

In the end he did find a new approach. He arranged with the makers of the telephone handset to put a lot of lead into the handset. This made the handset heavy and long calls became very tiring. Apparently the idea worked, and to this day Red Telephones are unusually heavy.

Even when no specific lateral thinking techniques are used, there is a high value in simply pausing at a point with the determination to find new ideas and a new way of doing things.

Such motivation arises from an understanding of the possibility of new ideas and an understanding of the creative potential of the human mind.

On many occasions you may not be able to find a new idea, but in the long run the habit of pausing and putting in the effort to find a new idea will pay off.

TOOLS AND TECHNIQUES

After reading the central section of this book the reader will be equipped with some specific tools that can be used systematically and deliberately in order to generate new ideas. Of course, skill in the use of such tools will depend on practice. The more the tools are used, the more skillful will the use become. It is also true that some people will be better at using the tools than others. That is always the way with skills. Nevertheless a valuable degree of creative skill can be acquired by anyone who sets out to acquire such skills.

I want to emphasize yet again that the tools are deliberate and can be used systematically. It is not a matter of inspiration or feeling in the mood or being "high." You can use the tools just as deliberately as you can add up a column of numbers.

Over the years many highly creative people have told me that they can usually rely on their own creative talent for new ideas. But when they want an outstanding idea they find it better to use some of the tools systematically instead of relying on natural talent. This has also been my experience. Whenever I use the techniques systematically and deliberately I usually surprise myself with an idea I have never had before. So these tools are not just crutches for those who cannot get going but useful techniques even for those who are highly creative. It is only fair to add that it does require some discipline and some effort to use the tools when your head is already full of possible ideas.

Many of the practitioners in the field deal with creativity from an inspirational point of view. If you get rid of your inhibitions you will be creative. If you learn to use your right brain you will be creative. If you trust your intuition you will be creative. If you get into a theta state you will be creative. If you get a creative "high" you will be creative. The emphasis is placed on altered mental states. From time to time these altered mental states may have a creative effect, but the same effect can be produced in a more reliable and systematic manner using deliberate tools. An altered mental state may indeed produce a provocation but provocations can be produced to order using the provocative tools and the word "po."

Ever since I devised the basic lateral thinking tools many years ago they have been plagiarized, borrowed, and altered, usually without permission or acknowledgment. Even the more prestigious institutions in the field are not above borrowing methods and material without acknowledging the source. For example, the word "po" is now widely used.

One of the purposes of this book is to clarify the tools so that the essential power of the tool is made clear and the assorted paraphernalia are stripped away.

So the reader of the book should be able to learn some basic lateral thinking techniques. There still has to be the motivation to practice them and the will to use them. What was remarkable about Peter Ueberroth was his strong motivation (and leadership). It is not enough just to learn the tools and then never use them.

Some of the methods, like the Six Thinking Hats, are now widely used by major corporations and have changed the thinking behavior of these corporations.

The third part of the book deals with the application of creative thinking and considers structures and settings that make it much easier to use the creative tools.

The Theoretical
Need for Creativity

Humor is by far the most significant behavior of the human brain.

I have said this many times before and I write it again without any sense of provocation. I mean it literally. Humor indicates, better than any other mental behavior, the nature of the information system that gives rise to perception. This is a self-organizing information system.

Humor not only clearly indicates the nature of the system but also shows how perceptions set up in one way can suddenly be reconfigured in another way. This is the essence of creativity, and I shall explore it later in this section.

The neglect of humor by traditional philosophers, psychologists, information scientists, and mathematicians clearly shows that they were only concerned with passive, externally organized information systems. It is only very recently that mathematicians have become interested in nonlinear and unstable systems (chaos, catastrophe theory, and so on).

We need to distinguish two very broad types of information systems: passive systems and active systems. In passive systems the information and the information-recording surface are inert or passive. All the activity comes from an external organizer that relates the information and moves it around. In an active system, however, the information and the surface are active and the information organizes itself without the help of an external organizer. That is why such systems are called *self-organizing*.

Imagine a table on which there are placed a number of small balls (perhaps ball bearings). You are given the task of placing the balls in two neat lines. You set out to do this. You are the external organizer. Figure 1.1 and Figure 1.2 show the before and after of your organizing activity.

Suppose that instead of the smooth table top there had been two parallel gutters as shown in Figure 1.3. If you were to drop the balls randomly over the table the balls would *entirely by them-*

THE
THEO-
RETICAL
NEED
FOR
CREATIVITY

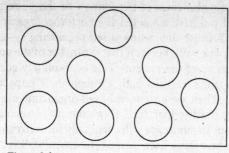

Figure 1.1

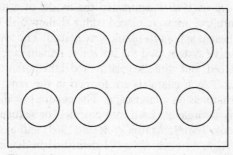

Figure 1.2

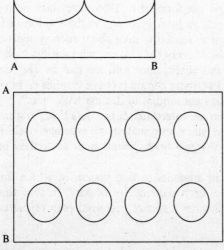

Figure 1.3

9

selves form two neat lines at the bottom of the gutters. In this second model you have not acted as an external organizer. There was no need because this is now a self-organizing system.

Of course, you would protest that the maker of the gutters was the real organizer of the system. This is absolutely correct. But suppose that previous balls had, through their impact, shaped these gutters. Then we have a truly self-organizing system.

We do not need to look far for an example of such a system. Rain falling onto a landscape will eventually form streams, rivers, and valleys. Once these have formed, future rainfall is channeled along these rivers and valleys. So the rain interacting with the landscape forms channels, which then affect the way future rain is collected and organized.

As far back as 1969 I contrasted the model of a towel onto which spoonfuls of ink were placed with a shallow dish of gelatin onto which heated spoonfuls of ink were placed. The towel represents the passive system, and the ink stains remain exactly where they were placed. But with the gelatin model the hot ink dissolves the gelatin and soon channels are formed in the same way that rain forms channels on a landscape. The gelatin has allowed the incoming ink to organize itself into channels or sequences.

In the book *The Mechanism of Mind* (1969) and again in the book *I Am Right You Are Wrong** I described in detail how the nerve networks in the brain allow incoming information to organize itself into a sequence of temporarily stable states that succeed each other to give a sequence. There is no magic or mysticism about it. This is the simple behavior of neural networks. The ideas first put forward in 1969 have since been elaborated by people such as John Hopfield at the California Institute of Technology, who started writing about such systems in 1979. In fact, Professor Murray Gell Mann, who got his Nobel prize for discovering the quark, once told me that in *The Mechanism of Mind* I was describing certain types of systems eight years before mathematicians got around to dealing with them.

Those who are interested in the details of how simple nerve networks can allow information to organize itself in patterns should read the two books mentioned, as well as other books in this field.

What it all amounts to is a system in which incoming information sets up a sequence of activity. In time this sequence of activity becomes a sort of preferred path or pattern. Neuro-

*Viking, London, 1990; Viking, New York, 1991.

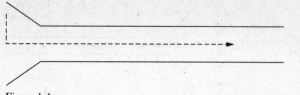

THE
THEO-
RETICAL
NEED
FOR
CREATIVITY

Figure 1.4

chemists and neurophysiologists will argue over the precise enzymes involved in the process, but the overall picture (in its broad aspects) will not be changed.

Once established, these patterns are most useful because they allow us to "recognize" things. Once the pattern has been triggered then we follow along it and see things in terms of previous experience. A simple pattern is suggested in Figure 1.4.

The difficulty with a simple pattern system is that there would have to be a huge number of patterns to deal with all manner of situations. Any new situation that did not lead directly into an existing pattern would have to be analyzed afresh. The brain handles this problem in a very simple way.

Like rivers, the patterns have large catchment areas. This means that any activity within the catchment area is unstable and will lead towards the established pattern. This follows directly from a very simple type of behavior. What computers find so hard to do (pattern recognition) the brain does instantly and automatically. The catchment area is shown as a sort of funnel in Figure 1.5.

So whenever we look at the world we are only too ready to see the world in terms of our existing patterns as suggested in Figure 1.6. This is what makes perception so powerful and so useful. We are rarely at a loss. We can recognize most situations. This is also why the analysis of information will not yield new ideas. The brain can only see what it is prepared to see (existing patterns). So when we analyze data we can only pick out the idea we already have. This is an important point with which I shall deal later.

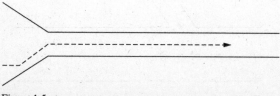

Figure 1.5

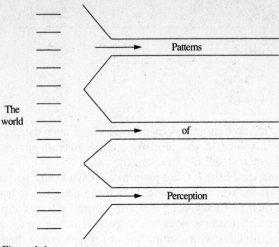

The
world

Figure 1.6

The point I want to make is that this pattern-forming and pattern-using behavior of the neural networks of the brain is magnificent. Without it, life would be impossible. Perception is the process of setting up and then using these patterns.

But what happens if there is a side pattern, as suggested in Figure 1.7? Do we have to stop and consider every side-track? If we had to do this, life would be impossibly slow. In practice the situation never arises because the way the nerves are wired up, the dominant track suppresses the other track which, for the moment, ceases to exist. So we go along the main track with full confidence.

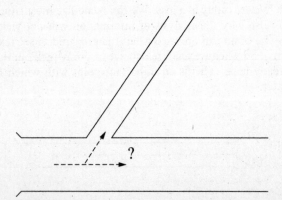

Figure 1.7

THE
THEO-
RETICAL
NEED
FOR
CREATIVITY

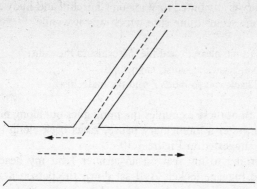

Figure 1.8

If, however, we were to enter the side-track from another point, then we could follow that side-track back to the starting point. This process is shown in Figure 1.8.

We now come to the classic asymmetry (lack of symmetry) of patterns. As shown in Figure 1.9 the route from B to A is very direct but the route from A to B may be very roundabout.

It is precisely this phenomenon of asymmetry which gives rise to both humor and creativity.

In the telling of a joke we are taken along the main track. Suddenly we are shifted to the end of the side-track and immediately we see the track we might have taken.

"If I were married to you, I should put poison in your coffee."
"And if I were married to you, I should drink the coffee."

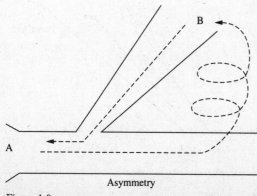

Asymmetry

Figure 1.9

13

(This story is attributed to Winston Churchill and Lady Asquith, but no one seems quite sure which way it went.)

"Hit me please," said the masochist to the sadist.
"No," said the sadist, enjoying it.
"Thank you so much," said the masochist.

In both of these examples the mind goes out along one track, and then, after a momentary pause, zings back along the other track as suggested in Figure 1.10.

Returning to my seat on an airliner I hit my head on the overhead luggage locker. As I sat down the person next to me said, "I also hit my head on that locker, it must be too low."

"On the contrary," I said, "the trouble is that the locker is placed too high."

There is nothing humorous about this exchange but there is the same sudden switch in perception—which eventually makes sense. If the luggage locker is really low then you see that you must duck your head. If the locker is placed really high, then it does not matter whether you duck or not. But if the locker is placed at a level that you do not think you need to duck, then you do not duck and you do hit your head.

MODEL FOR CREATIVITY

The humor model of the asymmetric pattern is also the model for creativity. The time sequence of our experience has set up the routine perception track. We see things in a certain way.

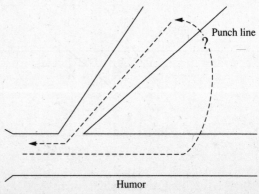

Figure 1.10

THE
THEO-
RETICAL
NEED
FOR
CREATIVITY

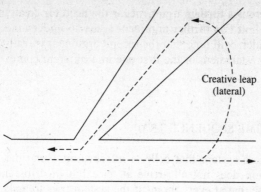

Creative leap
(lateral)

Figure 1.11

We expect things to be done in a certain way. If, somehow, we manage to cross over from the main track to the side-track then we can track back to the starting point and get our creative "insight" or new idea as suggested in Figure 1.11.

But how do we get to the "idea point" on the side-track? That is precisely where the techniques of provocation come in. They are methods of helping us to escape from the main track in order to increase our chances of getting to the side-track. That is also the basis of the expression *lateral thinking*. The "lateral" refers to moving sideways across the patterns instead of moving along them as in normal thinking.

Using the same model we can also see why every valuable creative idea must always be logical in hindsight. If we were to jump out of the main track in order to create a "new idea" at point C then we would have no way of fitting that idea into our existing value system. We would have no way of telling whether the idea was truly crazy or simply unrecognizable in our present state (patterns) of knowledge. So we can only recognize ideas that do have a logical link-back. It therefore follows that all valuable creative ideas must be logical in hindsight. To put it more simply: the word "valuable" automatically means logical in hindsight.

In summary, the brain is a wonderful device for allowing incoming information to organize itself into patterns. Once these patterns are formed, with their broad catchment areas, we use those patterns in the process known as perception. The patterns are not symmetric. This lack of symmetry gives rise both to humor and to creativity.

This then is the logical need for creativity. It is the logic of self-organizing patterning systems.

There is a further argument for the need for creativity; some people find this further argument easier to understand. Perceptive readers will note that the second argument is really no more than a restatement of the first one in a different context.

THE TIME SEQUENCE TRAP

Imagine a system that collects information over time. The information does not all arrive at once but in dribs and drabs. Suppose that at every moment the system tries to make the best use of the information available. Obviously this sort of system resembles individuals, institutions, corporations, cultures, and so on. Information is gathered over time and the system tries to make the best use of what has become available.

We can play a simple game in which letters are presented one at a time. The task is always to form a known word.

- The first letter is A.
- This is followed by T to give the word AT.
- The next letter is R, which is simply added to give RAT.

The letters represent incoming information and the total available information, is used to make up a word.

- The next letter is E to give the word RATE.
- The next letter is G, which gets added to give GRATE.

So far the new information has been easily added on to the existing structures.

- The next letter is T. There is no easy way this can be added on. A new word can only be formed by going back and disrupting existing structures to reassemble the letters to give TARGET.

In this simple example we can see how the time sequence of arrival of information sets up structures which have to be disrupted in order to put things together in a different way. This process is a useful definition of creativity. Without creativity we cannot move forward in such a system.

It might be argued that at each stage all the letters should be freed up and then the new letter added to the jumble and a new word formed. In real life, of course, it is impossible to disrupt all existing concepts, perceptions, words, or institutions in order to put the old information and the new information together in the best possible way.

After a while the items of information are no longer as separable as the letters in the game. For example, the cluster RAT has survived so long that it has now become a solid piece and resists disruption. In exactly the same way, basic perceptions resist disruption.

We need creativity in order to break free from the temporary structures that have been set up by a particular sequence of experience.

As I suggested, perceptive readers will see that the time sequence effect is the same as the patterning effect. It is the time sequence of experience that sets up the routine patterns of experience; we need to escape from these to put together new sequences.

Most people will accept these points. The difficulty arises when a person believes that it is a simple matter of rearranging the existing pieces into a new format. This might seem easy in the tabletop model of passive information systems but it is extremely difficult in self-organizing information systems because the information is no longer separable but becomes an integrated part of the pattern. Changing patterns is just as difficult as trying to give a word a totally new meaning whenever you choose to. Words are patterns of perception and experience.

So we see that there is an absolute need for creativity in any self-organizing system and, indeed, in any system in which new information is added to existing information in an integrating fashion.

If the human mind were to work like a library, new information could simply be stacked on empty shelves with no attempt to integrate it into the existing system. That would then be a waste of the new information. This, of course, is what we do when we do not use creativity and when the new information cannot be integrated into the old information.

Creativity is not simply a way to make things better. Without creativity we are unable to make full use of the information and experience that is already available to us and is locked up in old structures, old patterns, old concepts, and old perceptions.

The Practical
Need for Creativity

Life insurance is a very traditional industry controlled by tradition and regulations. One day Ron Barbaro, the chief executive of Prudential Canada, who is a strong user of lateral thinking, came up with a sort of provocation: why not pay out life insurance benefits before the policy-holder dies? This led to the concept of "living benefits"; any policy holder who falls sick with an illness that might be terminal is immediately entitled to 75 percent of the benefits that would have been payable on death. This concept has been a big success and has been imitated by many others because it makes life insurance much more attractive by turning it partially into catastrophic illness insurance. It was partly on the success of this idea and also on his skill in seeing the idea through that Ron Barbaro was soon chosen to be president of Prudential Insurance (USA).

Tony O'Reilly, the chief executive of Heinz, tells how a cost-cutting exercise so reduced the labor force in a tuna-processing factory that too much fish was being left on the bones. An increase in staff increased the costs again but saved enough tuna flesh to pay for the increased costs and add to the profit.

Singapore is one of the countries most determined to succeed. The government spends 20 percent of the budget on education. In 1965 the GNP of Singapore was $970 million; today the GNP is $23 billion. There is always a huge attendance whenever I give seminars in Singapore—but there used to be a problem. Effective seminars depend on participation from the audience: the offering of ideas, alternatives, and so on. In Latin countries this is never a problem since each member of the audience knows that his or her ideas are the best in the room. But in Singapore no one would offer any comment. In a subject like "creativity" you cannot easily point to a person and demand that the person be creative. This can be unfair and embarrassing.

I decided to use the "random word" technique in a formal manner. The random word was obtained from a list of 60 words by glancing at my watch and noting the position of the second hand. The word "gun" immediately suggested a specific aim. You did not usually just shoot a gun into the air and hope to hit something. From this came the idea of numbering the tables and lettering every position on the tables. So I could now ask for an output from table 12, position D. The response was wonderful and I now got as much feedback as I needed. It seems that the participants had not been shy but they saw no virtue in pushing themselves forward. The numbering of each position at once gave them an official status and they were then happy to share their thoughts.

Benetton is a highly successful company in a very crowded and competitive field. The company was started by three brothers and a sister in Italy. One of them was an ordinary accountant and she was a seamstress. Today they have 3,000 stores worldwide and the company is worth about $2 billion. The success of the company depended on some strong concepts. Traditionally garment makers make up garments and try to persuade store buyers to buy and stock the garments. Instead Benetton decided to get right next to the customer by opening small and simple stores. The next part of the concept was to sell "color," not "shape." So garments were left in their natural grey or undyed state. If customers started to buy red garments then the garments were dyed red. If the customers were buying mauve garments then the garments were dyed mauve. Sophisticated computer systems gave a flexibility of response almost as great as for mail order.

Each of these four examples indicates one aspect of the practical need for creativity.

In the case of the Singapore seminar, there was a problem and no standard way of solving that problem. Where there is no standard way or where the standard way is not available then there may be a practical need for creative thinking.

In the case of the Heinz tuna processors, a cost-cutting program had gone wrong. It is easy enough to cut costs just by slashing employment numbers and then hoping that the survivors will be able to cope. Today that approach is seen as dangerous and inefficient. There is a need to rethink and to restructure the work before cutting the numbers. This can require creativity.

The example of Benetton shows the great power of new concepts in a highly competitive industry. Doing the old things better is not going to be enough. There is a need to do things differently.

The Prudential example shows that even within a traditional industry it is possible to create a powerful new idea that opens up new opportunities. There was no need for Ron Barbaro to design a new idea. There was not a real problem to solve. But he is the sort of man who is driven by creativity to develop new concepts and so open up opportunities.

At this point we could say that the practical need for creativity falls into two areas:

1. Where there is a real need for a new idea and we cannot proceed without a new idea. It may be a problem, a crisis, or a conflict. Other approaches have failed. Creativity is the only hope.
2. Where there is no pressing need for a new idea but a new idea offers opportunity, advantage, and benefit.

COST-CUTTING AND QUALITY PROGRAMS

Many organizations give cost-cutting top priority. In many cases analysis will, by itself, help in the cost-cutting exercise. But there are times when design is also required. There is a need to re-design a function so that it can be done at lower cost. Do you simply buy cheaper materials to keep the cost down or find ways of reducing the wastage in order to let you continue to buy superior materials? It is a mistake to assume that cost-cutting is purely an analytical procedure.

A change in the way something is done may be much more effective than just doing less of it. A company that had huge bills for maintenance of its motorcycle fleet sold the bikes to their users and paid them a use fee. The cost savings were considerable.

The same sort of considerations apply to quality programs. There are times when creativity needs to be brought in as a tool in order to achieve some quality objective. There may be problems to be solved.

It also needs to be kept in mind that doing the old things with more quality may not be the right answer. There may need to be a change in what is being done. Quality programs can sometimes be misleading because they seem to start with the assumption that what is being done is what should be done and all that is required is to tune up the quality. Doing the old things with better and better quality will not suddenly lead to doing things differently. Nor should we devalue the word *quality* by making the word cover "all that needs to be done." Quality means doing what is now being done with better quality.

Another popular program is "continuous improvement." It is obvious that from time to time improvement may need some creative input. If something has always been done in the same way, then there may be a need for creative thinking to challenge that way and to suggest a better way of doing things. "Improvement" is one of the major areas of use for creative thinking and I shall be dealing with that later.

The main point is that wherever thinking is needed there is a need for information, for analysis, and for creativity. Concepts and perceptions are a basic part of all thinking that is not simple routine.

MAINTENANCE MANAGEMENT

Although it is rarely expressed, most managers have a "maintenance" attitude. They feel that their job is to keep things going and to solve problems as they arise. It is someone else's business to worry about products or strategy or financing. Deviations from this maintenance management would be high risk with the possibility of failure.

The success of an organization would depend on market muscle or a strong niche position. Backed up by competent management, this would be enough.

Maintenance management is strongly oriented toward problem solving. When problems arise they have to be solved. If there are no problems then everything is satisfactory.

Unfortunately, in a highly competitive world, maintenance management is no longer the sufficient concept that it might once have been. While you are seeking to maintain your current position your competitors are seeking to get ahead of you.

Even within maintenance management there is a need for creativity to solve the problems that arise from time to time. This is only the "fix-it" side of creativity. Fixing problems as they arise is not usually enough to ensure survival of an organization.

COMPETITION AND SUR/PETITION

Even classic competition itself is becoming part of maintenance management. There is a need to keep up with competitors in terms of price, quality, distribution, and promotion. There is a need for some product differentiation and marketing initiatives.

In the book *Sur/petition** I discuss how competition will no longer be enough in the future and why there will be a need to shift to sur/petition. The word *competition* means "seeking together." This means accepting that you are running in the same race as your competitors. Your behavior is quite largely determined by the behavior of the competitors. Sur/petition means "seeking above" or creating your own race. It means creating new "value monopolies."

These value monopolies will be largely based on "integrated values." For example, a car is no longer just a lump of engineering. The integrated values include the ability to buy, sell, and insure the car. They include safety and security against theft. Integrated values also include the ability to park in cities. I once suggested to Ford (UK) that they should buy up the company that owned most of the city center parks throughout the British Isles and then restrict parking in these to Ford cars. In Japan, Honda and Nissan have taken up this idea and I would not be surprised to see them spreading the idea around the world.

The first phase of business was "product or service."

The second phase of business was "competition."

The third phase of business will be "integrated values."

Sur/petition will be very highly dependent on concepts. To generate these concepts there will be a need for powerful creative thinking.

OTHER AREAS

I have focused here mainly on business areas because in my experience business has seen more need for creative thinking than other areas. I believe this is beginning to change. Other areas that have real problems and budget constraints will sooner or later come to see that creative thinking is an essential element in their way forward.

There is a need for new concepts in government and administration.

There is a need for new concepts in economics.

*HarperBusiness, New York, 1992.

There is a need for new concepts in education.

There is a need for new concepts in crime prevention.

There is a need for new concepts in the administration of the law.

There is a need for new concepts in health care provision.

There is a need for new concepts in conflict resolution.

There is a need for new concepts in the protection of the environment.

There is a need for new concepts in alleviating Third World poverty.

Is there any area that would not benefit from creative thinking, new concepts, and new perceptions?

What is being done to provide these new concepts? In some areas there are interesting initiatives, but on the whole there is still the belief that intelligent analysis, adequate information, and skilled argument will be enough. I do not agree.

Information and Creativity

What is the relationship between information and creativity? This is an important and fundamental question because the majority of people believe that sufficient information subjected to competent analysis and followed by logical decision making is enough—and there is therefore no need at all for creativity. Even those who will not openly admit this behave as if this is what they believe.

If you want to catch a plane from New York to London you had better check the timetables or ask your travel agent to do this for you. If you want to treat an infection with an antibiotic it helps to know what is causing the infection and also to check the antibiotic sensitivities. It also is useful to check whether the patient is allergic to any particular antibiotic. Thinking and guessing is not a substitute for information. When you need information, you need information.

It is quite true that if we had perfect information in a particular situation then thinking would be unnecessary. But our chances of getting perfect information are low. We assume, however, that as we get more and more information and approach the perfect state of complete knowledge, the need for thinking is lessened. On the contrary, the need for thinking becomes greater and greater because we have to make sense of the information.

If we do need thinking, then surely it is of the "analytical" type as we seek to make sense of the information. Where does creativity come in?

Most executives, many scientists, and almost all business school graduates believe that if you analyze data, this will give you new ideas. Unfortunately, this belief is totally wrong. The mind can only see what it is prepared to see. Analyzing data will enable the analyst to select from his or her repertoire of old ideas to find which one may fit. But analyzing data will not produce new ideas (see page 277). If you want a really new idea you have to be able to start it off in your head, with creativity, and then check it out against the data.

A scientist seeks to understand a phenomenon: for example, why do locust populations suddenly explode? There is a problem with the computer system and the analyst seeks to find out what has gone wrong. Sales of hamburgers are falling off—what is the explanation? There is a serious labor dispute over the sacking of a supervisor; what is really going on?

There are so many occasions when we need to understand what is going on in order to take appropriate action. We seek information and we seek clues. Then we put forward a hypothesis.

In some of my writings I point out the very harmful effect of classic Greek thinking (the gang of three) on Western thinking culture because it led to an obsession with argument and critical thinking and a general negative orientation. At the same time, it is only fair to point out that the "hypothesis" is also a Greek invention and a valuable contribution to human thinking. This is not as obvious as it might seem. Chinese technology was very far advanced about two thousand years ago but then it came to an abrupt end because the Chinese never developed the concept of the hypothesis. When everything had been labeled and described by the "scholars" there was no method of provocation or speculation. Possibly the Chinese did not develop the "hypothesis" because they never developed the concept of "God" as a super-designer of the world. A hypothesis is only a presumptuous guess as to what the underlying design might be.

A hypothesis is a guess or speculation. This has several merits. The hypothesis gives us a framework through which to look at the information so that we can begin to notice things we have not noticed. The hypothesis also gives us something to work towards—in proving it or disproving it.

Creativity is very much involved in constructing a hypothesis. If there is no creativity, then we can only use standard concepts. Science has been held back considerably by the notion that scientists simply have to be good analysts; this notion ignores the need to be creative about hypotheses.

Unfortunately, there is a serious dilemma associated with hypotheses. Without a hypothesis we flounder around. But when we have got a hypothesis then this can close down our minds to other possibilities. We now only look at the data through the hypothesis. If a detective on a difficult case forms an early hypothesis then that detective may ignore important clues as he or she only looks for what is relevant to the hypothesis.

A hypothesis should open up possibilities, but only too often it closes down possibilities. A marketing manager with a hypothesis of why hamburger sales are falling is not usually inclined to explore the matter further.

Traditional science falls into the same trap. There is supposed to be the most reasonable hypothesis. At first you seek evidence to support this hypothesis but once it is established you seek to destroy the hypothesis in order to move on further. Hypotheses are supposed to be reasonable. But when there is this "reasonable" hypothesis then we can only look at the data through this window. That is why paradigm changes can take so long to happen. The data may be available long before the paradigm change takes place. But we have looked at that data through the old hypothesis, which has sterilized the data. No matter how unreasonable they may seem, there is a need to hold several hypotheses in order to see the data in different ways.

Creativity is needed for generating these alternative and parallel hypotheses. There is a need for generous speculation, guessing, and the creation of hypotheses.

MARKET ANALYSIS

At least within Japan, the Japanese are not great believers in market analysis. They believe that consumers are the best test of new products. So they put out a large number of new products and then see which ones succeed. This sort of philosophy requires the ability to contemplate the failure of many products without great financial risk.

The opposite state of affairs prevails in the West. The actual cost and reputation cost of failure is so high that a person or a corporation must be convinced of a product's success before taking the risk. So there is a heavy dependence on market research. This research gives both the "logical" reasons for action and also the fall-back position if the product fails.

Market analysis shows that men drink whiskey and other strong drinks. So there is no point in spending money on advertising such drinks in women's magazines. Market analysis tells us "what is" rather than "what could be." It may be that a whiskey-drinking campaign directed to women would produce new whiskey drinkers. In any case, women do most of the buying of hard liquor, so even on that basis there might be a reason for advertising whiskey in women's magazines.

Traffic planners put in roads to meet the existing demand with some extrapolation factor. But as soon as the roads are opened they are crowded because the very existence of the road draws in traffic that was not there before. The danger of market analysis is that it is static and reflects neither interactive loops nor possibilities.

So there is a high need for creativity in interpreting data and looking at possibilities. What other ways can we look at this? What other explanations might there be? What else might be going on here? What sort of things might happen?

THE FUTURE

It might just be possible to get complete data about the past but it is certainly impossible to get complete data about the future. So where do we get our picture of the future?

We can extrapolate present trends. We can continue present cycles. We can foresee certain convergences that might produce new effects. We might make informed guesses and then try to refine these guesses with various scenario techniques. All these things are very valuable but all depend on an analysis of the present. What about the discontinuities? What happens if the future is not an extension of the present?

We need to use deliberate creativity in order to put forward certain future possibilities. There is no way of proving that these "possibilities" are actually going to happen. But having the possibilities enriches our concept map of the future. Planning and decisions based on the enriched concept map are likely to be more flexible. Possibilities should not be mistakenly elevated to certainties but given full value as possibilities.

Traffic congestion in cities is getting worse and commuting times are getting longer. People want to move into the countryside to get a better quality of life. Electronic technology allows people to work at home. What does this suggest? The obvious answer is working from home, at least in knowledge industries. But what are the other possibilities? This is where creativity comes in to generate other possibilities. Perhaps there might be workstations in the neighborhood. You walk to the work-station and have your electronic equipment there. Each person in the work-station might be working for an entirely different organization. The work-station provides an out-of-home environment and the social aspects of "going to work." In the United States a very high proportion of young people meet their future spouses at work. Alternatively there might be "city dormitories" where people live when they come into work for sustained bursts of two weeks followed by a week at home. Yet another idea is adding mini-offices on to houses and allowing a small group of workers to assemble and work there.

CONCEPT DRIVERS

The Wright brothers were the first to fly a heavier-than-air machine because they changed the prevailing concept. While everyone else was seeking a "stable" flying machine, the Wright brothers set out to cope with "unstable" machines. This was the driving concept. Through experimentation they found they could vary the lift on each wing by twisting or warping the wing. This resulted in "controls" and that is why they were the first to fly.

Sometimes we set out to analyze data in order to see the trends and what is happening. But at other times we develop a firm concept in our minds and then seek out data to develop and check out the concept. Here the concept comes before the data—though it may have been suggested by previous data.

It would be absurd to pretend that all concepts are the result of creativity. Nevertheless there is usually a strong creative contribution in the development of concepts. In the example of Benetton given earlier in the book, the driving concept was "flexibility." Those who sit back and wait for the analysis of information to give them their directions are going to miss out entirely on the value of concept drivers.

The creation of a new concept opens up a new window through which we can look at the world around us and the information that might be available. The new concept tells us where to look and what to look for. Without the concept to direct attention and to select information we would never have found evidence to support the value of the concept. This is the "active" use of information as contrasted with the more normal "passive" use. Do you know what sort of market there might be for home delivery of pasta?

INGREDIENTS

Surely the more information we have, the better will be our creative thinking. If there is more to play around with, then the result will be more valuable. If an artist has more colors on his or her palette, then the painting will be richer. So it must follow that the more information available to the "creating person" the better will be the results of the creativity. Unfortunately this is not so.

It is perfectly true that more information is valuable. If you know that certain metals will always return to a predetermined shape at a given temperature then you can use this phenomenon to invent useful control devices. If you know that there is a powerful membrane process for purifying water then you can be more creative about waste disposal.

The trouble is that information rarely comes purely as information. Usually the information comes wrapped in concepts and perceptions. When the creating person takes on board these existing concepts and perceptions then that person is forced to think along the same lines. I shall return to this point when considering the value of "innocence" as a source of fresh ideas.

So it does not automatically follow that more information will lead to better ideas.

COLLECTING INFORMATION

Creativity plays an important role even in the collecting of information. The design of questions in an opinion poll may require creativity. Getting access to certain people or segments of the population may require creativity. When you know the information you want there is a need for creativity in order to see how to get that information and how to get it in the cheapest and most accurate way.

Market researchers are always on the look-out for better ways of getting information. There is considerable scope for creativity here. There is usually a high cost involved in getting information from people and in getting information to people. There should be a creative effort to find cheaper ways of doing it.

"Do we know about . . . ."

"What would happen if . . . ."

"How would this be seen . . . ."

There is always a need for better ways of collecting information. Some of those better ways are going to come from creative thinking focused on information collecting.

29

Misperceptions About Creativity

At several points in the book I have made comments about the way creativity is sometimes regarded. At various points later in the book I shall very likely make further comments. I feel, however, that there is some value in bringing together in one place these various points. This may lead to a degree of repetition, but that in itself can be useful. Quite obviously the views I put forward here are personal opinions based on many years experience in the field of creative thinking and the teaching of creative thinking skills.

1. CREATIVITY IS A NATURAL TALENT AND CANNOT BE TAUGHT

This misperception is actually very convenient because it relieves everybody of the need to do anything about fostering creativity. If it is only available as a natural talent then there is no point in seeking to do anything about creativity.

The argument is usually set by pointing to rather extreme cases of creativity such as Mozart, Einstein, or Michelangelo. This is not unlike saying there is no point in teaching mathematics because mathematical geniuses like Poincaré cannot be produced to order. We do not give up teaching people to play the piano or violin because we cannot guarantee a Liszt or Paderewski from every pupil. Can you produce a Bjorn Borg or Martina Navratilova from every tennis pupil?

There are very useful levels of mathematical ability, piano playing, violin playing, and tennis playing, even when these fall short of genius.

Imagine a row of people lined up to run a race. The starting signal is given and the race is run. Someone comes first and someone comes last. Performance has depended on natural running ability. Now suppose someone invents the "roller skate" and gives all the runners some training on the roller skates. The race is run again. Everyone goes much faster than before. Someone will still come first and someone will still come last.

If we do nothing at all about creativity then obviously creative ability can only depend on "natural" talent. But if we provide training, structures, and systematic techniques, then we can raise the general level of creative ability. Some people will still be much better than others but everyone can acquire some creative skill. There is no contradiction at all between "talent" and "training." Any athletics or opera coach can make that point.

That some people are naturally creative does not mean that such people would not be even more creative with some training and techniques. Nor does it mean that other people can never become creative.

When I first started writing about creativity I half expected truly creative people to say that they did not need such matters. Quite the contrary happened. Many well-known creative people got in touch with me to say how useful they found some of the processes.

At this point in time there is also a wealth of experience to show how people have used deliberate lateral thinking techniques to develop powerful ideas. There is also a lot of experience from others to show that training in creative thinking can make a significant difference.

On an experimental basis, it is quite easy to show how even as simple a technique as the random word can immediately lead to more ideas; ideas that are different from those that have been offered before.

In my view, learning creative thinking is no different from learning mathematics or any sport. We do not sit back and say that natural talent is sufficient and nothing can be done. We know that we can train people to a useful level of competence. We know that natural talent, where it exists, will be enhanced by the training and processes.

In my view, and at this point in time, I think the view that creativity cannot be learned is no longer tenable.

It may not be possible to train genius—but there is an awful lot of useful creativity that takes place without genius.

2. CREATIVITY COMES FROM THE REBELS

At school the more intelligent youngsters seem to be conformists. They quickly learn the "game" that is required: how to please the teacher. How to pass exams with minimal effort. How to copy when necessary. In this way they ensure a peaceful life and the ability to get on with what really interests them. Then there are the rebels. The rebels, for reasons of temperament or the need to be noticed, do not want to play the going game.

It is only natural to assume that in later life creativity is going to have to come from the rebels. The conformists are busily learning the appropriate games, playing them, and adjusting to them. So it is up to the rebels to challenge existing concepts and to set out to do things differently. The rebels have the courage, the energy, and the different points of view.

This is our traditional view of creativity. But it could be changing.

Once we begin to understand the nature of creativity (or at least, lateral thinking) then we can start laying out the "game" and the steps in the game. Once society decides that this game is worth playing and should be rewarded then we might well get the "conformists" deciding that they want to play this new "game." So the conformists learn the game of creativity. Because they are adept at learning games and playing the games the conformists might soon become more creative than the rebels who do not want to learn or play any games.

So we might get the strange paradox that the conformists actually become more creative than the rebels. I think this is beginning to happen.

If it does happen I would expect to see much more constructive creativity. The rebel often achieves creativity by striking out against the prevailing ideas and going against current idioms. The momentum of the rebel is obtained by being "against" something. But the creativity of conformists (playing the creative game) does not need to be "against" anything—so it can be more constructive and can also build on existing ideas.

So creativity is certainly not restricted to rebels but creative skills can be acquired even by those who have always considered themselves conformists.

Japan has produced many highly creative people but on the whole the Japanese culture is oriented towards group behavior rather than individual eccentricity. Traditional Japanese culture has not put a high value on individual creativity (in contrast to the West). In a smooth arch it is not necessary to see the individual contribution of each stone.

Things are changing. The Japanese now know that creativity is central to their continued economic success. They have decided that the game of creativity is important. So they have now decided to learn to play the game. In my experience in teaching creativity in Japan I would have to say that they are going to be very good at this "new" game. Just as they learned to play the "quality" game very well, so they will also learn the creativity game and play it well.

The West will be left somewhat behind if those responsible for education in the West still believe that creativity cannot be taught and that critical thinking is enough.

3. RIGHT BRAIN/LEFT BRAIN

The simple geography of right brain/left brain has made it very appealing—to the point that there is almost a hemispheric racism:

"He's too left-brained. . . ."

"We need a right-brained person for this. . . ."

"We employed her to bring some right brain to bear on the matter. . . ."

While the right/left notation has some value in indicating that not all thinking is linear and symbolic the matter has been exaggerated to the point that it is dangerous and limiting and doing great harm to the cause of creativity.

In a right-handed person the left brain is the "educated" part of the brain and picks up on language, symbols, and seeing things as we know they should be. The right brain is the uneducated "innocent" that has learned nothing. So in matters of drawing, music, and the like, the right brain can see things with an innocent eye. You might draw things as they really look, not as you think they ought to be.

The right brain might allow a more holistic view instead of building things up point by point.

All these things have a value, but when we come to the creativity involved in changing concepts and perceptions, we have no choice but to use the left brain as well because that is where concepts and perceptions are formed and lodged. It is possible to see which parts of the brain are working at any given moment by doing a PET (Positive Emission Tomography) scan. Little flashes of radiation captured on a film show the activity. It seems clear that when a person is doing creative thinking both left and

33

right brains are active at the same time. This is much as one might expect.

So while there is some merit in the right/left brain notation and some value for innocence in certain activities (music, drawing) the basic concept is misleading when it comes to creative thinking. It is misleading because it suggests that creativity only takes place in the right brain. It is misleading because it suggests that in order to be creative all we need to do is to drop the left brain behavior and use right brain behavior.

4. ART, ARTISTS, AND CREATIVITY

Earlier I mentioned the confusion caused by the very broad usage of the word "creativity." Normally we see "creativity" most manifestly in the work of artists so we assume that creativity and art are synonymous. As a result of this confusion we believe that to teach creativity we must teach people to behave like artists. We also assume that artists might be the best people to teach creativity.

In this book I am concerned with the creativity involved in changing concepts and perceptions—that is why I sometimes prefer the much more specific term of lateral thinking. Not all artists are creative in my usage of the word "creative." Many artists are powerful stylists who have a valuable style of perception and expression. Indeed, many artists get trapped in a style because that is what the world comes to expect of them. If you employ I. M. Pei, the architect, to design a building for you then you expect an I. M. Pei-type of building. An Andy Warhol piece of art is expected to look like an Andy Warhol piece of art.

Artists, like children, can be fresh and original and very rigid all at the same time. There is not always the flexibility that is part of creative thinking.

Artists can also be much more analytical than most people suppose and artists do take great care with the technology of their work.

It is true that with artists there is a general interest in achieving something "new" as opposed to mere repetition. There is a willingness to play around with concepts and different perceptions. There is a readiness to let the end result justify the process of getting there instead of having to take a sequence of justified steps. All these are important aspects of the general creative mood. There are artists whom I would regard as creative even in my sense of the word and others whom I would not so regard.

The misperception consists of the notion that creativity has to do with art and therefore artists are the best people to deal with teaching creativity.

The second part of the misperception is that an artist (or indeed any creative person) is necessarily the best person to teach creativity. The grand prix racing driver is not the best designer of grand prix cars or the best driving instructor. There is this notion that through a sort of osmosis the attitudes of the artist will come through to the students who will therefore become creative. I am sure that there is some effect in this general direction but it is bound to be a rather weak effect because osmosis as a teaching process is too ineffectual.

There are some artists who are creative and are good teachers of creativity. These are people who are creative and are good teachers of creativity. They just happen to be artists.

I am not convinced that artists have any special merit in the teaching of creativity that has to do with changing concepts and perceptions.

The confusion of "creativity" with "art" is a language problem that can do considerable damage.

5. RELEASE

I have mentioned this point before. It is a very important point because much of the so-called "training" in creativity in North America is directed towards "freeing" people up and "releasing" the innate potential for creativity that is believed to be there.

Let me say at once that I fully agree that removing inhibitions, the fear of being wrong, or the fear of seeming ridiculous does have a limited value. You are certainly in a better position to be creative if you are free to play around with strange ideas and to express new thoughts. I would hardly be in favor of inhibition.

The "judgment" system is a very important part of our education as is the notion of the "one right answer" that the teacher has. So attempts to break people out of this mold are worthwhile.

It is precisely this limited value of the "release" idiom that is its greatest danger. There is the belief that that is all that needs doing. So organizations come to believe that if they have got someone to come and "free up" their people, that is all that is needed to develop creative skills. In the same way, "trainers" in creativity believe that creative training is no more than a series of exercises to get people to feel uninhibited and to say whatever comes into their minds.

As I have indicated earlier, the brain is not designed to be creative. The excellence of the human brain is that it is designed to form patterns from the world around us and then to stick to these patterns. That is how perception works and life would be totally impossible if the brain were to work differently. The purpose of the brain is to enable us to survive and to cope. The purpose of the brain is not to be creative. Cutting across established patterns to produce new ideas is not what the brain is designed to do.

Inhibitions depress us below our "normal" level of creativity as suggested in Figure 1.12. If we remove these inhibitions we come back to our "normal" level of creativity. But to be really creative we have to do some "not natural" things. Such things include the formal processes of provocation to be discussed later in the book.

It is true that some people are creative and that new ideas do occur from time to time. Surely this means that creativity is a natural activity of the brain? That does not follow. New ideas may be produced by an unusual coming together of events. New ideas may be produced by a chance provocation provided by nature (a sort of natural "random word" technique). Furthermore, people get sick from time to time but this does not mean that it is "natural" to be sick. So the fact that some people do have ideas and that ideas do occur does not mean that this must be a natural function of the brain. If it were a natural function then I should expect a very much higher output from natural creativity.

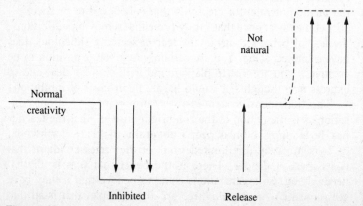

Normal
creativity

Not
natural

Inhibited

Release

36   Figure 1.12

Looking at matters purely from the point of view of the behavior of information systems it is very hard to see how any "memory" system could be creative—except by mistake.

6. INTUITION

I am often asked about the place of "intuition" in creative thinking. In the English language the word "intuition" seems to have two separate meanings. One meaning implies "insight" and the sudden viewing of something in a new way. This insight aspect is very similar to the humor phenomenon that I mentioned earlier as being the model for lateral thinking. If we do manage to get across to the side-track (see page 15) then in a flash we see the link-up with the starting point and the new perception is formed. For this meaning of the word "intuition" I would say the purpose of the specific creative techniques is precisely to help us get to this point of insight.

The second meaning of the word "intuition" covers a feeling that is generated from experience and considerations. The ingredients or steps leading to the feeling are not spelled out and so we call it "intuition" rather than "thought." In the case of previous experience we might find that we have a gut feeling on an issue. In the case of current considerations we feed in factors and then allow "intuition" to work on them to produce an output. Going to sleep on a problem is often cited as an example of this unconscious working of the "intuition."

The question is whether there is productive mental working which takes place outside our consciousness. Even if this is not the case there can be a sort of reorganization of information which we feed into the mind without any conscious effort to produce a result.

On a theoretical level it seems to me that this is best left as an open question. I suspect that some unconscious reorganization of information and experience does take place, once we feed contexts into the mind. This would hardly be surprising in a pattern-using system that is very prone to insight switching—if you enter a pattern at a slightly different point you can go in a totally different direction (like crossing the watershed between two river basins).

The more important point is the practical level. There is a danger in assuming that it "all happens" in intuition and therefore there is nothing that we need to do about it and nothing that we

37

can do about it. This is a sort of black-box approach which suggests that we abdicate all conscious effort and just hope that intuition does its job properly and when required. Needless to say I am very much against such abdication.

I believe that intuition does play an important part in the final stages of the systematic lateral thinking processes. I believe that from time to time intuition may make a valuable contribution quite apart from any deliberate creative techniques. I think, however, that we should treat these contributions of intuition as a "bonus." When the contribution is helpful we should be grateful. When there is no contribution we continue to make our deliberate creative efforts.

7. THE NEED FOR "CRAZINESS"

I have mentioned how the "crazy" aspect of creativity, which is pushed by some practitioners in the field, tends to relegate creative thinking to the periphery as something that cannot be serious.

Craziness is easy to encourage because it seems so different from normal thinking and it can also be fun. People feel their inhibitions slipping away as they compete to be more "crazy" than others in the group.

Obviously, creativity is not going to involve staying within the existing ideas, so any new ideas may, at first, seem crazy when compared with existing ideas. As a result it is very easy to make the false assumption and to give the false impression that creative thinking is based on craziness.

One of the legitimate techniques of lateral thinking is provocation. There is a need to set up a provocation that does not exist in experience and, perhaps, could never exist in experience. The purpose of this is to take us out of the normal perceptual pattern and to place our minds in an unstable position from which we can then "move" to a new idea. This process is deliberate, systematic, and logically based on the behavior of asymmetric patterning systems. There are formal ways of setting up these provocations: the formal word "po" to indicate that it is a provocation, and formal ways of getting "movement" from a provocation. All this is very different from having a crazy idea for the sake of having a crazy idea.

To explain to students the logical need for provocation and the ways of working with provocations is quite different from giving the impression that craziness is an end in itself and an essential part of creative thinking. As with so many of the points mentioned here, teachers of creativity fasten on this point of "craziness" and set forth to teach it as the essence of the process. This gives quite the wrong impression and puts off people who want to use creativity in a serious manner.

8. SCATTER-GUN SUCCESS

The traditional process of brainstorming sometimes gives the impression that deliberate creativity consists of shooting out a stream of crazy ideas in the hope that one of them might hit a useful target. It is just possible that in the advertising world, for which brainstorming was designed, scatter-gun ideas might produce something useful because novelty is what is being sought. But in almost every other field a scatter-gun approach to creativity makes no more sense than having a thousand monkeys banging away on typewriters in the hope that one of them might produce a Shakespeare play.

If deliberate creativity were no more than a hit-and-miss scatter-gun process then I should have no interest at all in the subject.

What actually happens is quite different. There are the main tracks of perception (see page 10) which, like river valleys, collect all information in the neighborhood. Everything flows into the existing "rivers." If only we can get out of the track or catchment area then we have a high chance of moving into a different catchment area. So far from being a scatter-gun approach, it is more like tearing yourself away from your usual restaurant in a street full of restaurants and so making it easier for you to explore a new restaurant.

There are new ideas waiting to be used if we can but escape from the usual pattern sequence that experience has set up for us. There is a reasonable possibility that such ideas exist and there is a reasonable chance that we might step into them if we but escape from our usual thinking.

Of course, the difficulty is that any valuable creative idea will be perfectly logical—and even obvious—in hindsight, so that the receiver of the new idea will claim that a little bit of logical thinking would have reached the idea without all that "messing about."

9. BIG JUMP AND SMALL JUMP CREATIVITY

It is said that Western creativity is obsessed with the big conceptual jump that sets a new paradigm, whereas Japanese creativity is content with a succession of small jump modifications
that produce new products without any sudden concept change.
Which is better?

There is undoubted value in small jump creativity and to
some extent the West has ignored this because of the ego-
preference for really new and "big" ideas; these are more self-
satisfying and more apt to impress others. The Western concern
with "genius" creativity has sometimes meant a neglect of "practical" creativity. Small jumps often take the form of modifications, improvements, and combinations of things. The full value
of a new idea may depend on a lot of small jump creativity that
squeezes the maximum amount out of the innovation.

At the same time, it must be said that a succession of small
jumps do not add up to a big jump. A big jump is usually a
paradigm change or a new concept. Because this can involve
a total reorganization of previous concepts, this is not likely to
come from an accumulation of small jumps.

There is a need for both big jump and small jump creativity. It
is a matter of balance. Perhaps there needs to be some emphasis
on small jump creativity in order to get creativity accepted as a
necessary part of the thinking of everyone in an organization. If
we look at creativity as only "big jump creativity" then this is
seen as only being suitable for research scientists or corporate
strategists.

10. GROUP OR INDIVIDUAL

I shall be returning to this point in the Application section of
the book.

Because brainstorming has been the traditional approach to
deliberate creative thinking, there has grown up the notion that
deliberate creative thinking must be a group process. After all,
if you sit on your own, what are you going to do? Are you just
going to hope for inspiration? The whole idea of brainstorming
was that other people's remarks would act to stimulate your own
ideas in a sort of chain reaction of ideas. So the group element
is an essential part of the process.

But groups are not at all necessary for deliberate creative thinking. Every one of the techniques put forward in this book can be used by an individual entirely on his or her own. There need not be a group in sight. The formal techniques of provocation (and "po") allow an individual to create provocative and stimulating ideas for himself or herself. There is absolutely no need to rely on other people to provide the stimulation.

In my experience, individuals working on their own produce far more ideas and a far wider range of ideas than when they are working together in a group. In a group you have to listen to others and you may spend time repeating your own ideas so they get sufficient attention. Very often the group takes a joint direction whereas individuals on their own can pursue individual directions.

It is quite true that the social aspects of a group have a value. It requires a lot of discipline to work creatively on your own. In practice I often recommend a mixture of group and individual work, as I shall explain in the Application section.

I believe that individuals are much better at generating ideas and fresh directions. Once the idea has been born then a group may be better able to develop the idea and take it in more directions than can the originator.

At this moment the point I want to make is that deliberate creativity does not have to be a group process as is so often believed.

11. INTELLIGENCE AND CREATIVITY

There is a classic study by Getzels and Jackson which claimed to show that up to an IQ of 120, creativity and IQ went together, but after that they diverged. Questions need to be asked about the methods used to test intelligence and creativity and also the expectations of the people involved.

People with a high IQ have often been encouraged not to speculate or guess and not to put forward frivolous ideas. This sort of background training can seriously affect the result of any comparisons. The highly intelligent person may know an idea is absurd and so not present it. The less intelligent person may not be smart enough to know the idea can never work and may therefore score a mark for an additional idea.

The practical question is whether you have to be super-smart to be creative, and whether being super-smart might make it more difficult for someone to be creative.

41

I look at intelligence as the potential of the mind. This may be determined by certain enzyme kinetics which allow faster mental reactions and so a faster rate of scan. This is equivalent to the horsepower of a car. The horsepower is the potential of the car. The performance of the car, however, depends on the skill of the driver. There may be a powerful car which is driven badly and a humble car which is driven well. In the same way, an "intelligent" person may be a poor thinker if that person has not acquired the skills of thinking. A less intelligent person may have better thinking skills.

The skills of creative thinking are part of the skills of thinking but have to be learned directly in their own right. An intelligent person who has not learned the skills of creative thinking might well be less creative than a less intelligent person because some of the thinking skills imparted by education may run counter to creative behavior (as I suggested earlier). If the intelligent person learned the skills of creative thinking then I would expect that person to be a good creative thinker.

So very much depends on habits, training, and expectations.

I do not think that being highly intelligent need prevent a person from being creative—if he or she has made an effort to learn the methods of creativity.

Above a certain basic level of intelligence I do not believe that a person has to be exceptionally intelligent in order to be creative.

Sources of Creativity

In this section I want to consider some of the traditional sources of creativity and also some other sources. These considerations will serve both to place the systematic techniques of lateral thinking in perspective and also to generate some practical points about creative thinking.

INNOCENCE

Innocence is the classic creativity of children. If you do not know the usual approach, the usual solution, the usual concepts involved, then you may come up with a fresh approach. Also, if you are not inhibited by knowing the constraints and knowing what cannot be done, then you are more free to suggest a novel approach.

When the Montgolfier brothers flew the first hot air balloon, word of this exciting event reached the king in Paris, who could immediately see the military potential. So he called for his chief scientific officer, M. Charles, and commanded him to produce a balloon. This considerable scientist racked his brains: "how could they have flown this contraption?" After a while he jumped up with the French equivalent of "Eureka." "They must be using this new gas called hydrogen, which is lighter than air!" he declared. So he proceeded to invent the hydrogen balloon, which is a totally different type of balloon.

Many years ago in the south of Sweden a group of high school children were brought together by Gunnar Wessman, who was then chief executive of the Perstorp Corporation. I gave them some training in lateral thinking. Then a number of government and industrial figures came down from Stockholm to put problems to the youngsters. One problem involved the difficulty of motivating workers to take the weekend shift in a plant that needed to be kept running over the weekend. In their innocence the children suggested that instead of motivating existing workers it would make sense to have a fresh workforce that always worked only Saturdays and Sundays. Apparently this idea was tried out and the number of applicants for these weekend jobs was far in excess of what was needed. Adults would have assumed that no one would want to do such weekend jobs, that the unions would never permit it, and so on.

Although children can be very fresh and original they can also be inflexible (as I have already mentioned) and they can refuse to put forward further alternatives. The creativity comes from the fresh or innocent approach rather than the seeking for a new approach.

Unfortunately, it is not easy to keep ignorant and innocent as we grow up. Nor is it possible to be innocent in one's own field. So what are the practical points that we can take from the creativity of innocence?

Perhaps, on certain occasions, we could actually listen to children. The children are unlikely to give full-fledged solutions, but if the listeners are prepared to pick up on principles then some new approaches might emerge.

Some industries, such as retailing and the motor industry, are traditionally very inbred and feel they have all the answers. There is the feeling that you have to grow up in the business to make any contribution. There is a point in such industries looking outwards and seeking ideas from outside. Such ideas may have the freshness that cannot be obtained from insiders no matter how experienced they may be.

A very important practical point concerns research. It is normal when entering a new field to read up all that there is to read about the new field. If you do not do so then you cannot make use of what is known and you risk wasting your time reinventing the wheel. But if you do all this reading you wreck your chances of being original. In the course of your reading you will take on board the existing concepts and perceptions. You may make an attempt to challenge these and even to go in an opposite direction but you can no longer be innocent of the existing ideas. You no longer have any chance of developing a concept which is but slightly different from the traditional concept. So if you want competence you must read everything but if you want originality you must not.

One way out of the dilemma is to start off reading just enough to get the feel of the new field. Then you stop and do your own thinking. When you have developed some ideas of your own then you read further. Then you stop and review your ideas and even develop new ones. Then you go back and complete your reading. In this way you have a chance to be original.

When a person joins a new organization there is a short window of freshness which runs from about the sixth month to the eighteenth month. Before the sixth month the new person does not yet have enough information to get the feel of the business (unless it is a very simple business). After the eighteenth month the person is so imbued with the local culture and the way things should be done that innocent freshness is no longer possible.

It should be noted that some of the most rigid businesses are soft businesses like advertising and television. In some other fields there are fixed regulations or even physical laws to guide behavior. Because these are virtually absent in the soft fields, the practitioners in such fields invent for themselves a whole lot of arbitrary rules and guidelines in order to feel more secure. If everything is possible then how do you know what to do? So the rigid guidelines become established by tradition and people now find themselves forced to work within these totally arbitrary rules. In such fields innocence is usually dismissed as ignorance.

EXPERIENCE

The creativity of experience is obviously the opposite of the creativity of innocence. With experience we know the things that work. We know from experience what will succeed, what will sell.

The first mode of operation of the creativity of experience is "bells and whistles." The idea that worked so well before is tarted up with some modifications in order for it to appear as a new idea. This is quite often the sort of product differentiation talked about in classic competitive behavior.

The second mode of operation of the creativity of experience is "son of Lassie." If something has worked well before then it can be repeated. If the film *Rocky* has worked then why not have *Rocky II* and then *III* and even *IV* and *V*. This strategy covers copying, borrowing, and me-too products. A new style in advertising will immediately spawn many imitators. This type of creativity is very common in North America, where there is considerable risk aversion. If you know that something works then repeat it again rather than try something new. This is because the personal costs of failure are so high. An executive is only as good as his or her last action. This makes for opportunism rather than true opportunity development.

The third mode of operation of the creativity of experience is disassembly followed by reassembly. Things that are known to work are packaged as a product, for example, a financial product. When the time comes to have a new product, the original package is taken apart and the ingredients repackaged in a different way. Usually the ingredients are mixed around amongst different packages so the combinations are always changing.

The creativity of experience is essentially low-risk creativity and seeks to build upon and to repeat past successes. Most commercial creativity is of this sort. There will be a steady and reliable output of moderately successful creativity but nothing really new. If someone were to think of something really new then it would be rejected because there would be insufficient evidence to guarantee the success that is needed. As Sam Goldwyn once said: "What we really need are some brand new clichés."

MOTIVATION

The creativity of motivation is very important because most people who are seen as being creative derive their creativity from this source.

Motivation means being willing to spend up to five hours a week trying to find a better way of doing something when other people perhaps spend five minutes a week. Motivation means looking for further alternatives when everyone else is satisfied with the obvious ones. Motivation means having the curiosity to look for explanations. Motivation means trying things out and tinkering about in the search for new ideas.

One very important aspect of motivation is the willingness to stop and to look at things that no one else has bothered to look at. This simple process of focusing on things that are normally taken for granted is a powerful source of creativity, even when no special creative talent is applied to the new focus. This is so important a point that I shall also be dealing with it later under creative techniques.

So motivation means putting in time and effort and attempting to be creative. Over time this investment does pay off in terms of new and creative ideas.

A lot of what passes for creative talent is not much more than creative motivation—and there is nothing wrong with that. If we can then add some creative skills to the existing motivation the combination can become powerful.

There is a difference between a photographer and a painter. The painter stands in front of the canvas with paints, brushes, and inspiration and proceeds to paint a picture. The photographer wanders around with a camera until some particular scene or object catches his or her eye. By choosing the angle, the composition, the lighting, and so on, the photographer converts the "promising" scene into a photograph.

The creativity of "tuned judgment" is similar to the creativity of the photographer. The person with tuned judgment does not initiate ideas. The person with tuned judgment recognizes the potential of an idea at a very early stage. Because that person's judgment is tuned to feasibility, the market, and the idiom of the field, the person picks up the idea and makes it happen.

Although this sort of creativity seems to lack the glamour and ego satisfaction of the originator of ideas, in practice it may be even more important. An idea that is developed and put into action is more important than an idea that exists only as an idea.

Many people who have achieved success with apparently new ideas have really borrowed the beginning of the idea from someone else but have put the creative energy into making the idea happen.

The ability to see the value of an idea is itself a creative act. If the idea is new then it is necessary to visualise the power of the idea. People who develop ideas in this way should get as much credit as those who initiate ideas.

CHANCE, ACCIDENT, MISTAKE, AND MADNESS

The history of ideas is full of examples of how important new ideas came about through chance, accident, mistake, or "madness."

Traditional thinking, which is a summary of history, is going along in one direction. Then something happens—which could not have been planned—and this takes thinking out in a new direction and a new discovery is made.

Many of the advances in medicine were the result of accidents, mistakes, or chance observations. The first antibiotic was discovered when Alexander Fleming noticed that a mold contamination of a Petri dish seemed to have killed off the bacteria; thus penicillin was born. The process of immunology was discovered by Pasteur when an assistant made a mistake and gave too weak a dose of cholera bacteria to some chickens. This weak dose seemed to protect them against the fuller dose that was given later.

Columbus only set off to sail westward to the Indies because he was using the wrong measurements. He was using the measurements derived from Ptolemy's erroneous measurement of the circumference of the globe. Had he been using the correct measurements, which had been worked out by Eratosthenes (who lived in Alexandria before Ptolemy), Columbus would probably never have set sail because he would have known his ships could not have carried sufficient provisions.

In some ways the whole of the electronics industry (about $150 billion a year in Japan alone) depended on a mistake made by Lee de Forrest. Lee de Forrest noted that when a spark jumped between two spheres in his laboratory, the gas flame flickered. He thought this was due to the "ionization" of the air. As a result he proceeded to invent the triode valve (also known as the vacuum tube or thermionic valve) in which the current to be amplified is applied to a grid and so controls the much larger current passing from the filament to the collector plate.

This superb invention provided the first real means of amplification and gave rise to the electronic industry. Before the invention of the transistor all electronic devices used such vacuum tubes.

It seems that the whole thing was a mistake and that the gas flame flickered because of the noise from the spark discharge.

Mistakes, anomalies, things that go wrong have often triggered new ideas and new insights. This is because such events take us outside the boundaries of "reasonableness" within which we are normally forced to work. These boundaries are the accepted summary of past experience and they are very jealously guarded, particularly by people who are themselves rather unlikely to have new ideas.

Apparent "madness" is a source of creativity when someone comes up with an idea that does not fit current paradigms. There is heavy condemnation of the idea. Most of the ideas are mad and do go away. But sometimes the new and mad idea proves to be right and the paradigm has to be changed, but not before there is fierce opposition from the defenders of the old paradigm.

So what is the practical point arising from this powerful source of creativity? Should we make mistakes on purpose?

One practical point is to pay close attention to mistakes and anomalies when things do not turn out as we had hoped.

The second practical point is the deliberate use of provocation. As we shall see later, the techniques of provocation allow us to be mad, in a controlled way, for 30 seconds at a time. In this way we can achieve those boundary jumps that otherwise have to depend on chance, accident, mistake, and madness.

Figure 1.13 suggests how the boundaries of past experience and "reasonableness" turn back our thinking. These boundaries can be jumped by chance, accident, mistake, madness—or deliberate provocation.

There is a further practical point that arises here. Individuals working on their own can hold and develop ideas that are at first "mad" or eccentric and only later become acceptable. If such a person is forced to work with a group from an early stage then it might not be possible to develop such ideas because the "reasonableness" of the group will force the new idea back within the boundaries of acceptability.

Cultures which rely heavily on group work (such as Italy and the United States) may be at a disadvantage in this regard. Countries like the U.K., with its tradition of eccentric individuals working away in corners, may have an advantage. Perhaps that is why M.I.T.I. in Japan found that 51 percent of the most significant concept breakthroughs of the twentieth century had come from the U.K. and only 21 percent from the United States, in spite of the much larger technical investment of the United States.

It has to be said, however, that the complexities of modern science make it much more difficult for individuals to contribute. Cross-disciplinary teamwork may be essential for idea

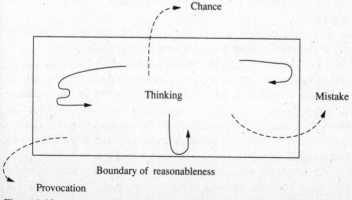

Figure 1.13

development in the future. Therefore there is an even greater need to develop the deliberate skills of provocation.

In 1970 I suggested to a meeting of oil executives that they should consider drilling oil wells horizontally instead of vertically—and even suggested the use of a hydraulic drilling head. At the time that idea seemed "mad." Today it is the most fashionable way of drilling for oil as it results in a much higher yield.

STYLE

I have already dealt at length with "style" as an apparent source of creativity. Working within a style can give a stream of new products which are new because they all partake of the same new style. There is not, however, an individual creative effort for each product except to apply the style. This sort of creativity can have a high practical value but is not the same as the generation of new ideas as such.

I have already commented that in some cases the creativity of artists is the creativity of a powerful and valuable style.

RELEASE

I have also commented extensively on the creativity that is produced as a result of release from traditional cautions and inhibitions. I have noted that this does have a limited value but is not sufficient because the brain is not naturally designed to be creative, so freeing up the brain only makes it a little bit more creative.

It should be said, however, that the change of culture in an organization can lead to a valuable output of creativity. If it is seen that creativity is a game that is permitted and even valued by top management, then people do start to become more creative.

In my experience, when the chief executive in an organization has shown a strong and concrete commitment (not just lip service) to creativity, the culture of the organization can change quite rapidly. Perhaps it is not so much a release from inhibitions but a quick appreciation of new values and a new "game."

Release from fears and inhibitions is an important part of creativity and will produce some useful results. But by itself it is only the very first stage and is not enough.

The systematic creative techniques of lateral thinking can be used formally and deliberately in order to generate new ideas and to change perceptions. These techniques and tools can be learned and practiced and applied when needed.

The tools are directly derived from a consideration of the logic of perception, which is the logic of a self-organizing information system that forms and then uses patterns.

The important practical point is that such techniques/tools can be learned and used. In this way a skill in creative thinking can be developed.

The practical value and importance of the lateral thinking techniques does not, of course, mean that creativity cannot continue to come from other sources as well.

Lateral Thinking

> What is 'Lateral Thinking'?
> How does 'Lateral Thinking' relate to creativity?
> Why is it called 'Lateral Thinking'?

My interest in thinking came from three sources. As a Rhodes Scholar I had studied psychology at Oxford and this gave me some interest in thinking. In the course of medical research I was using computers extensively to carry out Fourier analysis of blood pressure waves in order to estimate the impedance in the pulmonary artery. I became interested in the sort of thinking that computers could not do. This was creative and perceptual thinking. Continuing my medical research at Harvard, I was working on the complicated way in which the body regulated blood pressure and the general integration of systems in the human body. This led to an interest in self-organizing systems.

The three strands (thinking, perceptual thinking, self-organizing systems) came together and I wrote a manuscript in which I referred to "the other sort of thinking" meaning the thinking that was not linear, sequential, and logical. I was explaining this "other sort of thinking" in an interview with a magazine called London Life. As I explained it I described how you needed to move "laterally" to find other approaches and other alternatives. At once it occurred to me that this was the word I needed. So I went back to the manuscript and substituted the phrase "lateral thinking" for "the other sort of thinking."

That was in 1967. "Lateral thinking" now has an official entry in the Oxford English Dictionary, which is the arbiter of the English language. The entry in the Concise Oxford Dictionary reads: "seeking to solve problems by unorthodox or apparently illogical methods." The key word is "apparently." The methods may seem "illogical" in terms of normal logic but are derived from the logic of patterning systems where, for example, provocation is a necessity.

The simplest way to describe lateral thinking is to say: "You cannot dig a hole in a different place by digging the same hole deeper." This emphasizes the searching for different approaches and different ways of looking at things.

With "vertical thinking" you take a position and then you seek to build on that basis. The next step depends on where you are at this moment. The next step has to be related and logically derived from where you are at this moment. This suggests building up from a base or digging deeper the same hole as suggested in Figure 1.14.

With lateral thinking we move "sideways" to try different perceptions, different concepts, different points of entry. We can use various methods, including provocations, to get us out of the usual line of thought.

Granny is sitting knitting. Susan who is three years old is upsetting Granny by playing around with the ball of wool. One parent suggests that Susan ought to be put into the playpen to keep her from annoying Granny. The other parent suggests that it might be a better idea to put Granny into the playpen to protect her from Susan.

The true technical description of lateral thinking is based on a consideration of a self-organizing pattern-making information system: "cutting across patterns in a self-organizing information system." This "lateral" move across patterns is shown in Figure 1.15, which repeats the basic diagram of an asymmetric patterning system. Instead of following along patterns we seek to cut across them.

Lateral thinking has very much to do with perception. In lateral thinking we seek to put forward different views. All are correct and all can coexist. The different views are not derived each from the other but are independently produced. In this sense

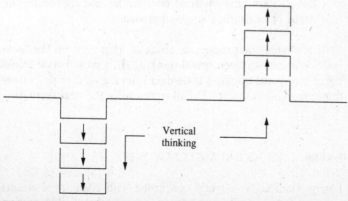

Vertical
thinking

Figure 1.14

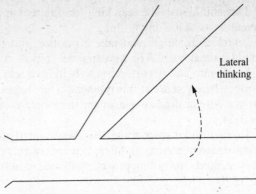

Figure 1.15

lateral thinking has to do with exploration just as perception has
to do with exploration. You walk around a building and take
photographs from different angles. All are equally valid.

Normal logic is very much concerned with "truth" and "what
is." Lateral thinking, like perception, is very much concerned
with "possibilities" and "what might be." We build up layers
of what might be and eventually arrive at a useful picture. Today this type of information processing is formally known in
the computer world as "fuzzy logic" because there are no sharp
right/wrong boundaries.

So the term "lateral thinking" can be used in two senses, one
of which is specific and the other more general.

Specific: A set of systematic techniques used for changing
concepts and perceptions and generating new ones.

General: Exploring multiple possibilities and approaches instead of pursuing a single approach.

It is obvious that there is a strong overlap between the "general" definition and perceptual thinking. In a sense lateral thinking is perceptual thinking as distinct from the logic of processing
thinking. This is a point I shall return to in the next section.

LATERAL THINKING AND CREATIVITY

Lateral thinking is directly concerned with changing concepts
and perceptions. In the second part of this book I shall be putting

forward systematic ways of doing this. This is the specific purpose of lateral thinking.

In some ways the changing of perceptions and concepts is the basis of the creativity that involves new ideas. This is not necessarily the same as the creativity that involves artistic expression. Many artists have told me that they find the techniques of lateral thinking useful to them but I make no claim for lateral thinking as the basis of artistic creativity.

As I have mentioned before, the word "creativity" has a very wide and confused meaning. There are elements of "new" and elements of "bringing something into being" and even elements of "value." There may be several entirely different processes involved in this wide definition of "creativity." The term "lateral thinking" is, however, very precise. Lateral thinking is concerned with changing concepts and perceptions. Lateral thinking is based on the behavior of self-organizing information systems.

In its general sense, lateral thinking is also concerned with exploring perceptions and concepts but the specific or creative sense is concerned with changing perceptions and concepts.

As we shall see when we come to the systematic techniques of lateral thinking, there are aspects which are perfectly logical (normal logic) and even "convergent" in nature. So lateral thinking is not just another term for "divergent" thinking. Divergent thinking is but one aspect of lateral thinking. Divergent thinking is interested in multiple possibilities, just like lateral thinking, but that is only one aspect of lateral thinking.

The relationship between lateral thinking and creativity is suggested in Figure 1.16. The degree of overlap is a matter of opinion.

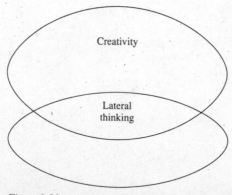

Figure 1.16

55

TERMINOLOGY

Throughout this book I use the terms "creative thinking" and "lateral thinking" at different points. This is because the term "creative thinking" is better known and I do not want to confuse readers. Furthermore, many of the points that are made in this first section of the book do refer to creative thinking in general. It should, however, be kept in mind that the book is concerned with the type of creative thinking that is concerned with new concepts and new ideas.

The term "lateral thinking" is reserved for the specific techniques and tools that are put forward as a systematic way of getting new ideas and new concepts. In mathematics there is the general term "mathematics" but also the specific methods that carry through the operations of mathematics.

Perception and Processing

You are in the kitchen. All the ingredients you need for the dinner party are piled up on the table: meat, vegetables, herbs, and the like. Your task is to process these ingredients to produce an excellent and memorable feast. You set about your task of processing.

Culturally, we have developed excellent methods for processing information. We have mathematics with its power and effectiveness. Mathematics is even beginning to move into nonlinear areas. We have statistics and the study of probabilities. We have computers and data processing. At first, computers were used to do mathematics, but today they are being used to do things beyond the capabilities of mathematics: iterative methods, simulations, modeling, and so on. This opens up whole new dimensions. Computers provide a world in which we can make things happen and then see what results. Processes that would have been impossibly tedious to work out mathematically can now be handled by computers. Then we have the various types of logic with which to process information. At the everyday level we have the simplicities of ordinary verbal logic in its Aristotelian form (identity, inclusion, exclusion, contradiction, and so on).

We are not short of processing tools. And they will get even better.

But in that kitchen with which I started this section, we might pause to wonder where the ingredients came from and how they got into the kitchen. How were the ingredients chosen? How did the ingredients come to be available in the store? How were the ingredients harvested? How did they come to be grown/produced in the first place?

The production of the ingredients for information processing is the role of perception. It is perception that organizes the world into the x's and y's that we then process with mathematics. It is perception that gives us the observations or propositions that we then handle with logic. It is perception that gives us the words and the choice of words with which we think about anything.

While we have developed excellent processing systems, we have done very little about perception—because we have not understood perception. We have always assumed that perception operates, like processing, in a passive, externally-organized information system. That makes perception impossible to understand. It is only in the last twenty years that we have begun to understand the behavior of self-organizing information systems and self-organizing neural networks. Now we have a conceptual model with which we can begin to understand perception, humor, and creativity.

It is obvious that creativity takes place in the perceptual phase of thinking. This is where our perceptions and concepts are formed and this is where they have to be changed. Readers of this book will by now have realized the central role of perception in creative thinking and how lateral thinking is closely related to perceptual thinking.

Outside technical matters, most ordinary thinking takes place in the perceptual phase. Most of the mistakes in thinking are inadequacies of perception rather than mistakes of logic. The astonishing thing is that traditionally we have always put the emphasis on logic rather than on perception. We have felt uncomfortable with the fluidities and "possibilities" of perception and have taken refuge in the apparent certainties and "truth" of logic. This has served us well when the input is as definite as a measurement or a number but much less well in those areas where the excellence of processing cannot make up for the inadequacies of perception.

With perception we do not see the world as it is but as we perceive it. The patterns of perception have been built up by a particular time sequence of experience. We perceive the world in terms of the established patterns that are triggered by what is now in front of us.

LIMITS OF PERCEPTION

A five-year-old in Australia, called Johnny, is offered a choice of two coins by his friends. There is the $1 coin and the smaller $2 coin. He is told he can take one of the coins and keep it. He picks the larger $1 coin. His friends consider him very stupid for not knowing that the smaller coin is twice as valuable. Whenever they want to make a fool of Johnny they offer him the usual choice of coins. He always takes the $1 coin and never seems to learn.

One day an adult who observes this transaction takes Johnny to one side and advises him that the smaller coin is actually worth more than the bigger coin—even though it may seem otherwise.

Johnny listens politely then says, "Yes, I know that. But how often would they have offered me the choice if I had taken the $2 coin the first time?"

A computer programmed for value would have had to take the $2 coin the first time. It was Johnny's human perception which allowed him to take a broader view and to consider the possibility of repeat business. This is a very complex perception. Johnny had to assess how often his friends would want to tease him; how many $1 coins they would be willing to lose; and how long before they realized what he was up to. There was also the risk factor. This is the difference between a computer and a human being. The computer is given its perceptions and then proceeds to process them. The human mind forms its perceptions by choosing to look at the world in a particular way.

Figure 1.17 shows a simple map with roads going in three directions. You are at point X and you want to go north. It seems pretty obvious and logical that you should take the road that heads north. All the information available to you suggests that this is the correct road.

Now look at Figure 1.18 where the first small map is placed in a larger map. At once we see that the road heading north is actually the worst road to take because it comes to a dead end. Both other roads link up with a ring road that eventually leads north.

Of course, in the first place, we did not have the full information and made a perfectly logical choice in terms of the information we had. It is the same with perception. If we have a limited perception then we can make a perfectly logical choice consistent with that limited perception.

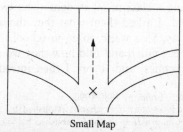

Small Map

Figure 1.17

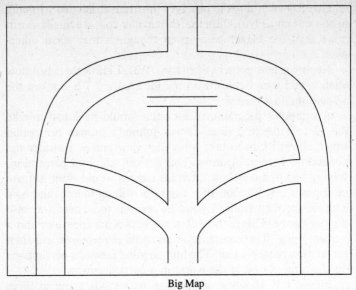

Big Map

Figure 1.18

In one of my earlier books, *Future Positive*,* I introduced the concept of a "logic bubble."

A "logic bubble" is that personal bubble of perceptions within which each person acts in a totally logical fashion. The logic is correct but if the perceptions are limited or faulty then the resulting action may be inappropriate. Different logic bubbles give rise to different behavior and conflicts. But each party is behaving very sensibly within that party's logic bubble.

In the direct teaching of thinking as a school subject one of the most important things is to provide the students with tools for broadening their perception. So the first lesson of the CoRT Program[†] is the PMI. This simple perceptual tool requires the students to scan first the Plus points, then the Minus points, and finally the Interesting points.

I was teaching a class of 30 students who were between 10 and 11 years old. I asked them what they thought of the idea of being paid, say, $5 a week, to go to school. All 30 students liked the idea very much and told how they would buy sweets, chewing gum, comics, and so on. I then introduced the PMI

*Penguin Books, London, 1980/1990.
†CoRT Thinking Lessons (for schools) published by S.R.A. (Chicago), also in *Teach Your Children How to Think* published by Viking/Penguin, New York, 1992.

and asked them systematically to go through each part in small groups of five students. At the end of four minutes I asked for their thinking. The Plus points were as before. But now there were Minus points. The bigger boys might attack the younger boys and take the money. The school might raise the charge for lunch. Parents would be less inclined to give presents. Where would the money come from? There would be less money for teachers, and so on. There were also some Interesting points. Would the payment be withheld if school performance was poor? Would older students get more?

At the end of this simple exercise, 29 of the 30 students had reversed their opinion and decided it was a bad idea. The important point to note is that I did not discuss the matter with the students or argue with them. I simply presented the students with a perceptual scanning tool and asked them to use it. As a result of using the tool they got a broader perception. As a result of the broader perception they changed their judgment. That is precisely what the teaching of thinking should be about: providing tools that students can use and that make a difference.

A friend shows you three upturned cups. Under one of them is a chocolate and under two of them are small stones. You are asked to make a choice. When you have put your finger on one of the cups to indicate your choice, your friend removes one of the other cups to show a stone. Should you now change your choice to the other cup or stay with your original choice? Logic might suggest that there is a fifty/fifty chance of the chocolate being either under the cup you originally chose or under the remaining cup—so there is little point in changing. But a different perception, followed by logic, will show that two times out of three you would be better off to change to the remaining cup. Why? I could reveal the explanation but it is more interesting if you figure it out.

WATER LOGIC

In the book *I Am Right You Are Wrong** I introduce the concept of "water logic" and contrast it with traditional "rock logic." Water logic is the logic of perception, rock logic is the logic of processing.

*Penguin Books, London, 1990; Viking Books, NY, 1991.

A rock has a fixed and permanent shape. Water fits the container, vessel, or circumstances. Perception depends on context, experience, emotions, point of view, framework, and so on.

If you add one rock to another rock you get two rocks. If you add water to water you get water. Perception builds up by layers. The layers do not remain separate but build up to give a total perception.

A rock is static; water is fluid and flows. Rock logic is concerned with "what is." Water logic and perception are concerned with "what might be."

A rock has a hard edge but water has a fluid edge. This relates to the "fuzzy logic" of perception.

Perception strives for meaning and attempts to make sense of what is present. Perception also seeks a stable state (in terms of the neural network in the brain). Water seeks to flow toward a stable state. A rock is immobile.

THE LOGIC OF PERCEPTION

If we look closely at the logic of perception we find that it is very different from traditional (rock) logic. We have ignored this difference because we have felt uncomfortable with the uncertainty of perception and always wanted the dogmatism of processing logic. So we have assumed that the words in language can handle the perception side and then we can proceed to process the words as if they were mathematical symbols.

This approach locks us into the inadequacies of words and also the traditional way of looking at things, since words are nothing if not history. In a sense, words are encyclopedias of ignorance because they freeze perceptions at one moment in history and then insist we continue to use these frozen perceptions when we should be doing better.

In order to be creative, it is important to realize the fluidity of perception and the possibility of multiple perceptions, all of which are valuable. This is an essential background for creative thinking. We need to replace "is" with "can be." At the end of our creative thinking, however, we need to come back to the world of rock logic to present ideas that are solid, workable, and of testable value. But to get to those ideas we need the fluidity of water logic and lateral thinking.

Design and Analysis

The traditions of Western thinking are based on analysis and argument. The major thrust of Western education is "analysis." In order to understand information, in order to understand situations, we need to analyze them. Through analysis we break down complex and unknown situations into bite-sized chunks that we can recognize and with which we can cope.

The emphasis on analysis is not unrelated to that search for the "truth" that is characteristic of Western thought.

We teach analysis because it is certainly important but also because it is much more convenient to teach. You can ask students to analyze situations. You can give students case studies and ask them to analyze the situations.

With analysis we are interested in "what is." With design we become interested in "what could be."

It is always assumed that if you reveal the truth with analysis then knowing what to do is very simple and obvious. We assume it is like finding a good map on which the roads are clearly marked and then all you have to do is to choose a road and follow it. Unfortunately, life is not like that. Life involves action as well as description. It is true that action is sometimes routine, standard, and obvious. But at other times we have to "design" appropriate action.

We ought to be giving equal weight to the design of ideas and the design of action as we give to analysis. We do not.

We claim to balance analysis with synthesis. Analysis breaks something down into elements and then synthesis combines elements to give an answer or an action. It is rather like a Lego™ set. You pull the plastic pieces apart in analysis and then you can build the pieces up again into anything you wish. Unfortunately, design is not just the putting together of elements in a sort of additive way. There is a need for concepts and these concepts will not come simply from the synthesis of separate elements.

It is for these reasons that intellectually we are much better at analysis rather than at design.

Analysis is our traditional method of problem solving. What is the cause of the problem? If you sit on a chair and experience a sharp pain you examine the cushion. You find a pin and remove

63

it. You have removed the cause of the problem—the problem is solved. You have a sore throat. A swab reveals a streptococcal infection. You take some penicillin, which kills the streptococcus. The cause of the problem has been removed, the problem is solved.

There are problems where we cannot find the cause. There are problems where there are so many causes that we cannot remove all of them. There are problems where we can find the cause but cannot remove it (the cause might happen to be human nature). Such problems cannot be solved by analysis. There is a need to "design a way forward." It is precisely because we have put so little emphasis on design in education that we are so feeble in the face of such problems.

Design uses information and design uses logic. Design also needs to use creativity in order to put forward possible concepts and to change existing perceptions. Sometimes we are trapped in problems by our fixed way of looking at things.

In general use, the word "design" has an element of visual design and graphic design. Sometimes design is seen as a sort of cosmetic luxury. We badly need to broaden the meaning of the word *design* to cover all those situations where we put things together in order to achieve some effect. Whenever standard routine is not enough, we need "design." Design is the basis for action.

So instead of assuming that analysis reveals a map with ready-made roads upon it, we should assume that the map only shows the terrain and we have to "design" the roads.

Like action, "design" always has a purpose. With action we set out to achieve something. With design we set out to achieve something.

We can design a concept. We can design an idea, which is to say we design a way of putting that concept into action. Analysis would seek to discover a relationship which might exist (as in science) but design seeks to put forward a relationship which does not exist and perhaps has never existed (as in a new concept). No amount of analysis can reveal a concept that is not there. Theoretically, there is only one truth and you approach nearer and nearer to that truth. With design there can be any number of designs providing all of them satisfy the design brief. Some designs will be better than others in all respects and some better in some respects.

Even in science we need to create and to design hypotheses and speculations. The notion that science has only to do with analysis is wrong and most good scientists have always known this. It is the poetry of speculation that makes the good scientist, provided the rigor of information collecting is also present.

In conflict situations we always think of argument and bargaining and the exertion of force. Design should play a much larger part in conflict resolution. There is a need to design an outcome which satisfies the values of both parties. There is a need to design interim stages. There is a need to design fall-back positions, sanctions, guarantees, and monitoring systems.

There is a very interesting type of conflict resolution that is prescribed by law in certain states in the United States but is not often used because it is not much liked by lawyers. In normal conflict situations, both parties start at extreme positions knowing that they will gradually bargain and fight their way to a middle or compromise position. A great deal of time, effort, and expense is involved. In the alternative method the conflicting parties never meet. Each party "designs" the most reasonable "outcome" or conclusion. Both outcomes are placed before a judge or arbitrator. This person has to choose the most "reasonable" of the proposed outcomes. Clearly if one suggested outcome is unreasonable and the other is reasonable then the reasonable outcome wins. So both parties try their hardest to "design" a reasonable outcome. All the effort which might previously have gone into fighting now goes into "design." If both parties do a good job of designing a reasonable outcome then it probably does not much matter which one is chosen by the judge. The interesting point about this procedure is that all the emphasis is placed on design instead of on argument.

MODES OF DESIGN

The normal mode of design is to set out the requirements to form a sort of "mold" and then seek to fit something into this mold. So if you were designing a car you might seek the following: attractive shape, adequate seating capacity, aerodynamic styling, fuel efficiency, ease of manufacture, use of standard parts, good handling, and some unique feature to advertise. The designer would seek to satisfy these requirements. The result would be adequate but probably rather bland. The result would be a sort of optimization and a putting together of known concepts to achieve the desired effect.

The second method is to develop some creative concepts in their own right and then to see how these concepts could be "shaped" and made to fit the design requirements. Here the requirements are brought in as shapers of the concept. There is a higher risk element in this second approach but a greater likelihood of a really new approach.

An architect may set out to meet each of the design requirements in a new building: space, lighting, communication, energy efficiency, attractive appearance, data-equipped, and so on. At each point, all the requirements are satisfied. Another architect may choose one fundamental requirement (which might be an imposing appearance or work space) and then develop concepts to further this requirement. Once the requirement has been fully satisfied, the designer then seeks to accommodate the other requirements. In military terms the difference is between a steady advance on all fronts or throwing forward a salient and then catching up with it.

It is not my purpose here to go into the fascinating and important process of design, which merits a book of its own. It is my intention to draw a sharp contrast between our obsession with analysis and the urgent need for design thinking. Along with this need for design thinking goes the need for creative thinking.

The Uses of
Creative Thinking

We have been considering various important aspects of the nature, background, and need for creative thinking. These are all important points and not just academic reflections. If you set out to use the systematic techniques of lateral thinking as a bag of tools you will be far less effective as a creative person than if you pay attention to the background points as well.

If you understand the "logic" of perception, the difference between design and analysis and all the other points then your motivation becomes much stronger and you will acquire the idiom of creative thinking.

The considerations put forward in the book up to now can stay with you for the rest of your life or be supplanted by better ones. It has been necessary to cover these points because of the misunderstandings about the nature of creativity. It has been necessary to cover these points because of the sad neglect of creative thinking in our educational system, which is convinced of the sufficiency of information, analysis, and argument. The points have been necessary to provide a solid base for the use of the specific creative tools.

From this point onward we can start to look at the practical use of creative thinking. The first thing I want to do is to consider some of the major uses of creative thinking. These uses are set out in broad terms. This is only one way of looking at the uses of creativity. There can be other ways which are equally valid.

I shall also return to some of these points in the third part of the book which is devoted to the application of creative thinking.

IMPROVEMENT

In volume terms, "improvement" is by far the biggest use of creative thinking. Perhaps I should qualify this by saying it is the biggest "potential" use of creative thinking. We can seek to apply creative thinking to anything at all that we are now doing with the hope of making an improvement or finding a "better" way of doing something. The potential is enormous—but for reasons I shall consider later, we do not make much use of this potential. We are generally too satisfied with the way we now do things.

What do we mean by "improvement"? What do we mean by finding a "better" way to do things? What does "better" mean?

There is a need to have a clear idea of what we mean by better. Better can mean at a lower cost or in less time. Better can mean with fewer errors and faults. Better can mean with less energy or with less pollution. Better can mean in a more humanly satisfying way. Better can mean with less wastage or with cheaper materials. In the future one very important direction of "better" is going to be "simpler." Simplicity has a very high value for users and consumers. Simplicity has a very high value for producers because it means that highly skilled workers are not essential.

It is very important to define the direction of improvement. There may, of course, be several directions that are important.

The Western notion of "improvement" has always been concerned with removing defects, overcoming problems, putting faults right. This is very much part of the general negative orientation of Western thinking. The Japanese are also concerned to remove faults—but this is only the beginning of improvement. The Japanese, unlike Westerners, are able to look at something which seems perfect and then set about improving it. The Japanese notion of improvement is not limited to putting things right. It is just that the Japanese never had the negative culture of Western thinking (proving someone wrong, solving problems, correcting faults, and so on). The Toyota Motor Company gets something like 300 suggestions per year per employee. The figure in a normal Western company would be below 10.

It is perfectly true that today Western companies are seeking to adopt the Japanese approach with such programs as "continuous improvement" and "total quality management." Such programs ask for improvement at all points—even when there are no faults to correct.

I know a large European company that has a successful suggestions scheme that has saved them millions of dollars (equivalent of local currency) but the company is not fond of the scheme. The difficulty is that no one has the time or wants to assess the suggestions. This is possibly because all suggestions move upward and centrally. The Japanese handle this problem by having councils at all levels that assess the suggestions at the level at which they arise. So there is no massive accumulation of suggestions at some central point. Setting up ways of dealing with suggestions is a vital part of any improvement program.

The key point about improvement is to be able to look at any procedure or method and to suppose that there might be a better way of doing it. I know corporations that have gone back and looked at processes which they had perfected over the years and with which they were totally happy. Further improvements in these "perfected" processes led to savings of millions of dollars.

There is now a general acknowledgment of the value of seeking to improve procedures even when there is no problem and no pressure of cost saving. Even so, it is not easy. Theoretically it is necessary to look at everything with this "improving" frame of mind. Since this is clearly not feasible it is very comfortable to slip back into looking only at problems and faults.

The key point to remember is that the removal of faults is only a small part of the improvement process.

There are improvements that can be made on the basis of experience, new technology, new information, analysis, and logic. Creative thinking is not always necessary. When there are faults then logical problem-solving can often be enough to remove the faults. But when there are no faults, there is a greater need for creative thinking to open up new possibilities.

PROBLEM SOLVING

Problem solving has always been a traditional area for the use of creative thinking. If the standard approaches cannot provide a solution then there is a need to use creative thinking. Even when the standard approach can provide a solution there is some point in trying creative thinking in order to find an even better solution. There is nothing to say that the standard solution or the first solution to be found is necessarily the best solution.

I have discussed already the analysis approach to problem solving and the design approach. Obviously the design approach demands creative thinking. But even the analysis approach may need creative thinking in order to imagine alternative possibilities that can then be checked out.

A great deal of fuss is usually made about "problem definition." Problem definition is very important: "What is the real problem here?" It has to be said, however, that the only time you can really find the best problem definition is after you have found the solution. That is not of much practical use. Nevertheless there needs to be an effort to consider alternative problem definitions, some broad and some narrow. The emphasis is not so much on the *right* problem definition but on *alternative* problem definitions. Sooner or later you will find a definition with which you are happy and that gives useful results.

A problem is like a headache or a stone in your shoe. You know it is there. A problem is provided by the world around you (government regulations, currency changes, disasters, ecological difficulties), by your competitors, or by a breakdown in your own systems (machinery, computers, labor relations). You do not have to go looking for problems.

But then there are the problems that you set for yourself. You could call this "problem finding" but I prefer the broader term of "task setting." You set yourself a task and then set about carrying out the task. If the task can be achieved in a routine way then there is no problem. If there is no routine way then you have set yourself a problem and it may need creative thinking to solve the problem. The more confident you become about your creative thinking the more willing you will be to set "apparently impossible" tasks.

Many years ago I was sitting next to Professor Littlewood (a famous English mathematician) at dinner in Trinity College, Cambridge University. We were discussing the playing of chess on computers. Chess achieves difficulty through having many pieces with different moves. I said it would be interesting to invent a game in which each player has only one piece. This was a self-imposed challenge. I went away and invented the "L" game in which each player has only an L-shaped piece. The game can be learned in twenty seconds but is a real game and can be played with a high degree of skill. It may, possibly, be the simplest real game.

Any inventor behaves in exactly the same way. The inventor sets himself or herself a task and then sets out to achieve this task. The same thing applies to a design with the only difference being that with a design, some sort of output is usually possible, whereas within an invention, unless there is a "breakthrough" there may be nothing at all.

There is an unfortunate tendency in North American psychology to call all purposeful thinking problem solving. This fails to distinguish the thinking involved in extracting ourselves from a difficult situation with the thinking involved in achieving something new.

In the techniques section we shall see that there are techniques, like the "concept fan," that are particularly suited to achievement thinking. With a problem or a self-imposed task we know where we want to go—we need to find a way of getting there. This is achievement thinking and it is broader than the "problem solving" heading that I have given to this subsection out of consideration for the normal usage of the term "problem."

It is well known that "problem avoidance" is an important part of problem solving. Instead of solving the problem you go upstream and alter the system so that the problem does not occur in the first place. This is a process of redesign. If people are always losing their keys you redesign the security system so that it does not use keys.

VALUE AND OPPORTUNITY

As competing organizations increase their competence, success and survival shift to what they can do with their core assets. The assets may be market position, qualified people, distribution systems, technical know-how (and patents), brand names, and so on. This third use of creative thinking is directly involved in adding value, in creating value, and in designing opportunities.

There was a time when efficiency and problem solving were enough, but today these just provide the baseline. What new products and services can we design? How can we position our products and services? How can we provide added value? What new markets and market segments might there be?

Earlier in the book I mentioned the need to switch from classic competition to the newer concept of sur/petition. I mentioned the importance of "integrated values" in providing the consumer with what is needed. These are all matters that are dealt with in detail in the book called *Sur/petition*.*

It is always possible to copy others, to devise me-too products and to take over innovative companies. These are valid strategies and seem to carry less risk than innovation. But why wait for other parties to do what you could have done first? In any competent and well-run corporation there are unused assets that only require creative thinking to be put to work.

Problems demand attention. Crises have to be survived. Improvement is often undertaken as part of a cost-cutting exercise. Unfortunately there is no simple spur that encourages people

*HarperBusiness, New York, 1992.

to look for opportunities. That requires entrepreneurial spirit. Where people are encouraged to be risk-averse there is little incentive to incur risk or extra hassle.

The design of opportunities requires creative thinking. The creation of new value requires new concepts. The "out of the blue" crafting of opportunities depends on someone making the effort to find them. If you simply wait for opportunities to occur, you will be one of the crowd. If you put in some creative ability you can be ahead of the crowd. Opportunity ideas do not lie around waiting to be discovered. Such ideas need to be produced. Organizations that are very good at producing things sometimes find it difficult to see the need to produce ideas.

THE FUTURE

Consideration of the future always requires thinking. We can never have full information about the future, and yet our actions are going to take place, and have consequences, in the future. So creative thinking can be required to foresee the consequences of action and to generate further alternatives for consideration.

Creativity is also required for laying out the possible future in which we may have to work. I have already mentioned how creativity is needed to produce the discontinuities that will not arise from the extrapolation of present trends.

Designing strategies, designing contingency, and fall-back positions are all part of a creative design process. Information and logic set the framework. Creative design offers the possibilities. Information and logic assess the possibilities.

In the future, instead of striving to be right at a high cost, it will be more appropriate to be flexible and plural at a lower cost. If you cannot accurately predict the future then you must flexibly be prepared to deal with various possible futures.

In my experience, strategy is too often seen solely as a reduction process in which various possibilities are reduced to a sensible course of action. There is a greater need for creativity in order to generate further possibilities and in order to devise ways of coping with multiple possibilities. A course of action that should be rejected by well-informed judgment can become a preferred strategy through a creative modification. Like a gold thread running the length of a garment, so creative thinking should continue as part of all thinking that is taking place about the future.

David Tanner, who used to run the Center for Creativity at Du Pont, tells me how the umbrella of "creativity" allows people to look at anything that they are doing with a view to rethinking it. Quite often this new attention turns up improvements that have depended more on logic than on creativity. But without the umbrella of creativity the new thinking would never have taken place.

Creativity is a great motivator because it makes people interested in what they are doing. Creativity gives hope that there can be a worthwhile idea. Creativity gives the possibility of some sort of achievement to everyone. Creativity makes life more fun and more interesting. Creativity provides a framework for working with others as a team.

All these motivating aspects of creativity are quite separate from the actual results of the creative effort.

The important thing is to encourage and to reward creative effort. If you wait to reward creative results you will get less effort. If you get lots of effort then you will, in time, get results.

I have considered here some of the main uses of creative thinking. It could have been simpler to say that wherever there is a need for thinking then there is also a need for creativity. This is not quite good enough, because there are occasions, as with improvement and opportunity design, where there is no apparent "need" for thinking unless we choose to set up that need. No one is forced to look for an opportunity until it is too late. No one is forced to make improvements until it is almost too late.

Fortunately, the thinking culture of business and some other organizations is now beginning to change. I was once told by the chief executive of a very large organization that he was very happy when there were no "problems" in any of his divisions. Today the mood is changing from purely reactive thinking to proactive thinking. This requires creativity.

PART 2

Lateral Thinking Tools and Techniques

The Six Thinking Hats

How do you get time for creative thinking?

How can you ask someone to make some creative effort?

How do you stop someone from being persistently negative?

How do you encourage people to look at the benefits of an idea?

How do you express your intuition and gut feeling in a serious meeting?

The six thinking hats method is extremely simple but it is powerful simplicity.

There was a breakfast meeting in Tokyo to launch the Japanese translation of the book *Six Thinking Hats*.* At this meeting were the chief executives of some of the best known Japanese corporations, including Mr. Hisashi Shinto, who was chief executive of NTT (Nippon Telephone and Telegraph). He had just been chosen as Japanese businessman of the year for his feat in privatizing this giant organization. At that time NTT had 350,000 employees and in stock market valuation was worth more than the top five U.S. corporations put together. Mr. Shinto liked the idea of the six hats and asked his executives to read the book. I met him again six months later and he told me the method had had a powerful effect on his executives who were now more creative and more constructive. He asked me to give a talk to his board and also to the top managers in NTT.

In 1990, IBM used the six hat method as part of the core of their training for their 40,000 managers worldwide. The method is widely used by Du Pont, Prudential, and many other major corporations. It is used because it is practical and makes a difference.

The method is fully described in the book *Six Thinking Hats,* and instruction in the training of the method is also available.†

---

*Little, Brown, New York, 1986, and also ICCT, New York. Published in London by Penguin Books.

†For training in the method please contact Kathy Myers, APT/T, Fax (515) 278-2245.

For the sake of completeness I shall give a simple overview of the method here.

WHITE HAT

Think of white paper, which is neutral and carries information.
The white hat has to do with data and information.

What information do we have here?

What information is missing?

What information would we like to have?

How are we going to get the information?

When you ask for white hat thinking at a meeting you are asking those present to put aside the proposals and arguments and to focus directly on the information. For the moment everyone at the meeting looks to see what information is available, what is needed, and how it might be obtained.

RED HAT

Think of red and fire and warm.
The red hat has to do with feelings, intuition, hunches, and emotions.
In a serious meeting you are not supposed to put forward your emotions, but people do this by disguising their emotions as logic.
The red hat gives people permission to put forward their feelings and intuitions without apology, without explanation, and without any need to justify them.

. . . Putting on my red hat, this is what I feel about the project.

. . . My gut-feeling is that it will not work.

. . . I don't like the way this is being done.

. . . My intuition tells me that prices will fall soon.

Because the red hat "signals" feelings as such, they can come into the discussion without pretending to be anything else. Intuition may be a composite judgment based on years of experience in the field and may be very valuable even if the reasons behind the intuition cannot be spelled out consciously. It should also be said that intuition is not always right, and it can be wrong.

It is sometimes valuable to get feelings out into the open.

BLACK HAT

Think of a stern judge wearing black robes who comes down heavily on wrong-doers.

The black hat is the "caution" hat.

The black hat prevents us from making mistakes, doing silly things, and doing things which might be illegal.

The black hat is for critical judgment.

The black hat points out why something cannot be done.

The black hat points out why something will not be profitable.

... The regulations do not permit us to do that.

... We do not have the production capacity to meet that order.

... When we tried a higher price the sales fell off.

... He has no experience in export management.

Mistakes can be disastrous. No one wants to make mistakes or do silly things. So the black hat is very valuable. It is the most used hat and possibly the most useful hat.

At the same time it is very easy to overuse the black hat. Some people feel that it is enough to be cautious and negative and that if you prevent all mistakes then everything will be fine. It is easy to kill creative ideas with early negativity. Wine is fine but overuse of alcohol can turn you into an alcoholic. It is the same with the black hat. The hat is very valuable but overuse of it can be a problem.

YELLOW HAT

Think of sunshine.

The yellow hat is for optimism and the logical positive view of things.

79

The yellow hat looks for feasibility and how something can be done.

The yellow hat looks for benefits—but they must be logically based.

> ... This might work if we moved the production plant nearer to the customers.

> ... The benefit would come from repeat purchases.

> ... The high cost of energy would make everyone more energy efficient.

The black hat is much more natural than the yellow hat because we need to avoid mistakes and danger for survival. Yellow hat thinking often requires a deliberate effort. Benefits are not always immediately obvious and we might have to search for them. Every creative idea deserves some yellow hat attention.

GREEN HAT

Think of vegetation and rich growth.

The green hat is for creative thinking.

The green hat is for new ideas.

The green hat is for additional alternatives.

The green hat is for putting forward possibilities and hypotheses.

The green hat covers "provocation" and "movement" (to be described later).

The green hat requests creative effort.

> ... We need some new ideas here.

> ... Are there any additional alternatives?

> ... Could we do this in a different way?

> ... Could there be another explanation?

The green hat makes it possible to ask directly for a creative effort. The green hat makes time and space available for creative thinking. Even if no creative ideas are forthcoming, the green hat asks for the creative effort.

Think of the sky and an overview.

The blue hat is for process-control. The blue hat thinks about the thinking being used.

The blue hat sets the agenda for thinking.

The blue hat suggests the next step in the thinking.

The blue hat can ask for other hats.

The blue hat asks for summaries, conclusions, and decisions.

The blue hat can comment on the thinking being used.

... We have spent far too much time looking for someone to blame.

... Could we have a summary of your views?

... I think we should take a look at the priorities.

... I suggest we try some green hat thinking to get some new ideas.

The blue hat is usually used by the chairperson or the organizer of the meeting, but other participants can put forward suggestions. The blue hat is for organizing and controlling the thinking process so that it becomes more productive. The blue hat is for thinking about thinking.

INSTEAD OF ARGUMENT

The Western tradition of argument insists that we try to move forward by means of position taking and argument. "A" has a point of view and "B" disagrees. The ensuing argument is supposed to give adequate exploration of the subject. Too often the protagonists get locked into their positions and become more interested in winning or losing the argument than in exploring the subject.

The six hats method allows us to get right away from argument in order to get more productive discussions. Both "A" and "B" can wear the black hat at the same time to find out the dangers. Both "A" and "B" can wear the yellow hat to explore the benefits. Both "A" and "B" can wear the green hat to open up possibilities. Instead of adversarial thinking there is cooperative exploration. That is why the method has been so eagerly taken up by those who have to run meetings. At last there is a way of breaking free from the traditional argument system.

EGO AND PERFORMANCE

Usually ego and performance in thinking are too closely bound together. Someone who does not like an idea will not make any effort to find points in favor of the idea—and the other way around. The hat method separates ego from performance. The thinker is challenged to use the different hats and actually experiences a sense of freedom because the thinker is no longer limited to one position.

A person who does not like an idea will now make an effort under the yellow hat to find some benefits. A person who is enthusiastic about an idea will be asked to look at the difficulties under the black hat. With the hats, quite often the thinker comes up with insights that change his or her opinion in the matter.

PERSISTENT NEGATIVITY

Some people are cautious by nature and feel that at every moment they have to put forward the possible dangers. In a normal discussion there is nothing to stop a person being persistently negative. With the hat system there is ample opportunity to be negative at the right moment (under the black hat) but at other times negativity is out of place. In this way the natural dominance of the black hat is reduced.

If a person is being negative, you say, "That is good black hat thinking; let us have some more of it." Then after a while you say, "We have had a lot of black hat thinking—now let's try some green hat thinking." The black hat wearer must now keep quiet or make a green hat effort.

SPACE FOR POSITIVE AND CREATIVE THINKING

The yellow and green hats make it possible to allocate time for deliberative creative effort and also a positive effort. I have seen Ron Barbaro, president of Prudential, listen to someone telling him why something cannot be done. After a while Ron would say: "Now for the yellow hat."

It is not natural to allow time for creativity. It is not natural to allow time for positive thinking unless we happen to like the idea. But once we do make the deliberate effort, this effort can be well rewarded. The natural flow of thinking and discussion allows insufficient time for creative effort (unless an idea immediately comes to mind) and insufficient time for a positive effort.

GAME

The more you invest in the six hats method as a "game" the more powerful the method becomes. People feel very foolish if they are seen not to be playing the game. If everyone is making a yellow hat effort then the person who comes out with some black hat comment feels out of place. If you invest in the game (using the hat colors) when you do not really need it then the method is available for use when you do really need it: fierce arguments, crises, conflicts, dogmatic views, and so on.

NOT CATEGORIES

It is perfectly true that some people are much better at one type of thinking than another. It is perfectly true that some people are much more comfortable with one type of thinking rather than another. But I want to emphasise very strongly that the hats are not categories or descriptions. I do not want someone considering himself "the black hat thinker in this group." I do not want someone considering herself "the green hat thinker in this group." That is exactly the opposite of the purpose of the six hats. Everyone must make an "effort" to use all of the hats. When a group is doing green hat thinking then everyone is "wearing" the green hat at that time. If a person chooses to keep quiet at all times other than when his or her favorite hat is in use then that person can be asked directly for some "green hat views" or "yellow hat views."

It is only too easy to see the hats as categories. They are categories of thinking behavior, but not of people. Just as every golfer needs to attempt to use all clubs, so every thinker must attempt to use all six hats.

OCCASIONAL USE

The most frequent use of the hats is the "occasional" use. This means that you ask for one hat at a time. This is to request a

83

certain type of thinking or to change out of a certain type of thinking. Before the use of the hat there is a normal discussion and after the use of the hat there is again normal discussion. A single hat is used as a convenient way to switch thinking. You can ask another person to put on or take off a particular hat. You can announce that you are putting on a particular hat ("Putting on my black hat, these are the difficulties I foresee"). You can ask a whole group to put on a particular hat ("I think it is time we had some green hat thinking. We need some new ideas").

The great virtue of the six hat method is that you can switch thinking immediately and without offense. If you tell someone to stop being "so negative" that person is likely to be offended. But if you ask that person to "try the yellow hat" then there is no offense.

After a while the six hats become part of corporate culture and are used freely and automatically to ask for different types of thinking.

SYSTEMATIC USE

There are times when a group, or an individual, wants a quick exploration of a subject. This can be done by putting together a formal sequence of the hats and then going through them, one by one, spending about four minutes on each hat.

There is no one correct sequence because the sequence will vary with the subject, whether it has been considered before, and who is doing the thinking. There are some formal guidelines that may help to select the sequence. For example, it is useful to use the black hat towards the end to seek out difficulties and dangers and to see whether the proposed idea is viable. This should then be followed with the red hat, which allows someone to say: "In its present form this idea will not work, but I still feel the idea has potential. So let us try to find a way of making it work." This allows a "feeling" to prevent total dismissal of an idea that in its present form is not usable. These guidelines would only be confusing at this point because readers would be forever trying to remember the correct sequence. The guidelines are more properly given in the formal training on the use of the six thinking hats.* For practical purposes it is enough to agree

*For training please contact Kathy Myers, APT/T, Fax (515) 278-2245.

on a sequence that seems sensible and then to use it. This gives good results.

I shall be returning to the six hats method in the Applications part of the book.

The Creative Pause

Unless there is some obstacle, gap, or hold-up, thinking and action flow along smoothly. The brain works to make life easy by making things routine. We form patterns of thinking and behavior and then we use these patterns. This makes good survival sense and the brain does an excellent job of what it is supposed to do.

Creative attitudes and motivation can be built up by exhortation, by praising the wonderful results of creativity, by showing examples, and by general inspiration. Creative attitudes can also be established in a more reliable manner with such simple techniques as the "creative pause."

CREATIVE EFFORT

At various points in this book I have emphasized the importance of asking for creative "effort." The green hat is a formal way of asking for creative "effort" during a meeting. I have suggested that, instead of rewarding creative results, it makes more sense to reward creative effort. You cannot demand that someone have a brilliant idea. But you can demand (request) that a person make a creative effort.

Once the effort is there, results will eventually follow. Once the effort is there, we can add skills to the effort by formal training in lateral thinking techniques.

The creative pause is the simplest of all creative techniques, but it can also be powerful.

The creative pause should become a mental habit for anyone who wants to be creative. The creative pause is the simplest way of making a creative effort.

THE PAUSE

There is no problem. There is no hold-up. But you pause in your thinking solely because you want to. The pause is not in reaction to anything. The pause is the result of your intention to pause.

"There should be a new idea here."

"There could be a new idea here."

"I want to pause to think about this."

If you do not pay attention to something then you are unlikely to think about it. The creative pause is an interruption in the smooth flow of routine in order to pay deliberate attention at some point.

Why stop here? Why not there? Why not everywhere?

There need be no reason at all for stopping at a certain point. It is better that there should be no reason because once you start looking for reasons then you will only pause when there is a reason to pause—that would destroy the whole purpose of the creative pause. It is quite true that there are times when the thinker may sense some possible value or opportunity or may sense that something is being done in a very complicated way. Those are legitimate reasons for a creative pause, but the creative pause should not depend on legitimate reasons. As we shall see in the next section on "focus," some of the best results come when people stop to think about things that no one else has stopped to think about.

The creative pause is very simple, but that does not mean that it is easy to do. It requires a lot of discipline to halt the smooth flow of thought for a creative pause.

MOTIVATION

Which comes first? Do we stop for a creative pause because we are motivated to be creative? Or, do we become motivated to be creative because we develop the deliberate habit of the creative pause? I believe it can work both ways, but there does have to be some initial motivation; otherwise a person would never bother to develop the habit.

I want to emphasize that the "creative pause" is a deliberate process. It is not the result of some sudden inspiration that has to be followed through. You pause because you want to. You pause in order to make a creative effort. You have the intention of being creative.

Hope is an important part of creativity and hope is also related to excitement. You pause because there is the possibility of a new idea if you make the effort to pause. You can walk quickly along the country road or you can pause to look at the wildflowers by the roadside. If you walk quickly along the road you will not notice the wildflowers unless there is a spectacular grouping of them. But if you make the effort to pause and to pay attention to the flowers, you may be rewarded by their simple beauty.

Why should you pause? Why should you hold things up? Why should you waste time in an effort that is likely to be futile? The answer to all these questions lies in an appreciation of the "investment" nature of creativity. You certainly cannot guarantee that every creative pause is going to be productive. But as you continue to invest in creative effort the rewards will start to flow. If you do not make any serious creative effort then it is rather unlikely that you are going to get any new ideas. If you do not spend time gardening you are certainly not going to grow a garden.

Obviously the creative pause should not be allowed to interfere with the main purpose of the thinking or meeting. The pause may be personal: "I wonder if there could be a different way of doing this?" The pause may involve the group: "Let's see if there are any other alternatives." The pause may only be momentary and no one else need even notice.

USE OF THE CREATIVE PAUSE

What happens in the creative pause? How long should the pause be?

There is no need to use any of the systematic tools of lateral thinking in the creative pause. You may look quickly for simple alternatives but that is about all. The main point of the pause is to give attention to something and to place that point in your mind as being worthy of attention. As you become more skilled at creative thinking, even a short pause may suggest a better way of doing things.

If a stream is temporarily blocked, the water may quickly find new channels of flow. Sometimes the mere interruption of the quick flow of thought can open up new lines of thought. The pause as such has a value. The value of the pause is not that it allows us to do things during that pause. If you pause when eating then you will savor the taste of what you are eating. If you pause in thinking then you will attend more closely to the point at which you pause. If you pause at a road junction you can read the signposts. If you drive past the junction at high speed then you will have no idea where the side roads may lead.

There are some occasions when it is important to think quickly but there are also occasions when it is much better to think slowly. Creativity is one of the occasions where thinking slowly is an advantage. As with driving slowly, you can notice things, you can pay attention to things. Instead of being obsessed only with the ultimate destination, you can examine the way you are getting there and note the possibility of different routes.

The pause should not be long. Nor should you cudgel your brains in a determined effort to come up with a new idea. You just pause to think and to wonder for a moment (perhaps twenty to thirty seconds as an individual and two minutes as a group) and then you move on. You can always return to the point later if you wish. There is no pressure to get an instant result. The creative pause is an end in itself. In fact, it is better not to strive too hard at each creative pause, because then the pauses will become burdensome and you will be less inclined to make them. The pauses should be almost casual. It is almost like saying, "That is interesting," and then moving along.

Although the creative pause involves both focus and intention, there is a clear distinction between the simple creative pause and the picking out of an important focus area followed by a determined and systematic attempt to generate new concepts. The deliberate definition of a focus and the sustained application of creative effort (whether or not the systematic tools of lateral thinking are involved) is a different order of magnitude.

Even as you listen to someone talking you can be making creative pauses or creative "attention points" with regard to what is being said.

PROACTIVE

So much of our thinking is reactive: responding to requests, solving problems, overcoming difficulties. There is little time for any other thinking and less motivation to give ourselves additional thinking tasks. The creative pause is an important proactive thinking habit. It is a brief pause in which the thinker says:

"I want to notice that."

"I want to pay attention to that."

"That needs thinking about."

"Is there another possibility here?"

"Is that the only way of doing it?"

If a person or an organization puts any value on creativity then that value justifies the proactive creative pause. The pause is a simple technique. The pause is a way of building up a creative attitude. The pause is a way of turning creative attention into a habit. The pause is a concrete way of showing creative effort, at least to yourself if not to others. The creative pause is an investment in creativity and an investment in the building up of creative skills.

It is important to realize that the creative pause is a simple and light procedure. It should never be turned into a heavy challenge or demanding task.

Focus

It is said that the outside inventor who invented the Black & Decker "Workmate" made millions from this simple and practical invention. Black & Decker was focusing on its power tools. The inventor focused on a different area: the place for using the tools.

Focus is a very important part of creativity. Focus is a much more important part of creativity than most creative people realize. Some creative people pretend not to believe in focus and just want to scatter ideas around as they occur.

SIMPLE FOCUS

"Focus" is not usually thought of as a creative tool, but it is. What I shall call "simple focus" is a very powerful creative tool.

Mostly we think of creativity as applied to serious problems and difficulties that seem incapable of solution without a creative breakthrough. In such cases, a high degree of creative skill may be needed.

Suppose, however, that you focus on something that no one else has bothered to think about. In such cases, even a very little creative thinking can produce spectacular results. There is no competition. It is virgin territory. There are inventors who succeed by tackling really difficult problems and coming up with the solution that everyone has been seeking. But there are other inventors who pick out areas that no one else has noticed and with a slight improvement develop a significant invention. Seeking out these unusual and unnoticed focus points is a creative technique. We know that concentrated detergents have been a big success because they take up less shelf-space in the store and are 45 percent cheaper to handle. Is there any way of making cereal packets less bulky? What about some easy way of reclosing cereal packets?

While you are eating at the table you choose to focus on the relationship between the cutlery and the plate. There is no problem to be overcome, no difficulty to be solved, no obvious value to be achieved. But you choose to focus on the matter.

You are putting a stamp on an envelope and you choose to focus on that operation. What new ideas might there be? Perhaps an advertising or health message in the space to be covered by the stamp. Perhaps a totally different way of attaching the stamp.

You are drinking from a glass. You focus just on the rim of the glass. Could it be a different shape? Could there be a detachable rim for hygiene purposes?

Lining up to check in at an airport, you focus on the line. How could that time be used for information or entertainment? Perhaps we could start making "silent" movies again for showing on TV in places where additional noise is not acceptable.

You focus on the payment of regular insurance premiums. What new ideas might there be around this operation?

The food is growing cold on your plate. What could be done? What about a hot-wired table cloth to keep plates warm? What other ideas?

These are all minor examples but serve to show that "simple focus" can fasten on any point whatever.

You can choose to focus on the interface or relationship between things, like a person getting in or out of a car.

You can modify something to meet needs better. An inventor developed the variable-speed windshield wiper and eventually made millions from it.

You can break down an operation into small steps and focus on some of these. You take your car in to be serviced. Can anything be done to make certain steps quicker or easier?

There are an infinite number of possible focus points. As with the creative pause, it is up to you. You choose to pause. You choose to focus.

The creative pause and the simple focus are not the same thing, but they do overlap. The creative pause is the willingness to pause during some thinking or discussion to pay creative attention. The simple focus is a deliberate effort to pick out a new focus point. There may be no ongoing thinking. What the two do have in common is the willingness to think about things that do not demand thinking. It is the choice of the creative thinker to pause or focus in this way.

Once a simple focus has been made, it can then be treated in a number of different ways.

1. A simple noting of the focus point for future attention. The putting together of a list of possible focus points is part of

the application of creative thinking and will be considered in the Application section.
2. A preliminary attempt to generate some alternatives and ideas. This is a sort of pretest. If interesting ideas turn up then the matter can be pursued more seriously. This pretest would take about three to five minutes.
3. Serious effort to generate ideas in the defined focus area. This serious attempt would use the formal techniques of lateral thinking.

Once a focus area has been defined, it can then be treated just as seriously as a real problem or a suspected opportunity area. There is no guarantee that the creative effort is going to produce a worthwhile result. There is an investment of time and effort that may have no immediate payoff. It is a matter of the willingness of a person or an organization to allocate resources to this type of investment.

It should be added that the "simple focus" has value as an exercise even if no attempt is made to develop any ideas within that focus area. The mere exercise of setting out to pick unusual focus areas has a high value. This can become a habit in itself even if no further creative action is attempted. In time a person can become very good at finding such focus points. Once the habit is developed then that person can choose to apply formal creative thinking to any chosen focus. In fact, to begin with, it is probably better to develop this habit of picking focus points as an end in itself—without trying to generate ideas. The attempt to generate ideas may lead to disappointment and may slow down the habit.

Skilled focus with a little creative skill is probably better than poor focus with great creative skill. So the importance of focus should not be forgotten—especially as it is relatively easy to develop the focus habit.

SPECIFIC FOCUS

There are two broad types of creative application:

1. *Everyday creativity.* This involves the attitudes, motivation, and habits of creativity. Here creativity becomes part of any person's thinking skill. The formal tools may be used

from time to time. Creativity is applied as required. There is a willingness to look for alternatives and a willingness to look for more alternatives. There is an effort to use the green hat and the yellow hat. The creative pause and the simple focus process are parts of this everyday creativity.

2. *Specific focus.* Here there is a defined focus. The focus may be defined by the individual or group doing the creative thinking or it may have been assigned to that group. These are matters that I shall consider in the Applications section. The important point is that there is a "defined creative task." There is a specific focus. The systematic techniques of lateral thinking are now applied seriously, deliberately, and formally in an effort to generate new concepts and new ideas.

This is the specific focus. We now need new ideas.

There are some creative people who have a high degree of creative skill but do not know where to apply this skill.

I am creative. What shall I be creative about?

There are other creative people who feel that a tightly defined focus will limit their thinking and so prefer to operate without a specific focus and to rely on inspiration.

In my seminars I have found that executives and others can pick up the formal techniques of lateral thinking quite easily but that they find it very difficult to pick out a creative focus. This is usually done in a weak and feeble way. Yet creative skill without focus is not very powerful. I suspect that the difficulty is that most thinking people have been trained to "react" to problems and difficulties. The problems present themselves and then you may try different ways of describing or defining the problem. But when there is no problem and nothing to react to then there is also nothing to look at.

The ability to pick and to define a creative focus is an essential part of the skill of creative thinking.

In order to simplify the focus procedure I have simplified the "types" of focus down to just two:

1. General-area-type focus
2. Purpose-type focus

This is an extremely important type of creative focus but, surprisingly, it is not well known. This is because most people have been trained to think only in terms of a defined purpose or objective. In fact, thinking is often treated as synonymous with "problem solving." This means that creative thinking is very limited in its scope. That is why there is a need for "general-area focus" and a need to emphasize the usefulness of this type of focus.

General-area focus is so easy and so obvious that most people find it difficult to understand. With general-area focus we simply define the general area in which we want some new ideas.

> I want some new ideas in the area of restaurants.
>
> I want some new ideas in the area of telephones.
>
> I want some new ideas in the area of the transfer of funds between banks.

The general-area type of focus does not put a purpose on the thinking. The only purpose is to generate ideas within a defined area. As soon as a purpose is included then it ceases to be a general area type focus. The general area may be broad or it may be very tight.

> I want some ideas in the area of running a resort hotel.
>
> I want some ideas on the color of the bedside table in each hotel room.
>
> I want some ideas in the area of messages left for guests at the hotel.

There are several reasons why we need a "general-area-type focus." The first reason is that this type of focus allows us to think creatively about anything at all. There does not need to be any problem or difficulty. There does not need to be any sense of potential benefit. You just choose to think creatively in a defined area. This doubles the scope of creative thinking. Instead of being confined to problem solving, it can be used absolutely anywhere.

The second reason is that the definition of a purpose or objective can preset the sort of ideas we might have. Contrast:

> We need ideas to reduce the cost of cabin service in airplanes.
>
> We need some ideas in the area of cabin service in airplanes.

95

With the first type of focus our thinking is limited to ways of reducing the cost of cabin service because we have predetermined the value of such a reduction. This is a perfectly valid task for creative thinking. In the second case we may come up with some ideas that can be used to reduce the cost of cabin service but we may also come up with ideas that so increase the value of cabin service that the increased cost is worthwhile. In fact there may even be ideas in which cabin service becomes a profit center rather than a cost center.

It is important to be on guard so that "problems" do not disguise themselves as "general-area-type focuses."

We need some ideas in the general area of absenteeism.
We need some ideas in the general area of speeding up check-in.

Both these are really purpose-type focuses. The word "absenteeism" defines a problem. Speeding up check-in indicates an improvement type of focus. It is perfectly possible to treat "absenteeism" as a general-area focus so long as it is clear that the purpose of the thinking is not to reduce absenteeism or overcome the problems caused by absenteeism. That would need to be made clear. It is quite possible that with such a focus we might develop the idea of "undertime" as contrasted with "overtime" which might mean a shorter working week at lower pay when demand was slack.

If there is no given purpose with general-area focus, then how do we get useful ideas?

1. We turn up ideas in the general area that are seen as being useful in their own right. Such ideas offer a value or benefit even though we did not set out to get that value.
2. We examine the ideas that turn up in order to see which ideas offer value in the directions that are of interest to us. We ignore those that do not offer value in these directions.
3. We attempt to see if an idea that has been generated can be shaped or entrained to be of use for a certain purpose.

The fact that the sense of purpose was not present at the beginning does not mean that it cannot be brought in later. We then see which ideas move us toward this purpose.

PURPOSE FOCUS

This is the type of focus with which everyone is most familiar. What is the purpose of our thinking? What are we trying to achieve? What is the goal? What is the target? With what do we want to end up?

Improvement

We can define the creative focus as an attempt to get improvement in a defined direction.

> We want ideas to speed up supermarket check-out.
>
> We want ideas to reduce the cost of staff training.
>
> We want ideas for simplifying the controls on this VCR.
>
> We want ideas to reduce the wastage of food in the restaurant.

If the direction of improvement is not defined then the focus becomes very similar to a general area focus:

> We want ways of improving customer service.

In practice this general type of focus would be broken down into subtasks. For each subtask there might be defined a direction for improvement.

Problem Solving

We have to solve a problem or overcome a difficulty. We know that we want to end up without the problem or difficulty.

> How can we reduce the losses due to shoplifting?
>
> We need ideas to prevent condensation on bathroom walls.
>
> How can we deal with street violence?
>
> We need ideas to reduce the noise from the transmission unit.

Some of these may sound like "improvements" because of words like "reduce." This is because we would really like to remove the problem completely but do not think that would be possible. There can also be a genuine overlap between improvement and problem solving. The main difference is that in problem solving a difficulty is defined, whereas in improvement a change in a general direction (cost, time, and so on) is desired.

Task

With a task, it is not just a matter of removing a problem but of reaching a desired point.

> I want to design a flat refrigerator.
>
> I want a way of communicating with 5,000 trainers out there.
>
> We need to get some highly skilled computer programmers.
>
> We want some powerful slogan to help us get elected.
>
> We need a chocolate that does not melt in the desert.

Again we see some overlap with problems. For example, we might consider the melting of chocolate in the desert as a problem to be overcome. In practice the philosophical distinction between the types of purpose is neither watertight nor so important. Too often it will depend on what wording is used ("We need to overcome the problem of chocolate melting at desert temperatures").

Opportunity

Here there is a sense of potential and opportunity. Opportunities can easily be tackled as general area focus: "We need some ideas in this opportunity area of high scenic beauty."

> How can we use this glue that never dries?
>
> People cannot afford to keep up large houses any more—can we see an opportunity there?
>
> Satellite TV transmission is getting cheaper—what opportunities can we see?
>
> There is a glut of grapes in Bulgaria this year.

Although the philosophical distinction between the different types of purpose is not watertight, there can be a value in expressing a type of purpose directly as part of the definition of the creative focus or task. This makes clear how we are looking at it and what our intentions might be.

With "purpose-type focus" we should not be timid about expressing a purpose explicitly. If we feel that this might limit or direct our creative thinking then we have two choices. We can either switch to a general-area-type focus. Or, we can put up alternative definitions of the purpose and also work with these.

I want some ideas to solve the problem of overbooking on aircraft due to no-show passengers.

I want ideas to improve the speed with which we handle insurance claims.

The task is to find a partner in Hungary. We need some ideas on how to do that.

This elastic fiber with wonderful stretch qualities should offer interesting opportunities. What might these be?

It does not matter if the inclusion of the type of purpose makes the focus seem rather formal. So much the better.

FOCUS OCCASIONS

We have looked at the types of focus and now can consider, briefly, focus occasions.

1. *Defined need or purpose*. There is a specific assigned purpose or task. This provides a clear occasion for the use of creative thinking. The task may be self-selected by an individual or group or may have been assigned.
2. *Routine review*. Here there is no specific task or problem. There is the intention to rethink some process or procedure. This procedure can be divided up into convenient attention areas and convenient focuses. Creative thinking is applied to each of these in turn. Any existing procedure can be treated in this way. The focus type may be both general area and also purpose type.
3. *Idea-sensitive point (i.s.p.)*. The word "sensitive" indicates that a new idea at this point would have a very significant effect. Sensitive steering in a car means that a small turn on the wheel produces a big change in direction. Sensitive photographic film means that it responds to even a little light. So we set out to find those points which would respond to a change in idea or concept. This search is an operation in itself. When we have found what seems to be an idea-sensitive point then we try to develop new ideas at that point. This differs from "Review" inasmuch as with review there is no special sense that a new idea will make a huge difference. We review something simply because it is there. (Note: I used to refer to this as an idea-sensitive

99

"area" but have since changed the word to idea-sensitive "point" to avoid confusion with general-area focus).

4. *Whim.* This relates to creative pause and simple focus. This relates to the investment side of creative thinking. From time to time we may focus on something for no reason at all than that we want to focus on that thing. In essence we want to be able to focus on things when there is no good reason for doing so. In this way we might be able to focus on matters that other people have not attended to.

MULTIPLE FOCUSES

We can choose to tackle a broad focus as such or choose to break it down into multiple subfocuses or subtasks.

We need some new ideas about bus services.

I want to break this down into: equipment, traffic control, scheduling, market, peak problems, driver training, configuration of the buses, and so on.

When breaking down a broad focus into multiple smaller focuses, it is possible to follow the general lines of analysis. But there is no need to follow the strict divisions of analysis. In fact, it is better if the focuses overlap considerably than if they are completely separate. The difference between separate and overlapping focuses is shown in Figure 2.1. For example, under the broad focus of "bus service" there might be such focuses as "comfort" and "convenience." Obviously these overlap with such focuses as "configuration" and "scheduling." This does not matter at all because different ideas will come up under the different headings.

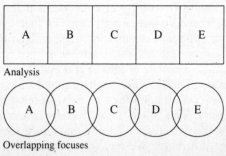

Analysis

Overlapping focuses

Figure 2.1

Just as it is useful to redefine problems and to set up alternative definitions of the problem, so it is also useful to consider alternative definitions of a creative focus.

We want ideas in the area of hotel management.

We want ideas in the area of the relationship between hotel management and the staff.

We want ways of assessing the quality of hotel management.

We want ideas to make hotel management less dependent on highly skilled managers.

We want ideas to set up a foolproof semiautomatic management system.

We want ways of involving all staff in the management function.

We want ideas on how we can build up a strong management team that all work together.

All these definitions are related to hotel management but the emphasis is different in each case. The definitions are not equivalent to each other. From such a list of alternative focus definitions, the group can choose which ones to use.

In any situation there is a value in compiling such a list of alternative focus definitions.

REPHRASING THE FOCUS

Anyone involved in teaching knows the importance of choosing words very carefully. One choice of words can encourage thinking in one direction and a slightly different choice of words can lead to a very different direction of thinking. Some phrasing can be ambiguous.

I want ways of reducing the paperwork.

This focus may elicit suggestions of E-mail and forms of communication that do not use paper. But if the real intention was to reduce the amount of items that need to be read and stored,

101

then simply shifting the communications from paper to electronic systems may not reduce the "reading load."

I want to reduce executives' reading load.

If this had been phrased as:

I want to reduce communication between executives.

then this would have caused some alarm because communication is seen as important.

Perhaps it could have been phrased:

I want ideas to reduce unnecessary communication between executives.

These are not so much alternative definitions but the use of alternative words: "paperwork," "reading load," "communication," "unnecessary communication."

Time spent on a careful choice of words is time well spent.

THE UNDERLYING PROBLEM

Sometimes in my seminars I invite participants to consider improving the design of an umbrella. There are usually some people in the audience who have had some experience with creativity. Such people are very reluctant to improve the design of the umbrella. Instead they want to consider the underlying problem of "protection from the rain." This may end up with a consideration of raincoats or even a new type of town design where there are arcades everywhere and umbrellas are no longer required. This may not be much use to the maker of umbrellas who is looking for an improved design.

Sometimes it is certainly necessary and useful to broaden the focus definition and to move towards "the underlying problem." This is a very useful habit.

We don't need drills—we just need holes.

Why do we need holes in the first place? Perhaps there are better forms of attachment, like super-bonding agents.

Nevertheless, there are times when we do need to focus on the focus point that is actually placed before us. To always refuse to

tackle the immediate problem in favor of some deeper problems
does not make sense. There is a need to be able to do both: to seek the underlying problem but also to deal with the focus as presented.

HOW MUCH INFORMATION?

How much information should be given along with the creative focus? There are those who demand more and more information in the hope that analysis applied to a mass of information will provide an answer without any need for creative thinking.

The creative focus itself should not carry much information. Background information should be available as required and requested.

The points I made about the creativity of innocence also apply here. Too much information bogs down creative thinking and leads back to existing ideas. It is usually better to deal with the matter at a level of "innocence." That is to say to deal with it in terms of concepts and principles. Once some ideas have started to emerge then it can be useful to feed in more information to see if these new concepts can be applied. It may be that some innovative concept is actually rendered useless by an existing regulation. But it is better to risk such wastage rather than just to shuffle information around in the hope that this will provide the new ideas.

Challenge

There is something very special about "the creative challenge."

Why is it done this way?

Why does it have to be done this way?

Are there other ways of doing it?

The first point about which it is important to be very clear is that the creative challenge is totally different from the critical challenge. The critical challenge sets out to assess ("critical" comes from the Greek "kritikos", which means *judge*) whether the current way of doing something is adequate. The critical challenge is a judgment challenge. We might set out to show that something is faulty or inadequate and then set about improving or changing the way something is done. This is normal improvement behavior.

The creative challenge does not set out to criticize, judge, or find fault. The creative challenge operates outside of judgment. The creative challenge is a challenge to "uniqueness."

No matter how excellent this may be, is it the only way of doing this?

The creative challenge is sometimes referred to as "creative dissatisfaction." In some ways this conveys the notion of not being happy with accepting something as the only possible way, but "dissatisfaction" may also suggest inadequacy.

We like to show that something is inadequate in order to give ourselves a reason for thinking of a better alternative. Without such a reason we do not feel justified in looking for a different idea. If something is fine, why look for a better way of doing it? This sort of guilt is all part of the negative orientation of Western thinking that I have mentioned so often.

Why is it important to be clear that the creative challenge is not a criticism? The first point is that if the challenge were a criticism then we should only be able to challenge those things that seemed inadequate. This would seriously limit the range of application of creativity. The second point is that if we could

104

not make a convincing case of inadequacy then we would be unable to suggest looking for other ideas. The third point is that attack engenders defense. If we set out to attack something, then others will rush to defend the existing way of doing things. A lot of unnecessary time is used in attack and defense. Even worse, there will be a polarization between those who defend the status quo and those who seem to be attacking it. So it is much better to avoid judgment and to indicate that there is no attack on the status quo but just an exploration of other possibilities. Such possibilities would never replace the existing methods unless the new ideas could be clearly shown to be superior.

The usual Western sequence is: attack and criticize, then set out to look for an alternative. The non-Western sequence is: acknowledge the existing, seek possible alternatives, and then compare the alternatives with the existing method.

There is often a supposition that the current way of doing things must be the best for the following reasons: the current method has survived over time and been tested by time; the current method has been in use for some time and so the faults have been removed; the current method is the result of a process of evolution, which has eliminated competing methods; the current method was selected from amongst many possibilities as the best method; the current method would have been replaced if it had not been the best method. So there is a sort of tacit agreement that unless proved otherwise the current way of doing things is very likely to be the best way of doing them.

The creative challenge simply refuses to accept that the current way is necessarily the best way. The creative challenge assumes that the current way is just one way which happens to be there for a variety of reasons. London taxis are of a peculiar shape because there is a law that there must be enough height for a passenger to wear a top hat. Some countries drive on the right hand side of the road because at the time of the French revolution, aristocrats left their carriages at home and chose to walk with pedestrians on the right hand side of the road.

Imagine that different ways of doing things are inscribed on slips of paper, which are put in a bag. Someone draws out a slip of paper, quite by chance, and that becomes the established way of doing things. Clearly this is a gross exaggeration, but it is a useful image to hold as a background to the creative challenge. In the creative challenge we assume that the current way of doing things is just one of many possible ways.

The creative challenge is usually expressed as "why."

Why do we do things in this way?

To some extent the creative challenge is interested in the reasons that might be given in answer to the "why" of the question. But these reasons are not essential. We may not know the reasons why something is done in a particular way. The reasons may be poor or the reasons may be good. The reasons may have made sense at one time but no longer today (like the top hat in the taxi).

Why are plates round?

Because at one time plates were made on a potter's wheel and this produces round objects.

Because people have become used to plates being round.

Because it is much easier to set them on a table because it does not matter in what orientation they are.

The last explanation is probably quite minor. The potter's wheel explanation is probably valid. But today many plates are not made on a potter's wheel but by compressing ceramic dust in a mold. So plates could just as easily be made in any shape.

There is no point in doing historic research to try to answer the "why" in the challenge. The actual explanations can be useful but they are not essential. If no explanation is forthcoming we still proceed to look for other ways of doing things.

The "why" is not only asking for explanations but also asking "why" it has to be the only way.

THE NEXT STEP

Once we have made the creative challenge then we move on to the next step. This is the search for alternative ways of doing things. There are three elements here. Each of them is illustrated in Figure 2.2.

1. *Block.* If we block the current path, road, or way of doing things then we are forced to find an alternative way.

Suppose we could no longer do it this way—how should we do it?

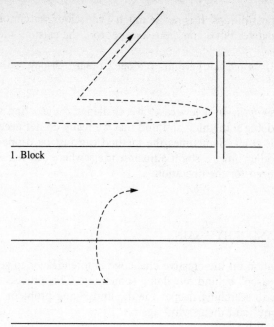

1. Block

2. Escape

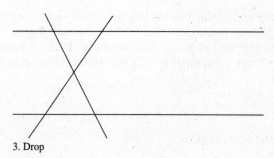

3. Drop

Figure 2.2

We proceed with a search for direct alternatives. This process will be described in more detail in the section on alternatives.

2. *Escape*. Here the emphasis is on escape. If we escape from some dominating idea or from the necessity to satisfy some condition then our minds are freed up to consider other

107

possibilities. It is not so much a conscious search for alternatives but a conscious escape from the existing method.

If we did not have to keep our customers happy, what could we do?

3. *Drop it.* In a few cases we challenge the existing way of doing something and find that we really do not need to do it at all. Sometimes the method can just be dropped. At other times a slight adjustment elsewhere can remove the need for the operation.

WHY AND WHY AGAIN

A variation on the creative challenge is to endeavor to seek the "real reason" behind our doing something. This process is very similar to searching deeper for the underlying problem. So we ask "why" and then "why" again.

Why do you have to fill in this form?
So that the manager can know what is going on.
Why does the manager need to know what is going on?
So that she can allocate resources as needed.

At the end of this process you may think of another method for allocating resources. The method has a value in untangling complicated bureaucratic procedures. It also relates to the "lock-in" type of continuity that will be described later in this section.

CONTINUITY ANALYSIS

Why do we do things as we do?
There are a number of possible answers to that question.

1. Because it was the best way of doing things and it still is the best way of doing things.
2. Because we have considered changing to a better way but the cost of change and the disruption of change are such that on balance we have chosen to stay with this way.

3. Because we have always done it this way and there has never been any need, any occasion, or any pressure for change.

The third answer brings in the notion of "continuity." Things continue because they continue. There are many possible reasons for continuity and I shall only consider four of them here.

The Continuity of Neglect

We continue to do things in a certain way simply because we have neglected to think about them. We have never looked to see if there might be a better way. Why have we neglected to think about the matter? Because the matter was never a problem and never presented any difficulty, so there was no reason to give it thinking time or thinking attention.

Our thinking is so problem-driven that if something is not a problem we do not think about it. There is the famous and very dangerous saying:

> If it ain't broke, don't fix it.

By itself, this saying was largely responsible for the decline of U.S. industry. Managers would think only of fixing their problems. Fixing the problems would, at best, bring them back to where they had been before the problem. Meanwhile, competitors like the Japanese were making changes at points that were not problems. Soon the problem fixers found that they were being left behind.

That is why in this book I have so repeatedly emphasized the need to look at things that are not problems (creative pause, simple focus, general area focus, creative challenge, and so on).

For about 40 years a direction change in a car would be indicated by an artificial arm that rose from the side of the car to imitate the direction indicating arm of the driver in early cars. This was not a very efficient way of indicating a direction change. But it continued because it was not a problem so no one bothered to look at it. Eventually there came a change to flashing lights. This change did not depend on any technical breakthrough but on someone bothering to look at the matter.

The Continuity of Lock-in

"Lock-in" means we do something because we have to satisfy someone else or fit in with some other requirements. Just as a

109

tent is tethered by tent-poles, so our behavior is fixed by the other parties that we have to satisfy.

There is an important aspect of "lock-in" that concerns other parties who were originally a help. In the early seventies, the U.S. auto makers started to make compact cars. The dealers did not like them and urged the makers to go back to full-sized cars. Then came the second OPEC oil price rise. The makers were locked into the dealers and were reluctant to go back to the smaller cars. This left the field clear for the Japanese imports, which established the foothold on which they have built.

When Coca-Cola announced "New Coke" they did not realize how strongly they were locked in to the expectations of the American public. Consumers of Coke welcomed the changes in taste, of which there had been several in the past. But they did not like being told that "traditional" Coke was being changed.

An organization sets up its computer department. After a while this department comes to run the whole organization. Certain changes are not possible because the system cannot cope, etc. The organization is locked into its DP structure and the DP structure may itself be locked into a certain architecture that is no longer up to date.

Declining organizations are locked into their loyal customers. They dare not change because they may upset their loyal customers and so decline faster. Because they are unable to change they cannot recover from the decline.

Organizations may be locked into their own strengths. A maker of bathroom fittings may have a superior technology in ceramics and may therefore be reluctant to venture into acrylics.

Artists get locked into their styles and their reputations.

Often "lock-in" is genuine and there may be no escape. For example, an architect is locked into building regulations. Sometimes the lock-in is treated more seriously than it need be. With early typewriters the mechanical arms would jam if two letters were hit in too rapid a sequence. So the classic QWERTY keyboard was designed to "slow down" typing. Today there is no jamming problem, but we are locked into the traditional keyboard because that is the way typists learned to type. I see no reason why there could not be the classic keyboard for those who had learned to type on it and a modern ergonomic board for those who learned to type today. A simple switch on the computer would allow either keyboard to be plugged in.

When a concept works and works, quite understandably, we come to believe that the idea is going to work forever. When things go wrong we never challenge the central concept but look for all sorts of peripheral reasons why the concept is not working. As a result, ideas that have been successful in the past usually continue long past the point when they could have been changed. At the moment of this writing, in the United States 23 percent of retail sales are through organizations that are in financial trouble. It is possible that the concept of the department store is really a dying concept. Others would argue that there is nothing wrong with the concept and that well-run department stores can still do well (Nordstroms).

When a concept has always done well then a certain sort of complacency surrounds that concept and protects it from further evaluation. IBM has done very well with the mainframe concept but there are some concerns as to whether the concept of distributed processing will seriously erode the mainframe market.

It is said that 70 percent of U.S. health care costs are incurred in the last month of life. This is mainly due to expensive heroic medicine which does not provide any quality of life. But we dare not move away from the concept of "staying alive at all costs."

There comes a time when we need to rethink central concepts no matter how successful they may have been in the past.

The Continuity of Time Sequence

This type of continuity has already been touched upon when I was considering the logical necessity for creativity. The time sequence in which our experience arrives allows that experience to arrange itself into structures, institutions, and concepts. Once established, these have a life of their own. Railways came before airlines, so when airlines started they were regarded as railways flying through the air. Many of the airline concepts are inappropriate railway concepts.

Figure 2.3 illustrates in a visual way how a time sequence of arrival of different shapes sets up a certain structure, which then has to be disrupted in order to make full use of later arriving pieces.

The history of banking set up certain banking concepts and regulations. Today many of the functions of traditional banks are being taken over by other financial institutions. There is an urgent need for the reconceptualization of banks. The time sequence of the medical profession set up professional bodies

111

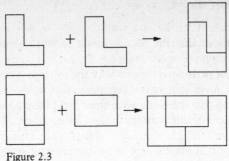

Figure 2.3

which now make it difficult for other medical professions, with lesser training, to develop. For example, there could be surgeons trained in a short time just to carry out a few defined operations very skillfully. The well-being of the patient would be looked after by the anesthetist and an after-care specialist.

The process of continuity analysis is a form of challenge. We look at the way something is being done and try to trace the elements of continuity. We might find examples of lock-in. We might find the influence of time sequence continuity. The purpose of the analysis is to allow us to break free from concepts and ideas that are only there through the process of continuity.

BREAKING FREE

We seek to break free from old concepts that are only there by reason of continuity. Concepts and ideas that might have made sense at one time may no longer be necessary and may not make sense now.

Technology Change

New technology, such as computers or easy air transport, may render some concepts obsolete as well as opening up the possibility of new concepts. Fax machines allow rapid communication.

Value Change

People drink less and smoke less. Concern for the environment is a new value. The place of women in society has changed. Mass communication through TV and recordings means that values are more uniform around the world. Travel has brought about marked changes in food tastes.

Circumstance Change

Changes in the former USSR and Eastern Europe and in Europe itself (EEC) must have an effect on the concepts we need. In most countries families are smaller and more women are at work.

Cost Change

People are becoming more and more expensive. The cost of pollution control is rising. Legal costs are rising.

All these types of change suggest that concepts that were valuable at one time may have now become obsolete. This suggests that continuity analysis and the creative challenge are not luxuries but have become necessities. All concepts need reexamining. Under the new sets of conditions, are there new concepts that would be more appropriate?

There is often a tendency to hope that the difficulties of the moment will pass and that the good old days will come back. It is sometimes difficult to distinguish between a temporary cyclical dip and a fundamental change in the nature of the game.

CONCEPT CHALLENGE AND IDEA CHALLENGE

We can challenge the basic concept behind an operation or we can challenge the particular way in which the concept is put into action (the idea). We might challenge the concept of a city center department store or we may just challenge the location of stores in city centers. In the section that deals with concepts I shall discuss the matter of concepts in detail.

What is the concept here?

Is this concept still valid?

Does the concept have to be carried through in this way?

Faced with mounting traffic congestion, the Singapore government has already challenged the assumed right of a citizen to buy what he or she can afford. You cannot just buy a car in Singapore. You first have to buy the right to buy a car. Should we be challenging the concept of traffic control in cities or the concept of personalized travel in cities? The concept of the free use of roads is being challenged. There are schemes to charge cars according to which roads they use and at what times. Sensors will record a car's passage and a bill will be sent to the driver.

There is no point in just challenging ideas when the fundamental concept behind the ideas needs challenging. At the same time it is wrong to assume that the underlying concept needs changing just because the way it is carried through needs challenging. In England the introduction of the poll tax was one of the causes of the downfall of Margaret Thatcher as prime minister. Was it the concept of the poll tax that was at fault or the way it was carried through?

CHALLENGING THE SHAPING FACTORS

At any moment our thinking is shaped by a number of factors. Sometimes we are aware of these factors and sometimes they are so much in the background that they exert their powerful influence in a hidden way. We can challenge these shaping factors just as we challenge existing methods, concepts, or ideas. But in this case we are not challenging something that already exists. We are challenging the factors and pressures that lead us to think in a certain way.

You may feel that you are free to choose what to put on in the morning when you get dressed. There are, however, background considerations that we take for granted: the sort of clothes you would wear to the office. You could challenge these considerations. That is what we are doing when we challenge the shaping factors of our thinking. We are not just challenging the thinking itself (the choice of clothes) but the background factors that actually limit our thinking (or set the range of choice of clothes).

This type of challenge can take place during a creative session when there is actual thinking about a subject. We stand back and take a look at the thinking itself. We pick out the shaping factors and challenge them.

Dominating Concept

Dominating concepts are very powerful. Sometimes they are obvious but at other times they exert their strong influence from the background.

What concept is dominating our thinking here?

What is the underlying concept that controls our thinking?

For example, in considering the problem of traffic congestion in cities, the dominating concept might be "discouraging motorists from driving into the city." All thinking tends to be along these lines. The concept is a valid one but it may still dominate the thinking.

We challenge the centrality of the concept. Might there be other concepts that should be given a change? Can we look for alternative concepts?

In most problem solving by analysis there is usually the dominating concept of the need to remove the "cause of the problem." This domination often makes it very difficult to think of other approaches.

Assumptions

Without assumptions we would never be able to think at all. Assumptions are based on experience and narrow down the range of possibilities in our thinking. There is absolutely nothing wrong with assumptions, which are most valuable. Nevertheless, it is useful to make ourselves aware of the assumptions so that we can choose to challenge them.

What are the background assumptions?

What are we assuming here?

In the problem of traffic congestion in cities we may be assuming that cars are driven by their owners. We may be assuming that a commuter car is not used for the rest of the day. We may assume that cars park on land (as distinct from being suspended in the air). We assume that all cars must have equal access. There are so many assumptions.

With the challenge we put the assumption aside. We seek to escape from the assumption.

Boundaries

Just as assumptions are essential for thinking, so too are boundaries. We work within the limits of what is feasible, what is permissible, and what is acceptable. If we wish our ideas to be reasonable then we must work within the boundaries of reason established by the present state of our knowledge. As we shall   115 see later the process of "provocation" is a deliberate method of jumping over the boundaries of reasonableness. At this point we are concerned with challenge.

As with assumptions we need to make the boundaries visible in order to challenge them.

What are the boundaries to our thinking?

What boundaries do we come up against?

In the problem of traffic congestion, we quickly come up against the boundaries of cost and of human acceptance. We come up against the boundaries of technology (could we really charge each car for the amount of city road it uses each day?). Then there are the physical boundaries of the existing towns and road layouts.

Sometimes the challenge to boundaries produces extreme ideas that are very like provocations. At other times the boundaries may produce a perfectly usable idea (every person is entitled to use his or her car as a taxi).

Essential Factors

Whatever clever thinking we may do about airlines, the factor of "safety" must always be included. Essential factors must be part of any solution. Usually the inclusion of such essential factors is fully justified. But since it is possible to challenge anything we can also challenge the essential factors.

What are the "essential factors" here?

Why do we always have to include these factors?

In looking at the traffic problem in cities we may feel that an essential factor is "supply of goods to stores." Another essential factor is a system that is "not easy to abuse." Sometimes an essential factor and a dominating concept may become very close. For example, the idea that traffic congestion can only be solved by some sort of "control, rules, or regulation" is both a dominating concept and an essential factor. The need to avoid a harmful environmental effect is, today, often an essential factor in all thinking—including the traffic problem. The need for perceived equality and equity is also usually an essential factor (rich people should not have an advantage over poorer people).

116

Even the most justified essential factors can be the subject of the creative challenge. This will seem difficult at the time.

Avoidance Factors

These are not boundaries since we know that we can use these factors if we wish to. But we spend our time trying to avoid these factors in our thinking. We steer clear of these factors. We shy away from them. We refuse to take any road that seems to lead in the direction of these factors. Sometimes an "essential factor" is no more than the need to "avoid" something (like "avoiding damage to the environment"). We know intuitively that these factors are not acceptable in any solution so we keep right away from them.

What things are we trying to avoid?

What are the things we do not want?

In the traffic problem we may want to avoid making driving in the city so easy that the congestion problem gets worse. We may want to avoid regulations that require a heavy policing effort or ones that will lose votes. We may want to avoid driving business and residents out of the city. We may want to avoid killing the city center.

Turned the other way around, such avoidance factors can become provocations ("Po, we kill the city center"). In the challenge process, however, we simply challenge the need to keep avoiding these factors.

Either/Or Polarizations

Very often in our thinking we are presented, by ourselves or by others, with an either/or polarization.

> We either have to accommodate the traffic or we have to keep cars out of the city.

Such polarizations give an appearance of broad thinking. They may also be very useful and fully justified. But there is a danger in either/or polarizations because they suggest that the situation can only be looked at in these two ways. This excludes in-between approaches or approaches that combine elements of other approaches. The forced separation of the either/or approach is one of its limitations.

117

What are the polarizations here?

What are the either/or approaches that are on offer?

In the traffic congestion problem we may get to the point where the either/or on offer is: "either we improve the flow on existing roads or we build better roads." This is a very reasonable approach, but it can still be challenged.

Because the creative challenge is not an attacking challenge, even the most useful polarizations can be challenged: is this the only way of looking at it?

In all cases of challenge to a shaping factor of our thinking, the process has two steps.

1. Being aware, making conscious and spelling out what the shaping factors seem to be.
2. Challenging those factors—even if they seem eminently sensible and fully justified.

Alternatives

The search for alternatives is the most basic of all creative operations.

Is there another way?

What are the alternatives?

What else can be done?

In some ways creativity can be defined as a search for alternatives. This is especially true when you set out to be creative about something that already exists.

Although the effort to find alternatives is so very basic to creativity, the process is not as easy as most people assume. Where do the alternatives come from? How do we get alternatives when we need them?

STOPPING TO LOOK FOR ALTERNATIVES

I have often repeated the true story of the alarm clock that I could not turn off. Systematically I went step by step through the procedure of turning off a hotel alarm clock that I had set to wake me up early enough to catch a 7:00 A.M. flight. Even when I pulled the electric connection out of the wall, the alarm clock continued its racket. In the end it turned out that the sound was coming from my travel alarm clock, which I had set and forgotten all about.

I tell that story so often because the point it makes is so important. If you are in a situation where the next logical step is easily available then you take that step. You do not look for alternatives. And if the next logical step is also available then you also take that step. In other words, it is extremely difficult to stop to look for alternatives when you do not need them. I had set up the hotel alarm clock and knew the sequence of steps to turn it off. There was no need to look for alternative sources of the sound.

119

When our line of action is clear and there are no hold-ups, then we proceed smoothly along that line without stopping to look for alternatives—because there is no apparent need to look for them.

I was once told by the chief executive of a major corporation how they had lost $800 million in this way. At board level there was the suggestion that the company should get into a certain field. This seemed a sensible suggestion. So they discussed each step. Each step was feasible and sensible. There was no need to look for alternatives. Some years later they had to pull out of the field, losing a great deal of money in the process. According to my informant, there was no consideration of alternative ways of entering the field.

I once spent a long time looking at an immobile cicada wondering how it could make so much noise with so little obvious movement. Only later did I realize that my cicada was actually mute and that there was an active cicada just on the other side of the branch.

It is extremely difficult to stop to look for alternatives when there is no hold-up and when there seems to be no need for alternatives.

This point has already been mentioned in many ways:

Simple focus: the willingness to focus on something that is not a problem in order to find alternative ideas

Creative pause: the pause to look for alternatives even when there is no need

Challenge: the willingness to challenge uniqueness and to see if there might be alternative ways of doing something

Continuity of neglect: things continue to be done in the same way because there was never any reason to look for alternatives

In spite of all this, it still remains difficult to stop to look for alternatives when there is no "need." It seems unnecessary. It seems a waste of time. It seems a luxury. We associated looking for alternatives with problem solving and difficulties.

The Western culture of thinking insists that we show inadequacy or fault before we have the right to seek alternatives. This inadequacy is the only justification for the search for alternatives. So we are into the usual attack/defense of argument with its time wasting and position taking. Because the Japanese never had the argument idiom (derived from the infamous Greek gang of three) they are able to look for alternatives any time they want to without having to show deficiency in anything. They can acknowledge that the present way of doing something is wonderful and yet still look for another way. When other ways are found they are compared with the existing way and if the new ways show no benefit they are not used.

THE ALTERNATIVES ARE PROVIDED

Which tie shall I wear this evening: the blue, the red, the striped one, the white polka dot on blue, the green dragon tie? I look at the tie rack. The alternatives are laid out before me. All I have to do is choose.

There are applicants for a certain job. I need to choose between them. The alternatives are provided. I may, of course, decide that none of the applicants are suitable and may readvertise the position.

I go into a restaurant. The alternatives are offered on the menu. All I need to do is to choose one of the alternatives. It is true that the menu offers the fixed alternatives but there is actually room for further alternatives. I can suggest two half-portions of two different dishes. I can ask if the shrimp can be kept away from the fish because I am allergic to shrimp. So there are some further alternatives if I can think of them and make the effort to ask for them.

A Boy Scout is lighting a fire. No matches are allowed. So what are the alternatives? The scout searches through his own experience and through the instructions given on the survival courses. What about a cigarette lighter? What about friction between two sticks? Might it be possible to focus the rays of the sun? The alternatives are not laid out as clearly as the ties in the rack or the dishes on the menu. There is a need to scan personal experience and to remember some instructions. There is more or less the normal procedure when we set out to find alternatives: we scan experience.

FINDING MORE ALTERNATIVES

When some alternatives are given or are available, why should we make an effort to find more alternatives? Why not just choose

121

from the available alternatives? Why not just assume that the available alternatives represent all possible alternatives (or, at least, the best ones)?

Why waste time in a futile search for even more alternatives?

You are asked to find a hidden spot on a piece of paper. Very sensibly you draw a line dividing the paper into two parts, A and B. You ask if the spot is in A. If it is not in A then it must surely be in B. There is nowhere else it could be. The alternatives of A and B cover all possibilities. Then we proceed to divide B into C and D. And so on. In the end we must find the point because at every moment we have covered all alternatives.

This simple example is actually very dangerous. It leads people to believe that the same procedure can be used in real-life situations.

> Either we raise the prices or we do not.
> We hold our position or we give in to the wage demands.

It is perfectly true that in some situations there are a limited number of alternatives. It is perfectly true that in some situations analysis can reveal the fixed number of alternatives in such closed situations. But most situations are open and there is no fixed number of alternatives. The alternatives we see are only limited by our imagination in designing them.

Once again the word "design" is very important. Too often we think only of "analysis" in finding alternatives. Design suggests that we make an effort to create new alternatives. This can be done by shifting the boundaries of the situation; by introducing new factors; by changing the values; by involving others.

"Either we raise the prices or we do not." We can raise the prices on some items and lower the prices on others. We can raise the basic prices and then give discounts. We can raise the price but give added service. We can totally change the product and set new prices. From a philosophical point of view some of these alternatives could be said to be ways of raising the price. But creativity is not concerned with philosophy as much as producing useful alternatives.

"We hold our position or we give in to wage demands." Clearly we can design many more alternatives. We can introduce the notion of productivity. We can introduce the notion of a shrinkage of the work force through attrition and voluntary redundancy. We can introduce the notion of benefits (such as health care) instead of wage increases. We can think of offering more leisure time instead of more money. We can consider bonus schemes and overtime work. The possibilities are only limited by our imagination.

At first sight the yes/no simplicity of the search for the hidden spot on the paper seems an attractive way of looking for alternatives, but this attraction is misleading. Where it is a matter of search and where the "no" answer has a real value (by closing a possibility) the process is valuable. But in generating ordinary alternatives it achieves nothing except to make a simple process more complex. Consider the Boy Scout with his fire lighting.

> I use matches or I do not.
> If I do not use matches then I could use a lighter or not.
> If I do not use a lighter I could rub sticks together or not.

It is obvious that this is simply a very lengthy way of saying: what are the alternatives here? It is far easier to put these down in a simple list.

In science we are always looking for further alternatives of explanation. No matter how perfect a hypothesis may seem and how fond of the hypothesis we may be, we should be looking for further explanations. The process is open-ended.

In market research, when we are seeking to understand the reason for certain consumer behavior, we have to generate as many possibilities as we can before seeking to test them.

In situations involving action or decision, we cannot sit around forever waiting for the "ultimate" alternative. We have to get on with things. There comes a point when we have to freeze the design in order to get going. The perfect idea is no good if it is too late.

So there has to be an element of practicality. We may need to set a cut-off point. You may decide to spend just one minute considering the possibility of further alternatives. Someone comes to you and says:

> There are only two possible ways of doing this.

You reply: "Maybe you are right, but let's spend one minute seeing if there might be some further alternatives."

It is the intention and effort to find other alternatives that matters in the long run. Where the matter is very serious you might decide to set the cut-off time at one week or even a month. At the end of that time there is a need to decide between the available alternatives.

123

Consider three possibilities:

1. "I can only think of these alternatives, therefore there cannot be any more."
2. "At the moment I can only think of these alternatives but I suggest we spend some time, with a cut-off, searching for further alternatives."
3. "We just have to keep on looking for alternatives."

The first possibility is limiting, arrogant, and most uncreative. The second one is practical. The third one is only possible in certain situations. For example, a police force is always looking for better ways of doing its work.

There is, however, a very practical reason why people are reluctant to even consider the possibility of further alternatives. This is not so much to do with the thinking time involved, because that can be short. If you believe that you have thought of all alternatives, then you can have full confidence in your choice from amongst these. But if you "admit" the possibility of further alternatives, you cannot have this confidence. And if you do not find better alternatives you have lessened the confidence with nothing to show for it. This is a valid practical point—but not valid enough to halt the search beyond the obvious alternatives.

There is a second, less valid, reason why people are disinclined to look for further alternatives.

"If I can usually think of two alternatives and you encourage me to think of four alternatives then you have doubled my work in deciding which one to choose."

This type of remark is often made to me in all seriousness. It is perfectly true that increasing the number of alternatives generated does increase the work needed to choose from amongst them. But the converse is absurd. You would have no decision work at all if you could never think of an alternative. The simple truth is that you cannot improve any decision by impoverishing the choice of alternatives. So you need to be able to generate alternatives and you also need to be able to choose between them.

If you find decision hard then you can be ruthless about it. You can discard any alternative that does not offer benefits that are obviously greater than the existing way of doing things. This may mean that you lose some good ideas that might have proved worthwhile on further scrutiny—but it does mean that you can make the decision process much easier. It is better to be able to generate many alternatives and to have a ruthless decision process than to generate but few alternatives and to have a thorough decision process. This is because the generating of more alternatives will often turn up alternatives that are so good and so obviously better than the others that decision will in fact be very easy. It can almost become an "insight" process.

FINDING AND CREATING ALTERNATIVES

As mentioned earlier (choice of ties) you may be presented with a fixed list of alternatives. At other times you may set out to find alternatives. You can use holiday brochures and the advice of friends to put together alternative holiday destinations. You can ask the concierge of the hotel for alternative restaurants in the neighborhood. You can look through the real estate advertisements to put together a list of possible apartments. There are times when alternatives are produced by conscious research and the conscious scanning of experience.

In all cases it makes sense to make an effort to find alternatives before setting out to create them. It is true that existing alternatives may be well known and standard and are unlikely to give you a really original idea. But as a general principle, at least be aware of the existing possible alternatives before setting out to develop some new ones. It does not make sense to seek an exotic way of doing something when there is a very good way available if you made the effort to find it. When you are aware of the standard ways, it does make sense to look for more creative ways.

I have mentioned the attitudes of "design" in the creation of new alternatives. This means refusing to consider the situation as a fixed one. It means changing the boundaries and ingredients, as suggested earlier in this section.

At this point I want to consider the deliberate creation of new alternatives. It may be said that this "creation" is only another form of "finding." This must always seem so because any acceptable alternative will seem reasonable in hindsight so it can be argued that a good search would have found it in the first place. Quibbles like this have no value. When you have put down the alternatives that come to mind then you need to do something to be able to put down further alternatives. Usually it is a mixture of find and create.

THE FIXED POINT

I want an alternative to a car steering wheel.

What about spaghetti as an alternative?

Because there is no obvious connection between a car steering wheel and spaghetti we do not accept this alternative. You may as well have said "walking stick" or "cockroach."

Whenever we set out to look for alternatives there is always a reference point.

Alternatives with respect to what?

Alternatives with reference to what?

We can call this reference point the "fixed point." Figure 2.4 suggests how we start off with an idea; then we pick out the "fixed point"; then we seek other ideas which will also relate to this fixed point. These other ideas are our alternatives.

It is true that the strict meaning of the word *alternatives* means one other choice. Throughout this book I am using the word in its common usage sense of meaning multiple choices or options or possibilities.

There are several possible types of fixed point.

Purpose

This is the most obvious and the most common type of fixed point.

What alternative ways of achieving this purpose are there?

What other ways are there of carrying out this function?

For the Boy Scout the fixed point purpose was "lighting" the fire. So he searched for alternative ways of lighting the fire. For the car steering wheel the purpose type of fixed point might have been "alternatives to carry out the steering function." Or

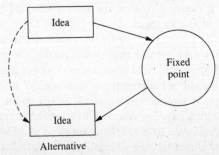

Alternative

Figure 2.4

the fixed point might have been "alternative ways of transmitting hand movements to the steering mechanism."

Whenever anything is achieving a purpose then the fixed point can be the achievement of that purpose.

What is the purpose here? That is the fixed point.

Groups

What is an alternative to an orange? We might say an apple, a pear, a banana, and so on. In this case we are offering other members of the group that might be called "normal domestic fruit." You might have preferred to think of "citrus fruit" as the group and then offered lemon or grapefruit as alternatives. That is why it is so important to define the fixed point very specifically. You might have thought of the group being "refreshing drinks" and might then have also considered beer. In this last instance there is a clear overlap with purpose.

> What other shellfish are here on the menu?
> What other four-wheel drive vehicles do you have?
> What other three-bedroom apartments overlooking the sea do you have?

We can give a group name or list some specifications. These become the fixed points and we search for members of the named group or items that satisfy the specifications of this new ad hoc group.

Resemblance

> What other leaves look like this?
> What other painters resemble this style?
> What other illnesses give a rash all over the body?

In effect, "resemblance" is only a particular way of specifying a group. But physical resemblance and perceptual resemblance deserve their own position as possible "fixed points." An innovative cook is always looking for alternative ways of achieving a certain taste.

Concepts

It could be said, and I should be in favor of saying it, that all fixed points are really "concepts." There might be a concept of purpose or a concept of group characteristics.

127

We move from the actual idea to the concept behind it and then seek for other ways of carrying through the concept. It is just like going from a child to the parents in order to find the child's brothers and sisters.

The "idea" is a practical way of doing something. The concept is the "general method" involved. You can say that you are going to "travel" along a certain road. That is a concept. But you have to do something specific: walk, ride a bicycle, drive a car, catch a bus. The specific mode of travel is the "idea."

> The fixed point is the concept of reward: how are we going to reward our salesmen?
>
> I think the fixed point should be "motivate" and that is not the same as "reward."
>
> My fixed point is the concept of "giving commission" to the salespeople. What are the alternative ways of doing that?

It is important to be very clear and specific about the precise concept and expression of the concept that is to be used as the fixed point.

In general, when we set out to look for alternatives we are very sloppy. There is a vague sense of a fixed point (usually as a purpose) and then we search around for alternatives. If the fixed point is defined as "motivation" then fear is an alternative. But if the fixed point is "reward" then fear is not an alternative. If the fixed point is "commission" then random reward is not an alternative.

We might be looking for alternatives to promotion. What might the fixed points be: money, power, status, recognition, responsibility, sense of achievement, social position, and so on. Some of these could be satisfied with "job titles" as an alternative, but others would not be satisfied.

It is not a matter of finding the "correct" fixed point but of trying several fixed points.

Sometimes we can look for a linking concept that makes two different things into alternatives. Is there a concept which could link up "steering wheel" and "spaghetti" so that they could be seen as alternatives? Such a concept might be "flexibility." Then we have the interesting difference that spaghetti is flexible in all directions whereas the steering wheel is flexible only in one direction. That leads to interesting possibilities.

The Concept Fan

You want to attach something to the ceiling in a room of normal height. The solution is simple. You look for a ladder. But you cannot find a ladder anywhere. What do you do? Do you give up and say the task cannot be done?

A ladder is only one way of "raising me off the ground." So the concept "raising me above the ground" becomes the fixed point. Alternative ways of satisfying this fixed point include standing on a table or having people lift me up.

But "raising me above the ground" is itself only one way of "reducing the distance between the object and the ceiling." This becomes the new fixed point and we look for alternatives. This time, however, the alternatives are themselves concepts. One concept is to "lengthen my arm." That concept can itself be carried out by "using a stick." Another concept alternative is to "have the object travel by itself." This can be carried out by attaching the object to a ball and throwing it up to the ceiling.

In this example we can see that there are two layers of alternatives as shown in Figure 2.5. We go from an idea (the ladder) to a concept which becomes the fixed point for other ideas. But we also go from the concept itself to a "broader concept," which then becomes the fixed point for alternative concepts. Each of these new alternative concepts becomes a fixed point for alternative ideas. So we use the two layers of concepts to cascade alternative ideas. This process is called a "concept fan."

At one end of the concept fan we have the purpose or objective of the thinking. The concept fan is an achievement technique. How do we solve the problem? How do we achieve the task? How do we get somewhere we want to go?

Moving backwards from the purpose of the thinking we then have the "broad concepts," approaches, or "directions" that would lead us to the objective. So if the objective was "coping with a water shortage" then the approaches or directions might be:

129

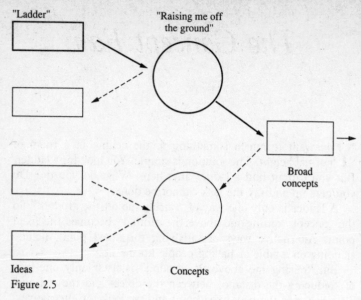

"Ladder"

"Raising me off
the ground"

Broad
concepts

Ideas

Concepts

Figure 2.5

reduce consumption

increase supply

do without

Each of these broad concepts or "directions" now becomes the fixed point for the finding of alternative "concepts." So we now move to the left and create the concept level. Each concept is a way of achieving either one of the "directions."

For "reduce consumption of water" we might have as concepts:

increased efficiency of use

less wastage

discourage use

education

For "increased supply of water" we might have:

new sources

recycling

less wastage from sources

For "do without water" we might have:

stop water-using processes

substitute other substances

avoid need to use water

At the end of this stage we have nine alternative "concepts" in the concept layer. Each of these concepts now becomes a fixed point for the next layer. For each concept we now seek alternative ways of carrying through the concept. We seek alternative ideas.

For example, for the concept "discourage use" we might get as alternative ideas:

meter the water

charge for water use

raise charge for water use

water only obtainable from public sources

water only at certain times

put a harmless bad smell into the water

restrict use for gardens, pools, and the like

publish names of heavy users

threaten to ration water

The same process could be undertaken for each of the concepts in the concept level.

The total process is illustrated in Figure 2.6.

The three levels of the concept fan are:

Directions

These are very broad concepts or approaches. The broadest concept you can conceive becomes the direction.

Concepts

General methods or ways of doing something.

Ideas

Specific concrete ways of putting a concept to work. An idea must be specific. It must be possible to put an idea directly into practice.

131

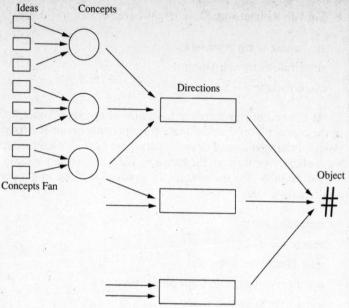

Figure 2.6

We can use the analogy I mentioned earlier. If you are driving north then this is the "direction." There are many roads, all of which are heading north. These roads are the ways of proceeding north and they become the "concepts." But you have to do something specific to travel along one of the roads (car, bus, walk) and this specific action is the "idea."

Many people get worried about the difference between "concepts" and "directions." This is because the difference is relative. A "direction" is simply the broadest concept you can think of. If you think of an even broader concept, then that becomes the direction.

There is no magic in the three layers of the concept fan. In practice there are times when there may be many layers of concepts between the directions and the ideas. The direction is always the broadest concept and the idea is always the specific way of doing something. Everything in between becomes a "concept."

MAKING A CONCEPT FAN

In making a concept fan, you are supposed to start at the "purpose" and then work backwards. At each point you ask: "Now how do I get to this point?" So you work backwards from directions to concepts to end up with a whole lot of alternative ideas—which is the point of the exercise.

Unfortunately the brain does not like behaving in this tidy way. Quite often, when you set out to make a concept fan the brain will immediately jump to a practical idea. For example, suppose we were making a concept fan on traffic congestion in cities. Your brain might immediately suggest "working at home." You then say to yourself: "How would this help in this matter?" The answer is that working at home would "reduce the need to travel." Now how would that help? By reducing the traffic load. So "reducing the traffic load" is a direction. Reducing the need to travel is a concept. And working at home is an "idea." (In this case "working at home" is also a concept, so we would need to find practical ideas for carrying this through).

You might think of "car pooling." How does this help? By increasing the "density of people per vehicle." How does this help? By reducing the traffic. Increasing the "density per vehicle" is a concept and another way of carrying this through would be "public transport."

You might think of "staggering working hours." How does this help? By "reducing the peak load." How does this help? By "improving flow along existing roads." This then provides a second "direction" or approach to the problem.

So if you think of an idea (or even a concept) you seek to move upstream by asking, "How does this help?" If you think of a direction (or a concept) you can seek to move downstream by asking, "How can this be carried through?"

So from whatever points you start you will gradually construct a concept fan.

It needs to be said that a concept fan is an "achievement fan." It is concerned with "how do we get there?" It is not an analysis tree that simply divides a subject into its sections and subsections. The emphasis is on action, not on description or analysis.

Exactly the same point can occur as many times as you wish on the concept fan. For example, in the concept fan on "coping with a water shortage" one of the directions was "do without." It is obvious that this is also a concept for "reducing the consumption of water." So the same point can occur at more than one place and also at more than one level. If you cannot decide in which of two places to put something, put it in both.

The purpose of the concept fan is to provide a framework for generating alternative ideas. The framework forces the alternatives by providing a succession of fixed points. The concept fan can also provide new focus points. For example, you might conceive of a concept but not yet have an idea for putting the concept into action. In the traffic problem the concept might be "rewarding people who could drive into the city for choosing not to do so." There may not yet be a feasible way of doing this. So it becomes a creative focus point. We now set out to find ways of doing this.

People who live in the countryside often give directions as follows: "If you find your way to the village of XXX then it is easy to get to our house." So the traveler seeks to get to XXX. Next, the countryfolk say, "If you get to the town of YYY then it is easy to get to the village of XXX because it will be sign-posted." So instructions are given by working backwards. Get to YYY then get to XXX then get to our house. This is exactly the same process as the concept fan. The concept fan is a way of working backwards from our objective to practical alternative ways of achieving that objective.

The difference between a concept fan and the direct listing of alternatives is shown in Figure 2.7. It is easy to see the cascade effect of the concept and direction layers.

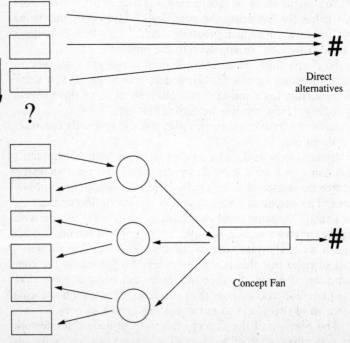

Direct
alternatives

Concept Fan

Figure 2.7

Normally when we look for alternatives we seek ideas that are useful and have obvious value. Warning signs are usually red in color. If we were to look for alternative colors we might suggest "yellow" or "orange." Yellow is a bright color and is also easier to see in the dark than is red. Orange can also be a striking color that is more unusual than red or yellow. So "yellow" and "orange" are serious alternatives that have a justifiable value.

There may be times, however, when we put forward a deliberate alternative without suggesting that it has value. For example we might suggest that warning signs be "blue." We say this because "blue" is an alternative color to "red." In fact "blue" is another primary color. There is no suggestion of special value attached to blue as a warning color. We suggest blue and then look around to see if this color might have some value. This is a provocative alternative because the reason for choosing blue may only become obvious *after* you have suggested blue.

It should be clear that there is a big difference between putting forward alternatives because they already have some value and putting forward alternatives to "see what effect they have."

This is part of the general process of provocation. The logic and techniques of provocation will be considered in detail in a later section. The provocative technique can, however, be used quite simply on its own:

> Here is a provocative alternative: let us see if we can find value in it.

There is no guarantee whatsoever that you will find value in the provocative alternative.

EVALUATION

When we have generated the alternatives, how do we evaluate them? Evaluation is a full subject in its own right and I intend to return to it later in the Applications section. In principle the evaluation of ideas generated by creative techniques should be no different from the evaluation of any other ideas. The process of evaluation is logical and judgmental and is not directly part of creativity—nor should it be.

Before creative ideas are presented to the judgment stage there may need to be further work done on the ideas in order to shape them, tailor them, improve their power, and remove their weaknesses. This process applies to all ideas that have been creatively generated and will therefore be considered at a later stage.

In general, evaluation is along four lines:

Feasible. Does the idea actually work? Can the idea be made to work?

Benefits. What are the benefits? How large are the benefits? Where do the benefits come from? How durable are the benefits? Without a strong showing in the "benefit" area an idea has no immediate value.

Resources. Are the resources available for implementing the idea? The resources may include time, money, people, technology, mechanisms, and motivation. An idea may be feasible in itself, but the resources may not be available to make the idea work.

Fit. Does the idea "fit" the needs of whomever is supposed to implement the idea? The concept of "fit" includes strategy, policy, personalities, agendas, and so on.

This very abbreviated checklist can be applied as a preliminary evaluation to any alternatives that are generated.

Concepts

The ability to form abstract "concepts" is probably the basis of man's ability to reason. The Boy Scout who looked around for another "way to light the fire" was using this general concept to search for alternatives. We use concepts all the time, both explicitly and implicitly. Yet many people, particularly in North America, are very uncomfortable when dealing with concepts. For such people, concepts seem vague, academic, and unnecessary. They want to rush to the "hands-on" practicality of concrete action.

North America was a pioneer society; in a pioneer society, action is always more important than thinking. The man of action did things while the man of thought sat at home musing. So the wonderful culture of action evolved in North America. But today the world is a place crowded with competition and saturated with goods and services. Thinking now matters almost as much as action.

A bank in California was one of the first to install automatic teller machines (ATMs) in its banks. The concept was that this would provide "convenience" to people who were too busy to line up inside the bank for personal teller attention and sophisticated enough to use such machines. After the ATMs had been operated for some time they took a look at what was happening. Apparently one of the major groups of users of the machines was Mexican immigrants (legal and illegal) who were not too happy with speaking English and who preferred the anonymity of the ATMs. The operating concept here was "anonymity."

Whenever we do anything and within every business there is an implicit concept. Is it an academic exercise to seek to extract that concept and to make it visible?

There may be many concepts present. Different people may see the concept differently. How do we know we have extracted the "right" concept? Why should we want to make the concept visible? Is it not enough that the concept seems to be working?

There are a number of reasons why it is useful to be able to extract and make visible a concept.

137

Alternatives

If we can extract the concept then we can use this concept as a "fixed point" to find alternative ways of carrying out the concept. Some of these alternatives might be more powerful than the ideas we are currently using.

Strengthen

When we extract a concept we can strengthen it through a deliberate improvement effort. We can remove faults and weaknesses and enhance the apparent power of the concept.

Change

Once we know the concept we can decide to change it. We may want to do this if things are not going well, if there is a competitive threat, or if we feel that we are not making full use of advantageous market conditions.

We can extract several concepts from the general business of "fast food:"

speed of service

standardized products and prices and quality

cheap

place for youngsters to meet

We can now "challenge" each of these concepts.

We can keep "speed of service" for those who need it. But we can also seek to keep customers longer so that we can sell them more things: salads, ice cream, and so on. In this way we might get more revenue per customer. We could find another way of providing "standardized products and price and quality." We could produce food packages with standardized prices and quality. Any restaurant that sold such standardized packages would display a sign indicating this. The range of items might be limited to frozen foods that could be microwaved to remove the risk of poor cooking.

The concept of "cheap" has already been widely challenged with fast-food-type places that are not at all cheap and may sell seafood or other high-priced specialty items.

The concept of fast food places as a sort of club for young people could be enhanced in different ways—or discouraged if this was not a profitable use of the space.

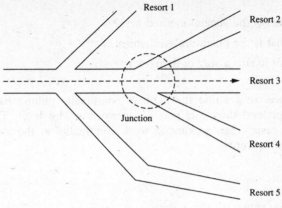

Figure 2.8

FROM IDEA TO CONCEPT

In general, it is difficult to work at the concept level. So it makes sense to work at the idea level and then keep "pulling back" to find the concept.

What is the concept here?

What concept is being carried out by this idea?

Figure 2.8 shows a road that leads to a seaside resort. You drive to the resort as quickly as you can. You go straight through the road junction without really noticing it as you follow the direct signs to your chosen destination. For some reason you are dissatisfied once you get there—perhaps the place is too crowded. You would consider driving back to the junction and then choosing some other route out of that junction to a different resort.

Concepts are very like road junctions. We pull back to the junction to find another way forward. This is why concepts are such good fixed points for the generation of alternatives.

With any idea that turns up in creative thinking it is worth making an effort to pull back to see what the underlying concept might be. There may be several concepts involved and there may also be different opinions as to what the concept really is. This does not matter, since the purpose of the pull-back is to generate new ideas and these are what matter.

139

The "pull-back" to concept level can be facilitated by a number of questions:

What is the general method here?

What is the operating mechanism?

This idea is a way of doing what?

Once we get into the habit of continually pulling back to concept level then it is possible to work at idea level. This is much easier than seeking to work continually at the abstract level of concepts.

THE NATURE OF CONCEPTS

In most of our thinking we are encouraged to be precise and to be definite. Concepts are the exception. With concepts we need to be general, nonspecific, vague, and "blurry." The more specific we are, the more we limit the usefulness of the concept.

At this point we run into a difficulty. There are many levels of concepts, ranging from the rather specific to the very general.

We are in the business of selling gold-plated pencils.

We are in the business of selling gold-plated writing instruments.

We are in the business of selling prestige writing instruments.

We are in the business of luxury personal items.

We are in the business of luxury goods.

We are in the business of selling people what they want.

We are in the business of making profits.

Here we see seven "concept levels" regarding the nature of a particular business. It is obvious that the first one is very specific and simply describes what is being done. The last one is far too general and could apply to any business whatsoever. The trick is to find the most useful concept level. This is not at all easy. Nor is there any magic formula that will find the correct concept level for you. It is a matter of "feel", which you have to acquire over time.

The best way of finding a useful concept level is to think of a concept and then to make this concept more general and also to make it more specific. So you "spread" around the chosen concept.

You are looking at the car rental business and the concept you extract may be "providing people with their own transport on a temporary basis." A more specific concept formulation might be "having cars available for rent where and when people want them and at a profit-making price." A more general concept formulation might be "matching customers transport needs."

By spreading upward and downward around an extracted concept we can get a feel as to whether we are at a useful concept level.

There are times when a concept may seem very close to a "definition" of a product or service.

Concept of a toothbrush: "a handle with a bunch of bristles at one end onto which the toothpaste is placed."

At other times the concept may be no more than a word.

Concept of a toothbrush: "a convenient way of using toothpaste."

Simple words like "convenient," "flexible," "commission," and "balance" are all concepts. There are times when a single word is enough. At other times a phrase is needed. Too much detail is always unnecessary.

TYPES OF CONCEPTS

There are general concepts which can be "included" within the concept of any product or service. Such concepts might be "convenience," "adjustable," "powerful," and so on. Then there are "defining" concepts, which capture the unique aspect of the situation. The test of a defining concept is to say, "could this be describing something else?"

Consider the following attempts to describe the "concept of a ladder:"

a way of getting to a higher place

This is too broad. The concept could cover an elevator, an escalator, a crane, or even climbing boots.

a method of using human muscle power to move vertically.

This is getting close but could also apply to steep steps.

a structure to allow steps in a vertical direction

This is probably a close enough concept description.
Note that a physical description of a ladder might have been:

two parallel vertical uprights with horizontal cross pieces at regular intervals.

Consider the following possible "concepts" of general insurance:

a method of compensation

making good the losses from accidents or disasters

protection from unexpected losses

those exposed to potential losses contribute to a fund that compensates such losses

risk reduction

paying a premium to earn the right to compensation for losses

spreading the risk

mutual financial protection

All of these are correct. But some of them leave out essential features such as the contributing element. For example, "risk reduction" could equally apply to staying at home or putting a lock on the garage door. At other times a single word like "mutual" can include a whole lot of elements that really need to be spelled out.

From the point of view of philosophical definition, dealing with concepts is very frustrating because there are different levels of concepts. There is no point whatsoever in getting bogged down in philosophical gymnastics. From a practical point of view you simply try different versions of the possible concepts and then chose whichever one seems most useful to you.

Sometimes we try to bundle purpose, mechanism, and value all into one single concept. Some of the concept definitions of insurance tried to do this. In general this can be useful. At other times we content ourselves with separating out three basic types of concept.

Purpose Concepts

What are we trying to do? What is the purpose of the activity or operation? This is really no more than a statement of purpose in general concept terms.

The purpose of an umbrella is to "provide protection against rain."

Mechanism Concepts

How does it work? How is the purpose achieved? What is the operating mechanism? What is happening? We try to see what mechanism is being used or proposed in order to achieve an effect.

Protection from the rain is achieved in an umbrella with a sheet of material that can be held open or stored folded.

There can of course be levels of detail when describing the mechanism.

Value Concepts

Why is this useful? What value does this provide? Where is the value? Why is this worthwhile?

The value of an umbrella is to have a portable and conveniently packaged rain protection device.

These are the three most useful types of concept. To these could be added "descriptive concepts" where the concept does no more than describe something. Most words are descriptive concepts. The word "mountain" describes a large vertical elevation of land. In practice we are more interested in "function" than description and the three concepts given above (purpose, mechanism, value) cover this function aspect.

WORKING WITH CONCEPTS

The main thing about working with concepts is to make the effort. In time it becomes much easier as you get a "feel" for useful concept levels. It is not a matter of finding the "right" concept but of trying different concept descriptions (as with problem

143

definitions) until you find a useful one. The use of a concept is determined by what you can then do with it in terms of generating further ideas or changing the concept.

There should be the continual movement from idea to concept and from concept to idea. This is characteristic of people who are naturally creative.

Provocation

Einstein used to carry out what he called "thought experiments." He would say: "What would I see if I were traveling at the speed of light?"

The child who places one block upon another "to see what happens" is carrying out an experiment.

Provocation has everything to do with experiments in the mind.

In an earlier section I described how many important new ideas came about through chance, accident, mistake, or "madness." All these provided a sort of discontinuity, which forced us outside the usual boundaries of "reasonableness" that had been established by our experience. With deliberate provocation we have a systematic method that can produce the same effects. We do not have to wait for change, accident, or mistake. We can be temporarily "mad" for just thirty seconds at a time in a controllable fashion. We can switch the madness on and off as we wish. That is why provocation is such a fundamental aspect of lateral thinking and of creativity in general.

We were considering river pollution.

Po, the factory is downstream of itself.

That is a provocation. It seems utterly impossible. How could the factory be in two places at once? We use the symbolic word "po" to indicate that this is intended as a provocation and not as a serious suggestion (the origin and nature of "po" will be described later).

From this provocation comes a consideration of the input and output of the factory. It would be normal to take in water upstream and put out effluent downstream. The provocation suggests that we might legislate that if a factory is built on a river then the input must be downstream of the output so the factory is the first to sample its own pollution and must therefore be more concerned to minimize effluent pollution. In hindsight this idea is perfectly logical. I am told it has become legislation in some countries.

145

At Du Pont there was some discussion about how to handle a new product. David Tanner put in a provocation.

Po, we sell the product to our competitors.

That provocation led to a change in the normal way of handling such a product, and a huge reduction in development time.

Po, cars should have square wheels

Po, planes should land upside down

Po, letters should be closed after they have been posted

All the above statements seem highly illogical and even "crazy." In fact, they are perfectly logical statements in the context of a patterning information system.

The definition of a provocation is simple:

> With a provocation there may not be a reason for saying something until after it has been said.

This contrasts strongly with our normal thinking habits in which there must be a reason for saying something before that thing is said. With a provocation we make the statement and then the effect of that statement will provide the retro-justification for making the statement.

At first it might seem that provocation is simply a scatter-gun approach in which you say anything that comes to mind in the hope that something might just prove useful. To some extent this is the way brainstorming is used by some people. Such an approach would be weak and very wasteful.

In fact, provocation is a logical necessity in any self-organizing system. Mathematical papers have been written to this effect. Such systems "bed down" into stable states. A provocation introduces instability and allows a new stable state to be reached.

The brain forms asymmetric patterns as shown in the basic Figure 2.9. Humor occurs when we are taken from the main track and deposited at the end of the side-track. From there we can see our way back to the starting point. Creativity occurs in exactly the same way. But how do we get across from the main track to the side-track? This is where the systematic provocation methods of lateral thinking come in.

Figure 2.10 shows how we set up as a provocation a concept or an idea that does not exist in our experience. So this provocation lies outside the patterns of our experience.

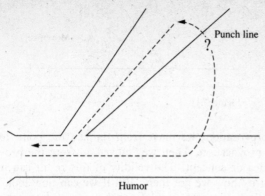

Humor

Figure 2.9

Figure 2.11 shows how we then "move" from the main track to the provocation and then on to the side-track. Once on the side-track we can trace our way back to the starting point and so open up the side-track as a new idea.

There is no magic in the process. In chemistry, if we want to move from one stable compound to another we may have first to move to an unstable compound which then re-stabilizes as the new compound. In physics, the changing of an atomic configuration may go through the same unstable step.

In normal thinking, each step that we take is firmly based on the preceding step (vertical thinking). When we arrive at a solution then the validity of that solution is proved by the validity of every step that has taken us from the starting point to the solution. This step-by-justified-step process is illustrated in Figure 2.12.

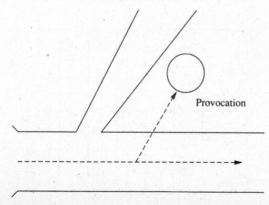

Provocation

Figure 2.10

147

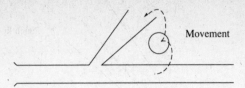

Figure 2.11

In provocation, we move from the starting point to an arbitrary provocation. Then we "move" on from the provocation to an idea or concept. The validity of this result can never be justified by how we got there. But if we can now look back to the starting point (the problem or the area of concern) we may see, in hindsight, how the new position has a real value. If this value can be shown, logically, in hindsight then the value is just as useful as if it had been achieved through a succession of valid steps. Hindsight justification of an idea is every bit as valid as any other form of justification.

But why do we need to use this "jump" method? Why should we have to justify by working backwards? The reason is very simple. In any pattern-forming system we have to take the established pattern forward at any point. So the established or traditional line of thinking takes us forward. There is no choice and we are not even aware of other possibilities.

It is only by working backwards that we are able to open up and use these other tracks—which have been there the whole time. This process is shown in Figure 2.13.

The purpose of the provocation is precisely to get us out of the usual maintrack of thinking. From the provocation we move on to find a new point which in hindsight seems to offer value. It

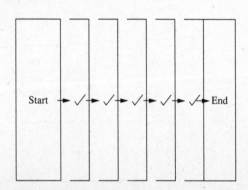

Figure 2.12

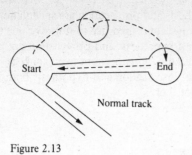

Figure 2.13

is the escape from the established main track that is so important. The brain has to work to establish the main tracks. That is the very essence of the excellence of the brain. At the same time we need ways of getting out of those main tracks in order to be creative. That is why provocation plays so central a role in lateral thinking.

PROVOCATION AND HYPOTHESIS

I have already mentioned the great value of the "hypothesis" mechanism that allows us to guess at an underlying mechanism. This guess then provides direction and a framework for our thinking about the situation. A provocation also provides us with a novel framework for looking at things. But a provocation goes much beyond a hypothesis. A hypothesis tries to be reasonable. A provocation usually tries to be "unreasonable" in order to jerk our thinking out of its usual channels.

We seek to reach, justify, and prove a hypothesis, which then moves from being a guess to being a provisional truth. We never seek to reach or justify a provocation. We never seek to prove that square wheels would be useful on a car or that planes should really land upside down. We seek to get to a useful idea that is quite separate and different from the provocation. The provocation is just a way of getting there.

Both hypothesis and provocation seek to change our perceptions. A hypothesis seeks to guide our perceptions in a certain direction. A provocation seeks to take our perceptions away from their usual direction.

149

Both hypothesis and provocation are speculations that we construct in our minds and then use to improve our thinking about a situation. Both hypothesis and provocation are part of the creative process and are quite different from analysis. Analysis looks at what is there. Provocation and hypothesis both bring in something that is not there.

TWO-STAGE PROCESS

The formal and deliberate technique of provocation is a two-stage process. The first stage involves the setting up of the provocation. The second stage involves the use of the provocation to move forward to a useful new idea.

Obviously, the first stage precedes the second stage when we come to apply the technique of provocation. The sequence has to be:

1. Choosing the creative focus
2. Setting up the provocation
3. Using the provocation

In practical terms, however, it makes sense to learn how to use provocations before learning how to set them up. In this way we know how to use provocations when we learn how to set them up. There would not be much point in setting up strange-looking provocations without any sense of how to use them. This general process of learning backwards is very powerful and very logical and is described elsewhere.*

Using provocations involves a special mental operation called "movement." This is an active mental operation. It is also completely different from judgment. Movement is an operation that we have to learn and practice in order to build up skill and fluency.

When we have considered the operation of movement then we can proceed with the methods of setting up provocations.

*Mentioned in the book *I Am Right, You Are Wrong* published by Viking, New York, 1991, and Penguin Books, London, 1990.

Movement

Movement is an extremely important mental operation. It is central to the whole of creativity. It is almost impossible to be creative without having some skill at "movement." Yet movement is not a normal part of our thinking behavior except, perhaps, in poetry. In poetry we move forward from images and metaphors to meaning and feelings.

The brain acts as a self-organizing system which allows incoming information to organize itself as patterns, tracks, channels, sequences, and so on. This is why the brain does such a very good job of allowing us to cope with the complex world around us. This patterning behavior is not in any sense a defect of the brain. On the contrary, it is the main strength of the brain as an information mechanism.

Perception is the original formation and subsequent use of the patterns. This involves "recognizing" the appropriate patterns and being sure that we follow along the pattern. This is where judgment comes in. Judgment is an essential part of perception.

There is judgment that is exercised consciously, as with a judge in court or with a teacher marking a paper or an interior designer choosing from amongst some fabrics. But there is also the judgment that happens automatically and unconsciously in the brain: what have we here?

Judgment has two main roles in perception. The first role is to find, identify, match, or recognize the appropriate pattern. This happens almost automatically but may need to be helped by conscious analysis which breaks down a situation into more easily recognizable parts.

The second role of judgment is to be sure that we do not wander off the track. Judgment points out the mistake, the wandering, the deviation, or the mismatch and hastens us back to the established track. This second aspect of judgment deals with the rejection of ideas that are wrong and contrary to experience.

If provocations such as "cars with square wheels" or "planes landing upside down" are presented to judgment then clearly they are, and should be, rejected immediately. Judgment has its job to do and should do it properly. Black hat thinking should be efficient black hat thinking. It is at this point, and for obvious reasons, that teachers of creative thinking start talking about "suspending judgment," "deferring judgment," "delaying judgment," and so on. This is the traditional approach of brainstorming. Unfortunately this is far too weak. Telling people not to use judgment does not tell them what to do. Telling people not to eat fried eggs for breakfast does not provide them with any breakfast.

We come now to "movement," which is an active mental operation. This operation can be learned, practiced, and used deliberately. Movement is not just an absence of judgment. Movement is providing you with oatmeal for breakfast instead of the fried eggs.

The difference between judgment and movement is suggested in Figure 2.14. In judgment, when we come to an idea we compare the idea with our existing patterns of experience. If the idea does not fit, we reject the idea. That is good black hat thinking. In movement, we come to an idea and we are totally uninterested in whether the idea is right or wrong or whether it fits our experience. We are solely interested in where we can "move" to from the idea. We seek to move forward.

Judgment is static and is concerned with "is" and "is not." Judgment is part of traditional rock logic. Movement is fluid and is concerned with "to": where does this lead to? Movement is part of water logic with its flow and fluidity. Movement comes under the green hat.

It is very important to appreciate that movement and judgment are totally different "games." Someone teaches you to play contract bridge. Then someone else teaches you to play poker. When you are playing bridge you are playing good bridge and not bad poker. When you are playing poker you are playing good poker and not bad bridge. So when you are using judgment you use good judgment. But when you switch to movement you use

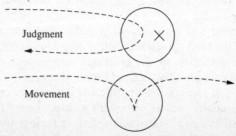

Figure 2.14

good movement. They are two separate mental operations and there is no compromise, in-between position.

THE USE OF "MOVEMENT"

At this moment we are considering the use of movement in order to move forward from a provocation to a useful new idea or concept. Without movement there is no sense in using provocation.

It should be said, however, that the use of movement in creativity is much wider than this. The use of movement with provocations is the most extreme form of movement. How do we move forward from an "impossible" provocation to something useful? But there are other occasions when the use of movement is not so extreme. We can use movement to move forward from a weak idea to a stronger one. We can use movement to move forward from a suggestion to a concrete idea. We can use movement to move forward from a concept to an idea.

The general sense of "movement" means the willingness to move forward in a positive exploring way rather than stopping to judge whether something is right or wrong. In creativity we are indeed interested in arriving at practical, useful, valid ideas. The difference is that creativity accepts many ways of getting there. Every step in the process does not have to be accepted by judgment.

The general attitude of movement is important. Someone says something. One person is quick to judge whether what is said is correct and even seeks to find some small aspect of it that is not correct. Another person is interested in what the statement leads to. The difference is a matter of sequence. The first person uses the black hat at once. The second person uses the green hat (movement) and only later uses the black hat to assess a conclusion.

There are two broad ways of using movement: general attitude and systematic techniques.

General Attitude

This is the general willingness to move forward from a statement or provocation. There are new ideas that may occur at once. A person who has practiced movement and who is aware of the systematic techniques of movement will often get useful movement just by using this general attitude. The general attitude is always

153

worth trying first. If the general attitude does not yield any useful results then it is worth trying the systematic techniques of movement. When learning lateral thinking it makes sense to use the systematic techniques in order to build up a general skill of movement.

Systematic Techniques

There are five systematic techniques for getting movement from a provocation or statement. Each of these can be learned, practiced, and applied in a deliberate fashion. There is no need to use all of them on every occasion—but they are there to be used. All this is very different from just telling people to "delay judgment."

TECHNIQUES OF MOVEMENT

Five techniques that can be used systematically to get movement will be described here. This does not mean that there are not other techniques or that the five given here cannot be subdivided into others. In some cases the different techniques can overlap. This does not matter at all since the sole purpose of movement is to move forward to a new idea or concept.

1. Extract a Principle

You look at the provocation (provided by yourself or by others) and you seek to extract a principle from the provocation. What you extract may be a "principle" or a "concept" or a "feature" or an "aspect". The choice of word is not important. You take something from the provocation. You completely ignore the rest and now proceed to work only with what you have "extracted." You seek to build a usable idea around this principle.

An advertising agency was seeking a "new advertising medium." A provocation was suggested: Po, bring back the town crier.

In a modern city with high-rise buildings, sealed ventilation, and a lot of traffic, a town crier would not be much good—but this is only a provocation. What principles, concepts, or features do we see in a town crier?

the town crier can go to where the people are

the town crier can change the message according to the audience the town crier can answer questions

the town crier is a respected official figure

the town crier is always up to date

you cannot switch the town crier off

Each one of these items could be "extracted" and used. The principle that was used was that you "could not switch the town crier off." So now you forget all about the town crier and look around for a medium that you would be unable (or at least, unwilling) to turn off. The telephone comes to mind. The idea would be to have public telephones that made no charge for a call because the conversation was interspersed with advertising messages. Advertisers would pay for the insertion of these taped messages and the caller would get free calls. This could be limited to local calls.

So we see how it is possible to move forward from a provocation to develop an original idea which could have a real value.

2. Focus on the Difference

Here the provocation is compared with the existing idea or way of doing things. The points of difference are spelled out and pursued to see if they might lead to an interesting new idea. Even if the provocation appears to be very similar to what is already being done, a conscious effort is made to focus on the difference. Even if the difference is only one percent, this one percent can be explored.

There is a "general-area-type" focus regarding a postage stamp. Someone puts forward a provocation: "Po, stamps should be long and very thin."

We focus on the "difference:"

you could put messages on the stamps

the stamp would leave more space for the address

you could use the stamp to seal the envelope

stamps might be sold in self-adhesive rolls

the length of the stamp might be proportional to the value

the stamp could be folded around to be on the back of the envelope, too

The suggestion that the length of the stamp might indicate the value follows directly from the "difference" of the long dimension now available. This suggests that a unit of length might represent a unit of value. So there would be no need to put a value on the stamp, which would just be divided into "postal units." These postal units would be purchased at the prevailing price like units of electricity or gas. This concept could now be carried back to stamps of normal shape which would carry no value but would be designated "internal mail," "first class mail," and so on. Such stamps would be purchased at the going price.

So we see that an idea stimulated by the provocation can be applied back to normal stamps. There are other ideas that might be worth pursuing. Some of these might require the long thin stamp of the provocation. Occasionally the provocation itself turns out to have a direct value even though this is not the purpose of a provocation.

3. Moment to Moment

This is possibly the most powerful of the techniques of movement. We imagine the provocation being put into effect — even if this involves fantasy. We visualize what would happen "moment to moment." We are not interested in the final result but only in the moment-to-moment happenings. It is like watching a videotape frame by frame to watch what is going on. From this observation we seek to develop some interesting concept or idea.

Po, cars have square wheels.

We imagine a car with square wheels. We imagine this car starting to roll. The square wheel rises up on its corner. This would lead to a very bumpy ride. But the suspension could anticipate this rise and could adjust by getting shorter. This leads to the concept of an adjusting suspension. This in turn leads to the idea of a vehicle for going over rough ground. A jockey wheel would signal back the state of the ground to the suspension which would then adjust so that the wheel was raised to follow the "profile" of the ground. In this way the car would "flow" over the ground rather than bump over the ground. This was an idea I first suggested about twenty years ago. Today several companies such as Lotus (part of GM) are working on "intelligent suspension" which behaves in a similar way.

Po, planes land upside down.

This seems totally absurd except that provocations are never absurd. Someone remarks that when a plane was coming in to

land the pilot would get a better view of the landing area. This is
typical moment-to-moment movement. From this comes a consideration of where pilots are placed in aircraft. When planes
were very small the pilot had to sit on top. This has remained
the chosen place. Is it the best place? Is it the best place at all
times? The Concorde comes in at so steep an angle that the pilot
cannot see anything. So there is a mechanism to drop the nose
of the plane to allow the pilot vision. Perhaps the pilot could be
placed somewhere else for landing? There could also be video
cameras at selected points.

4. Positive Aspects

This is the simplest of the movement techniques. It is more
yellow hat than green hat. We look directly for any benefits or
positive aspects in the provocation. What values are immediately
present? Here we are interested in what is directly present rather
than what the provocation might lead to. We then take this value
and seek to move forward with it to a new idea.

Po, cars should have their engines on the roof.

There would be trouble with transmission and the high center
of gravity but there are many positive aspects as well:

ease of access to the engine for maintenance

less risk of engine damage in a collision

equal weight distribution on both axles

more space in the car or a shorter car

less impeded air flow for cooling

From this might come the idea of a shorter mid-engined car
with the passengers sitting above the engine platform.
When a value is turned up by the provocation then we try
to find ways of achieving the same value in a more practical
fashion. We concern ourselves with the value and try to build
an idea around it.

5. Circumstances

Under what circumstances would this provocation have a direct
value? In flooded conditions a car with the engine on the roof
would have a direct value because it would be possible to drive

157

in deeper water without affecting the engine. In this method of getting movement we look around for special circumstances that would give value to the provocation.

Po, drinking glasses should have rounded bottoms.

Under what circumstances would rounded bottoms have a direct value? You could not put down the glass until you had finished your drink so perhaps bars could sell more drinks. You could not put down the glass unless you placed it in a special holder so perhaps polished furniture would not get white rings on it because all glasses would need to be placed in special holders — rather than being placed anywhere.

It is obvious that there is a great deal of overlap. For example, with the round bottom glasses there is an element of "moment-to-moment" movement as you visualize someone putting down an emptied glass. There is also an element of positive aspects when we examine the long thin shape of the provocative stamp.

We can consider a final example.

Po, everyone who wants to be promoted should wear a yellow shirt or blouse.

We can take each of the movement methods and put down just one point for each.

Extract a principle: the principle that the employee should be able to indicate his or her career ambitions in an unmistakable way.

Focus on the difference: ambitious people could now make themselves visible. Is it better to try to give ambition to the talented or to try to give talent to the already ambitious? This is an interesting training question.

Moment to moment: when a worker gets dressed in the morning the spouse might say, "why no yellow shirt (blouse) today?" So there might be the beginning of an idea to involve families in motivating workers.

Positive aspects: anyone wearing a yellow shirt or blouse has made a declaration to himself or herself and may try to live up to this.

Circumstances: anyone being served would prefer to go to a server wearing a yellow shirt or blouse both because service

might be better and also because a complaint would have MOVEMENT
more meaning.

It may be noted that certain aspects of the movement techniques are analytical and "convergent." This is why a general "divergent" attitude of thinking is not sufficient for effective creativity. Moment to moment involves both fantasy but also an analytical attempt to see what might happen. The search for positive aspects is also analytical. Extracting a principle has an analytical aspect.

POSSIBLE RESULTS OF MOVEMENT

As we proceed with "movement" a number of things may happen.

Negatives

When we focus on the difference or when we proceed "moment to moment" there may well be some genuinely negative points that arise. Such negative points should never be put forward because it becomes so easy to fall back into simple judgment. The negative points should be observed and a conscious attempt made to move forward from them to a useful idea. For example it might be said that a person who persistently wore the yellow shirt but never got promoted might get rather fed up. This is perfectly true. But perhaps it would be better for that person to know at once that he is not going to get promoted (as soon as he put on the yellow shirt) rather than to wait for years in a false hope.

Old Ideas

Sometimes movement tracks back into old ideas. When this occurs, a conscious effort needs to be made to develop other routes. There is no virtue at all in simply connecting a provocation to an already known idea.

Interesting Point

Movement may take the thinker to an "interesting point." This sense of "interesting" is important. The point need not have

159

value but there is the sense that it has potential. As skill builds in creative thinking, students get better at noting interest: "I feel there is something here." There is a sense of potential. So you pause and look around. It is the same feeling as the one you get driving around the countryside and coming across an "interesting" village. There is no hurry in movement. It is one of the times when it is better to think very slowly because that way you notice more.

Difference

"Difference" is itself a strong point of interest. You notice that a concept or idea is different from what has gone before. You notice that your own thinking is taking a different line. Difference is always worth exploring to see if it leads to any significant value. You can explore for difference and you can follow up difference. Points of difference or change in thinking are always worth noting even if they do not lead anywhere useful at the moment.

Value

This is a prize "catch." When you come across a point of value or obvious benefit then you treasure it. You dwell on the value and appreciate it. Then you look around to compare this new value with what existed before. Finally you make an effort to see if this same value can be obtained in another, more practical way.

Whenever you reach a final idea in lateral thinking you should always look around to see if the "value" can be obtained in a simpler or more practical way. Value becomes the fixed point. What alternative ways of providing this value might there be?

Reaching a Concept

Whatever the provocation, it is usually possible to reach some interesting concepts even if they do not immediately offer value. There is a need to spell out such concepts in order to become more aware of them. Fresh concepts are compared with old established concepts. There is an attempt to redefine and to strengthen the concept.

It may not always be possible to go forward from a concept to a practical way of putting the concept into action. So concepts should be listed and stored as part of the output of the provocative exercise. Concepts have a right to exist on their own. A concept is not just a step in the process of getting an idea.

Finally, an attempt is made to move from the concept to practical ideas for putting the concept into effect. Sometimes these may be realistic ideas, but at other times they may be no more than "for instance" ideas to show how the concept might be applied.

Reaching an Idea

The desired output of any creative session is a usable new idea. Occasionally, such an idea may occur directly as a result of the application of the provocative technique. More often there is a hint of an idea or the beginning of an idea that needs a lot more work done on it before it can be considered usable or fit for judgment. This treatment of ideas will be considered in a later section.

Sometimes movement reaches an idea which is obviously impractical or unusable in its present form. In such cases there is an attempt to pull back from the idea to the concept behind the idea. This concept can be stored as such. An attempt may also be made to seek another way of carrying through the concept. There is always some value in "for instance" ideas because they show some concept in action.

Nowhere

Sometimes movement gets nowhere. Thinking always seems to come back to established ideas. In such cases an attempt should be made to "harvest" as much as possible from the thinking session (the processing of harvesting will be described later). It is also useful to acknowledge, "I have not gotten anywhere useful." There is little point in continuing to think about the matter. Try again later with a different provocation or a different technique. There is nothing which promises that every time you set out to be creative you will get a wonderful idea. You will build up more confidence through acknowledging that you have not gotten anywhere than by trying even harder and still failing.

CONFIDENCE

What is important is to try to build up a fluency, skill, and confidence in the movement process so that whenever you wish

161

you can set out to use movement. As you build up skill and confidence then results will occur more frequently.

You cannot be confident that you will get a wonderful idea every time you seek one. But you can become confident that you can use the process of movement with skill and fluency.

When you become confident in the mental operation of movement, you will find that you can apply movement to any provocation whatsoever, no matter how illogical or bizarre it may seem.

It is now time to see where provocations come from and how to set up provocations.

Setting Up Provocations

I invented the word "po" in 1968. Since then many people have used and borrowed the word, usually without either acknowledgment or a proper understanding of what it is about.

Why do we need the word "po"?

Provocation covers a very wide spectrum. With provocation we put forward statements not to describe what is but to make things happen in our minds. At the milder end of the spectrum we have phrases like "what if . . ."; "suppose . . ."; "what would happen if. . . ." These are sufficient to put forward reasonable statements that suggest certain conditions. We then see what would happen. But there is nothing in language to cover the more extreme end of the spectrum, where a provocation can be something we know to be impossible, contradictory, or logical nonsense. There is no word in language to allow us to use such provocations because language is there to describe reality and such things could not exist in reality. The word *po* could not exist in any language and is, in a sense, an anti-language word.

The logical basis for "po" arises from consideration of the asymmetric nature of self-organizing pattern-making and pattern-using information systems. Such systems demand the "po" function. So it was necessary to invent the word "po" to indicate when something was being used deliberately as a provocation.

There is a need for some sort of signal; otherwise, a great deal of time would be wasted in normal judgment. If you were to suggest that cars should have square wheels, everyone would spend a lot of energy criticizing such a mad idea. At the very least, you would be asked to justify the suggestions. But as soon as you say, "Po, cars have square wheels," you can proceed at once to movement. It is now clear what you intend.

Words like *hy(po)thesis, sup(po)se, (po)ssible*, and *(po)etry* all indicate the "forward use" of a statement. We make the statement and then see where it takes us. This is the opposite of prose and description, in which we seek to show something as it is now. The syllable *po* is therefore extracted from such words and formalized as a symbol for provocation.

163

In ancient Polynesian, and in Maori, "po" represents the original formless chaos from which everything was then formed. This is not an unsuitable meaning.

In general, "po" can be taken as meaning:

(p)rovoking (o)peration

(p)rovocative (o)peration

(p)rovocation (o)peration

SOURCES OF PROVOCATIONS

There are two main sources of provocation. There are provocations that "arise" and are never intended as provocations. Then there are deliberate and formal ways of setting up provocations.

Provocations can happen by chance, accident, or mistake, and history offers many examples of such provocations. Such provocations may change our thinking whether we are cooperative or not.

Then there are statements that are not intended as provocations but that can be treated as provocations—if the listener chooses to treat them as such. These may be both serious remarks or silly remarks.

Someone says something with which you do not agree. You can disagree and judge the remark. That may be the end of it. But there is always the additional option of choosing to treat the remark as a provocation. You can do this after judgment or before judgment. It does not matter whether the author of the remark intended it as a provocation or even understands the provocative process. The choice is entirely yours.

There is a story that some crank wrote to Robert Watson Watt in the late 1930s and suggested that the Ministry of Defense should consider making a radio wave strong enough to shoot down aircraft. According to the story, Watson Watt rejected the idea for the crank idea that it was (the amount of energy in a radio transmission is rather small). According to the story, it was Watson Watt's assistant who used the idea as a provocation and suggested that perhaps the reflection of the radio wave might help detect aircraft. Thus was born the concept of radar, which proved so valuable in the war that was to start a few years later.

Like all such stories it is difficult to verify the actual happenings, but it is a good illustration of someone's willingness to treat an idea as a provocation no matter how absurd the idea may be.

Statements may arise in private conversations or in meetings. Ideas may be put forward by people informally or in formal reports. You may read an idea you consider to be mad. Any of these can be treated as a provocation—if you wish.

I once asked a classroom for ideas on how to estimate the height of a tall building in the town. I was given many sensible suggestions. Then one young fellow, trying to be facetious, said, "Put the building on its side, walk along its length and remember to count your steps." Although this was intended to be funny, we can choose to treat it as a provocation, "Po, put the building on its side." The first obvious idea is to measure the length of the shadow and use this to estimate the height of the building (by comparing your shadow with your height). Another idea is to take a photograph of the building and then put the building on its side from the photograph. But before taking the picture we would have a large box exactly twenty yards from the base of the building. The distance shown between the base of the building and the box in the photo would represent twenty yards and would thus provide a scale. There are other ideas that come from the same provocation.

In practice it is rather difficult to choose to treat as provocations ideas which we know to be unworkable and which we do not like. Nevertheless, we should be prepared to treat any idea as a provocation. The choice is ours. No one else needs to know anything at all about it.

We come now to the deliberate and formal ways of setting up provocations. These provide the systematic provocation tools of lateral thinking. They allow us to do in a controlled and deliberate way what would otherwise have to await chance, accident, or mistake. It is important to realize that provocation has a logical basis and is not just a matter of being "crazy" and hoping that something useful happens. We set up a formal provocation and then use the systematic methods of movement to go forward from the provocation to a new idea or concept. The process is done step by step.

THE ESCAPE METHOD

This is a simple and straightforward way of creating provocations. In any situation there are many "normal" things that we take for granted. We take for granted that a cup has a saucer and a handle. We take for granted that the rim of a cup is circular. We

165

take for granted that a cup stands upright. I prefer the term "take for granted" rather than "assume" because we sometimes feel that assumptions may not be justified. Features that we "take for granted" need not be present on every occasion but are "usually" present and part of the situation.

You must never put down a problem, a complaint, or a negative feature as a "take-for-granted" item. The escape method does not work from negatives because escaping from a negative has no provocative effect.

Sometimes the "take-for-granted" features are obvious. For example, we take for granted that shoes have soles. At other times we make an effort to find "hidden" items. For instance, we take for granted that there are left shoes and right shoes. We take for granted that the heel slightly elevates the foot.

So the first step is to spell out something we take for granted. This should be done formally and specifically. We take for granted that restaurants have food.

The next step is the "escape" from what we have taken for granted. This means canceling, negating, dropping, removing, denying, or escaping from what we have taken for granted.

We take for granted that restaurants have food.

Po, restaurants do not have food.

There we have our provocation.

The next step is movement. Using the moment-to-moment technique we imagine people sitting in this very nice restaurant but with no food. Next time they come they will remember to bring sandwiches with them. For this develops the idea of a restaurant as an elegant place for indoor picnics. You bring your friends and your food and pay a service charge to the restaurant owner. Perhaps, by arrangement, the picnic hampers can be packed by another restaurant at off-peak times. So just as you entertain your friends to a picnic on a river bank, so you can entertain your friends to an indoor picnic in elegant surroundings.

We take for granted that restaurants charge for the food.

Po, restaurants do not charge for the food.

Perhaps restaurants could charge for "time" instead of food. You paid a certain sum for every minute but the food was free. This might make sense in cafes where patrons could sit for a long time and just order one cup of coffee. Instead of the coffee being very expensive in order to cover the overhead, the coffee would be cheap, but a sort of parking meter in the middle of the table would charge for time. More simply, the bill handed you by the waiter would be time-stamped and on the way out, the time charge be assessed.

It is interesting to note that an "escape" from the necessity of having to pay the bill then and there led to the concept behind Diners Club many years ago.

We take for granted that restaurants have menus.

Po, restaurants do not have menus.

From this provocation we could go in many different directions. We could imagine a restaurant where the chef prepares a menu as for a dinner party and you trust the chef enough to eat what is set before you. Some such restaurants do now exist. Or you could go another route and imagine a restaurant that printed a list of available ingredients and you could order what you wanted within those limits.

We take for granted that waiters are polite (not always).

Po, waiters are not polite.

This leads to an idea for waiters to be actors and actresses. The menu indicates the "character" of the waiter. You can order whichever waiter you wanted: belligerent, humorous, obsequious, and so on. You might order a belligerent waiter and enjoy having a fight with him. The waiters and waitresses would act out the assigned role.

We take for granted that restaurants provide plates and cutlery.

Po, restaurants do not provide plates and cutlery.

So you take your own. But you do not want to keep taking your own plates and cutlery so you leave them in the restaurant. But your plates can now be special plates with your own monogram or corporate logo on them. You have your guests served on your own special plates. This would mean that you always tended to return to the same restaurant to entertain your clients.

Anything at all that we take for granted can be "escaped from" in order to create a provocation. It does not matter how impossible or absurd the resulting provocation may appear.

167

You can get the "take-for-granted" items by having people put down such items on slips of paper that are put into a bag. One of the slips is drawn out of the bag and this is the one to be escaped from. Another way is to ask everyone to write down a list of "take-for-granted items," one under the other. You then call out an arbitrary number, say, number five. Each person must then attempt to escape from the number five item on his or her list. Or you may simply suggest items that are taken for granted and then pick one of these for the escape.

The escape technique is particularly useful for looking at established methods, procedures, or systems where everything seems in order and has evolved over time to a stable state. If you wish to make improvements or changes you may not know where to start. The escape process suddenly upsets the existing procedures, so you are forced to think afresh about things.

The escape technique is quite easy to use but there are some difficulties. Sometimes the escape may simply block one path and the thinker then chooses a simple alternative.

We take for granted that we drive in to work.

Po, you cannot drive in to work.

At the simplest level we would just accept that cars were banned and so we would suggest taking a bus or a train. In other words, if one possibility is blocked, we just look around for other possibilities. Although the ideas may be useful, they are unlikely to be very original. We could take other directions from the same provocation. We might imagine having to sleep at work for extended periods at a time and then having a very long weekend. We might imagine working at home or having work drive to meet you at home. We might imagine that you had to drive "out" to work instead of "in" to work. This might suggest that in the mornings only traffic out of towns would be permitted. This would encourage the relocation of work places to the periphery of towns.

THE STEPPING-STONE METHOD

The difficulty with setting up provocations is that the thinker has to set up the provocation but the provocation must provoke the thinker. There is a danger of "choosing" a provocation that fits in with ideas or concepts that you already have. That is useless, as the technique will not provoke new ideas. In setting up provocations some people have a general idea of where an idea might lie and then set up a provocation leading in that direction. That has very little value. A provocation should be bold and mechanical. You should not have any idea where the provocation might lead you.

It is for this reason that many of the methods of setting up provocations are semimechanical. With escape you spell out the "take-for-granted" item and then you negate it. That is mechanical. With most of the stepping stone methods you carry out some mechanical operation on something that exists.

Visualize that on a walk you come to a stream that you need to cross. Your first action is to pick up a large stone and throw it into the middle of the stream. The second action is to use the stepping-stone to get across. I mention this analogy to indicate that setting up the stepping-stone and using the stepping-stone are two distinct operations.

A good test of whether your provocations are provocative and mechanical enough is to see how many of your provocations you can use successfully. There should be at least 40 percent that you are unable to use. If you can use them all successfully then either you must be exceptionally skilled at movement — or you are just creating provocations to fit ideas you already have.

Po, planes land upside down.

This is a mechanical provocation of the "reversal type." I have already mentioned how one idea leads to a consideration of the pilot's position. Another line of thinking focuses on the difference and observes that the wings would now give a downward thrust. This leads to the concept of "positive landing." This leads to the idea of some small winglets which did give downward thrust. Under what circumstances would these have a direct value? If the pilot needed instant life in an emergency then this downward thrust would be cancelled by flexing the winglets upwards. The result would be an instant reservoir of lift.

The purpose of provocations is to arrive at ideas you have not had before — not to reconfirm already held ideas.

Four formal and deliberate ways of creating stepping-stone provocations will be considered here.

Reversal

This means looking at the "normal" or usual direction in which something is done and then going in the reverse or opposite direction. Planes landing upside down and cars with square wheels are both examples of "reversal type" provocation.

In previous Olympic Games the organizing committees had been reluctant to encourage television because they had felt that showing it all on television would reduce the live attendances. One of the changes in concept of the 1984 Olympics was to reverse the normal attitude and to treat the Olympics as television shows. It was this concept that made them financially viable. In this case the provocation becomes the idea.

Very often people assume that "doing without something" is a reversal. It is not. Doing without something is an escape.

I have orange juice for breakfast.

Po, I do not have orange juice for breakfast.

That is not a reversal but an escape. So what would a reversal type provocation be, in this instance?

Po, the orange juice has me for breakfast.

Visualize a huge glass of orange juice into which I fall. I come out smelling of orange juice. That leads to an idea of an attachment on a shower head which would take sticks of perfume so that the bather could choose the perfume that would scent the shower water.

The telephone rings when there is a call to be answered.

Po, the telephone rings all the time and falls silent when there is a call.

This is a good reversal provocation but seems difficult to use because it is so absurd. From it come two useful ideas. If the telephone was ringing all the time then at least you would know that the phone was live and working. This leads to the idea of a small red light on the phone that indicates that the phone is live. The second idea is that the phone should be linked up to the television set. When there is a phone call then the television set goes mute. At once you know there is a call. The set might remain mute until you had completed the call (this last part is optional).

The caller pays for the telephone call.

Po, the receiver is paid for answering the phone.

A different reversal might have suggested the receiver paid for the call. Paying the receiver for receiving the call is an interesting idea in itself. Technically it should not be difficult to add an extra sum to the caller's bill and to subtract this sum from the receiver's bill. So the more calls you got the less would be your telephone bill. You might give your friends a special number that did not have this feature—or you might not.

Exaggeration

The second formal way of creating a stepping-stone type of provocation is exaggeration. This method is directly related to measurements and dimensions: number, frequency, volume, temperature, duration, and so on. There is a normal range of measurement to be found in any situation. Exaggeration means suggesting a measurement that falls far outside this normal range. The exaggeration may be upward in terms of an increase in the measurement or it may be downward in terms of a diminution in the measurement.

Po, every household has 100 phones.

Po, there is only one dialing button on a phone.

When the exaggeration takes the downward direction the diminution should never quite reach zero because this becomes a simple escape.

Po, toothpaste is a single drop of liquid.

Po, there is no toothpaste.

The single drop might suggest something that is put onto food and carries out its cleaning function even as the food is being chewed.

The exaggeration creates the typical instability of a provocation. We cannot stay with the exaggeration so we "move" forward to some idea.

Many years ago, *New York Magazine* arranged for me to be given some problems from the mayor's office. One of them was a lack of police to patrol the streets.

Po, police have six eyes.

171

From that simple exaggeration came the suggestion that individuals act as extra eyes and ears for the police. This was written up as part of the cover story in *New York Magazine* in April 1971. Subsequently this concept became widely used as "neighborhood watch."

Po, students are examined every minute.

This leads to the idea of a stand-alone computer unit that a student can use at any time. The computer presents questions and the student answers the questions. When the ratio of successes to failure exceeds a certain point, the student is deemed to know enough about the subject. The student can access the machine at any time. There would be ways of preventing fraud or abuse.

Po, telephones are too heavy to lift.

Po, telephones are small enough to be worn as a button.

Po, each phone call must last one hour.

Po, each call can only last ten seconds.

Po, you have to dial one hundred digits.

Po, you only dial one digit.

Po, a call always costs $100.

Po, calls cost a maximum of 10 cents.

Po, you can only reach one person by phone.

Po, you can talk to one thousand people at once.

The Swedish film institute once came to see me to see how they might raise money for films.

Po, each cinema ticket costs $100.

This leads to the idea that for first-run films there is a simple mechanism whereby viewers can go back to the box office and invest money directly in the film they have just seen. They would now have had a chance to assess the product—as distinct from investing in advance. They would also become ambassadors for the film and would encourage others to see the film. This investment would pay back the initial risk takers so reducing their risk and encouraging initial investment.

I am always surprised that some people find the exaggeration-type provocation difficult to use. I suspect it is because this type of provocation is very pure. You set up the provocation and have no idea where it is going to lead you. Those who have difficulty prefer to form a provocation around ideas they have already.

It is important to emphasize that exaggeration-type provocations are always based on some dimension or measurement. There is not the usual broad meaning of exaggeration, which also includes anything outrageous.

Distortion

In any situation there are normal relationships between parties. There are also normal time sequences of action. The distortion type of provocation is obtained by taking these normal arrangements and changing them. This "distorts" the situation to create a provocation.

In a seminar I set the exercise of creating provocations of each type around the postal system.

Po, you close the letter after you post it.

This very good example of a distortion provocation (distorting the sequence of operations) was suggested by a participant. An interesting idea comes from it. If you do not want to pay postage you post your letter open. A direct mail advertiser then inserts a leaflet or other message into your envelope, closes it, and pays the postage for you. Your benefit is free postage. The advertiser's benefit is direct access to potential clients. Obviously there would be a need to select postal districts in order to get the sort of clients one might want.

Po, students examine each other.

This provocation leads to a simple idea that an excellent question in any examination would be to ask students to set out examination questions and to explain why they had set such questions. You need to know a subject well to design good questions. These could also be used subsequently by the examiners in future examinations.

Po, you die before you die.

This was the sort of provocation that led Ron Barbaro of the Prudential Insurance company to develop the very successful idea of "living benefits." In reverse mortgages you really receive the benefits first and then pay the premiums later.

Po, you vote on behalf of your neighbor.

Po, the post office writes your letters for you.

Po, interest on your investment is paid to a third party.

Po, criminals pay for the police force.

Po, you can pour a soft drink before you open it.

Po, in an airplane you land before you take off.

Po, TV chooses what to show you.

Po, children decide who the parents should marry.

Where only two parties are involved, distortion and reversal come to exactly the same thing.

What is the normal arrangement (relationships, time sequence, and so on)? Now let us change that around.

The distortion method is probably the most difficult of the stepping-stone methods but it can yield powerful ideas because the provocations tend to be very provocative and we cannot easily slip back to existing ideas.

Wishful Thinking

The example of the factory that was going to be "downstream of itself" is an instance of "wishful thinking" provocation.

Wouldn't it be nice if. . . .

We put forward a fantasy wish knowing that it is impossible to achieve. It is important that the provocation be a fantasy. It is much too weak just to put forward a normal desire, objective, or task.

I would like to make this pencil for half the cost.

That is an objective or task toward which you can work even if it may seem very difficult. But it is not a provocation.

Po, the pencil should write by itself.

This is more obviously a fantasy and more obviously a provocation.

I was once asked to suggest a scheme for a small town that had all its central parking taken up by commuter cars, which remained in place all day.

Po, cars should limit their own parking.

(Wouldn't it be nice if cars limited their own parking)

From this comes the simple idea that you can park anywhere so long as you leave your headlights full on. This would run down your battery if you stayed for any length of time. The same idea could be applied in cities when you parked at a meter. If you left your headlights on you did not need to pay the meter. This would give a quicker turnover of meter spaces in central areas.

The three other ways of getting stepping-stone provocations all work by "pushing against" something that now exists (reversing it, exaggerating it, distorting it) but with the stepping-stone method we have to pull the provocation out of the air. Some people find this more difficult because it is less mechanical. Other people find that putting down a dream fantasy is not difficult at all.

Po, shoplifters identify themselves.

(Wouldn't it be nice if shoplifters were to identify themselves)

This is hardly likely to happen. We visualize a shoplifter raising an arm and saying, "I am a shoplifter." Perhaps they could identify themselves by their clothes. This leads to the idea of a hygienic shopping gown to be worn over normal clothes. This gown has no openings and no pockets so shoplifting would be more difficult. Anyone wearing a gown gets a small discount. Those who choose not to wear the gown can be observed more closely. Behind this idea there is a concept. There may be better ways of carrying through that concept. The concept is that shoplifters may resist some request that others find unimportant.

The more of a fantasy it is, the more provocative will be the provocation.

Po, you step into the plane as soon as you arrive at the airport.

Po, each passenger has his or her own plane and pilot.

Po, the plane will take you where you want to go when you want to go.

Po, there is member of the cabin staff just to look after you.

Po, you always sleep when in flight.

Po, you always sit next to the most interesting people.

Po, the airline provides you with all the baggage you need.

Po, you buy shares in the airline with your ticket.

Po, delays are enjoyable and worthwhile.

Po, whenever you want to fly is the cheapest time.

Po, the plane waits for you if you are held up in traffic.

Even if some of these seem utterly impossible they can all be used as provocations. The more confident you become of your "movement" skills the more able you will be to take any provocation whatsoever and to get some value out of it. The more able you are to use extreme provocations the more bold will you be at setting up provocations. Weak provocations do not have much provocative value.

Po, the plane waits for you if you are held up in traffic.

This leads to the idea that all flights are scheduled half an hour ahead of actual departure time. If you turn up late you get a surcharge but still get on the plane. Or, you get a discount voucher if you check in early. Another idea is automatically to rebook missing passengers on the next flight but that booking only lasts for one hour.

It is a useful procedure, and good stepping stone practice, to set up a whole number of stepping-stone provocations as an operation in itself when you are trying to be creative about some matter. Just set up the stepping-stones without making any attempt to use them. This exercise of setting up stepping-stones can free up the mind. You may then find that you are tempted to use one of the stepping-stones. The purpose of the exercise, however, is simply to put down as many stepping-stones as you can around the creative focus.

The Random Input

This is the simplest of all creative techniques. It is now widely used by new product groups, advertising agencies, rock groups, playwrights, and many others. I developed the technique in 1968 and it has been borrowed or plagiarized extensively, usually by people who do not know why and how it works.

The technique is very powerful but seems totally illogical.

There is a creative focus where we need new ideas. So we obtain a word which has no connection whatsoever with the situation and hold the two together.

Office copier po nose

From this juxtaposition we seek to develop new ideas.

Any person using traditional logic would point out the absurdity. If the "word" is truly random then that word would serve to help with any subject matter whatsoever. Similarly, any word whatsoever would work with the given focus. So any word is of value with any subject. This seems the height of illogicality.

It is only when we understand how the brain works as a self-organizing patterning system that the process makes sense. Figure 2.15 shows your home in a small town. You always take the same road when leaving your house. But if, one day, you are given a lift to the edge of the town and then find your way home, you are likely to use a road you would not have taken when leaving your house. Quite simply, the pattern probabilities are different in the center from what they are at the periphery. There is no magic at all about this.

The brain is so very good at making connections that even if the random word (or input) seems very remote, the brain will make the needed connections back to the focus area. It has never happened to me that the random word is too remote. On the contrary, what happens quite often is that the random word is so closely connected to the focus that there is little provocative effect.

The history of ideas shows many examples of instances where a chance event seemed to trigger an important new idea. Of

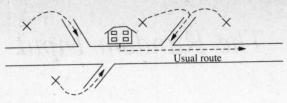

Figure 2.15

course, this happens only in a "prepared" mind which has been thinking about the subject. There is the story of how Newton was sitting reading under a tree in Woolsthorpe, Lincolnshire, England, and an apple fell on his head. This is supposed to have "triggered" the idea of gravity as a "force." Even if this story is not true, there are many other examples.

Do we have to sit around under trees and wait for apples to fall on our heads? Even if we choose to sit under apple-laden trees in a high wind the process is rather passive. Can we not get up and shake the tree whenever we want a new idea? We can do just this and that is what the random input technique is all about.

The random input technique is one of the provocative techniques but the way it works is slightly different from the other provocative techniques. As shown in Figure 2.16, with the other techniques we fashion a provocation (po) and then use this to get out of the main track in order to increase our chance of "moving" to the new track. With the random input technique we start at a new point and this immediately increases our chances of hitting the new track. Once we have done this we connect back to the focus and can now use this new line of thinking.

Starting from a new entry point is a well-established process in creative thinking. Sometimes we can switch our attention from the winner to the losers in a tennis tournament, from the criminals we catch to the ones we do not catch, from the readers who are interested to the ones who are bored, and so on. In certain cases there are clearly defined possible entry points. The random input technique is much broader and covers all cases, whether or not there are other obvious entry points.

We cannot really "choose" a random entry point because it would be chosen according to our existing thinking and would not provide provocation. So we need to use a chance method to get the provocation. There are many practical ways of doing this.

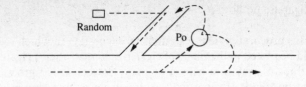

Figure 2.16

1. Compile a list of 60 words (fire, desk, shoes, nose, dog, plane, hamburger, tiger, etc.). When you need a random word you just glance at your watch and note the seconds reading. Use that number to get a word from your list. If you have a watch with the capacity for hundredths of a second then you can have a list of 100 words. Change the list about once every six months in order to get fresh words.
2. Use a dictionary. Think of a page number (say, page 82) and then think of a position of the word on that page (say, the eighth word down). Open the dictionary at page 82 and proceed to the eighth word down. If this word is not a noun then carry on until you come to the first noun.
3. A Canadian once produced a large plastic sphere with 13,000 words in it. You turn a handle, which shuffles the words and then you read off the word that appears in the window.
4. You close your eyes and stab your finger at a page of a newspaper or book. You take the word nearest to your finger.

All of these are practical ways of obtaining a "random word." The random input technique is easier to use than the other provocative techniques because the provocation is obtained so easily and does not have to be "constructed."

Cigarette po traffic light

Within a few seconds this led to the idea of printing a red band around a cigarette some distance from the butt end. This band would serve as a "danger zone." If you stopped smoking before you reached the band then your smoking is safer (because the last part of the cigarette is the more harmful). If you smoked through the "danger zone" you might feel guilty. If you wanted to reduce your smoking you would buy cigarettes with the band placed further and further along the cigarette.

Cigarette po flower

This provocation led to an unusual suggestion in which seeds would be placed in the filters of cigarettes so that when a cigarette was thrown away in a garden or park, flowers would grow out of the butt end. If a particular type of flower was chosen this would become a sort of advertising for that cigarette.

Unemployment po false teeth

False teeth have to fit. There is usually some sort of guarantee with false teeth. So individuals can be given a guaranteed type of employment to fit their needs. If they want a long-term guarantee then the wages are lower than if they want higher wages but the risk of being laid off first. Priorities can be decided and employment tailored to fit them.

We can now return to the provocation suggested earlier in this section.

Office copiers po nose

At once we think of smell. How could smell be of use? Perhaps we could design a simple cartridge to be slipped into a copier so that any malfunction would give a distinctive "smell." If you are standing by the copier and it is not working, you sniff. If you smell lavender then you know that there is a need for more paper. If you sniff camphor you know that the ink cartridge needs changing. The technology would be simple. An advantage is that you do not need to be standing by the copier. If you are working at your desk and smell lavender then you get up and put more paper into the copier. The concept of using smell to indicate the state of complex machinery is a powerful concept in itself and could be applied to many types of machinery.

It is obvious that the random input technique is very good for producing new lines of thought and ideas that would never have been reached by any sort of logical design or analytical process.

The random word technique is particularly useful in the following types of situations.

Stagnation

You feel that you have completely run out of ideas. You have tried to be creative for a long time but keep coming back to the same ideas and concepts. It seems impossible to get any fresh ideas. You put in a random word and this opens up new lines of thinking immediately.

Blank Sheet (Greenfield)

You are given a project that needs new ideas. You do not know where to start. You have no ideas at all. There is nothing existing that you can work upon. In such cases the random input technique is especially useful in getting your creative ideas working. The random input gives a starting point.

Additional Ideas

When you already have a number of ideas but have the feeling that there may be a completely different line of thinking which has not yet appeared, it is useful to spend a little time with the random input technique to see if some really new line of thinking can be found.

Blocked

When you are truly blocked and cannot find any way forward, since you are not making any progress it is worth using the random input method. There is no guarantee that it will work, but the investment of time and effort is fully justified. The random input technique may not provide the needed solution but it should open up new lines of thought and enable you to make some progress.

Although the random input technique is so very simple to use, there are a number of points to remember when using the technique: that is, a number of pitfalls to avoid.

1. There is no point whatsoever in showing how clever you are in linking the random input to an idea that you have already. This is totally pointless and usually shows. The purpose of the technique is to get new ideas, not to provide an excuse for putting forward old ideas.
2. Use the word as given and do not rearrange the letters or take part of the word to give another word. This is simply changing the random word to find one which fits better with your existing ideas. The provocative effect is lost.
3. Do not take too many steps: this suggests this . . . which leads to this . . . and that reminds me of this . . . and so on. If you take too many steps you will arrive at any existing ideas you have and will miss out on the provocation.

181

4. Do not list all the characteristics of the random word. If you do this you will simply go down the list to find something that "fits" very easily and so lose the provocative effect. Take the first characteristic that comes to mind and try to make it work.

5. Do not decide that the present word is unusable and immediately seek another one. In this way you would just be waiting for a word that "fits" existing ideas. The only time it is permissible to seek another random word is when the connection between the focus and the first word is so strong and direct that no provocation is taking place.

All the above points are important in order to preserve the "provocative" effect of the method. It is not a matter of finding a way of connecting the random word to existing ideas—but of provoking new ideas.

There is an interesting phenomenon that sometimes occurs with the random word technique. At first people are skeptical as to how such a simple method can possibly work. Then when these people see that the method does work, they become greedy.

If this random word has produced such interesting ideas, how do we know that a different random word will not produce even better ideas? How do we find the "best" random word?

The simple answer is that you cannot. The process has to be open-ended. It is quite true that another random word might produce even better ideas. There is no way of finding the "best" random word because it would then no longer be random. Be happy that you have some new ideas.

You should not use a succession of random words in an effort to extract every possible idea. Use the random input technique and then move on to other techniques. Return to it later on another occasion. If you use too many random inputs you run the risk of not trying hard enough with any one of them and just waiting for an easy one to come up.

It needs to be said that the random input technique does not apply only to random words. You can use random pictures instead of words. You shuffle some pictures and pick one at random. You can also use objects. Pick up an object or buy something in a store and use it as a stimulus. The random input process also covers going to exhibitions of fields other than your own and talking to people in other fields. The random input technique can mean picking up and reading journals dealing with other fields.

The general principle of the random input is the willingness to look for unconnected inputs and to use these to open up new lines of thinking. Some part of everyone's reading should also be random. If you always stick within what seems relevant then you are only reinforcing your existing ideas and not opening up the possibilities of new ideas.

The random word is a most convenient form of random input because it is so practical and so easy to use. A word is a package of functions, concepts, details, and associations. Other random inputs tend to be less powerful because they are more limited. It is also important to change around the random inputs because if you always use the same ones, your mind will find its way back to the same grooves each time.

The random input technique takes its place as one of the systematic techniques for using provocation in a deliberate way.

Sensitizing Techniques

We come now to some new "sensitizing" techniques. Although these are not provocations in the strict sense of that word, they are provocative in the sense that something is put forward "in order to see what happens." There is also an element of randomness since there is no attempt to be either analytical or comprehensive.

As a patterning system the brain is very susceptible to sensitization. If certain areas are stimulated then those areas become more ready to take part in the following sequences of thought. This readiness is sensitization. If you declare that you are going to pick out people wearing yellow clothes at a sport stadium, then as you sweep your eye over the crowd those wearing yellow will stand out from the others. The brain has been "sensitized" to yellow.

The purpose of sensitizing techniques is to feed ideas into the mind in order to allow our thinking to take new and creative lines. The techniques are not as strong or as powerful as the deliberate provocative techniques but they can generate new concepts and ideas.

STRATALS

Stratals is a new word that I invented for use in my book *I Am Right You Are Wrong*. Stratals refer to strata or layers. A stratal is a number of parallel statements or observations that are put together as a whole. The statements need not be connected in any way whatsoever. There is no attempt to be comprehensive. There is no attempt to cover all aspects or to be descriptive. There is no attempt to be analytical. Just as a random word is used because you want to use it, different statements are put together as a "stratal" simply because you want to put them together in this way. A stratal is a number of unconnected statements put together solely to form a stratal. The purpose of a stratal is to sensitize the mind so that new ideas can come forward.

184

A stratal could consist of any number of lines but for the sake of formality I have chosen five. So a stratal consists of five lines. Five is large enough to have some richness but not so large that the stratal cannot be considered as a whole. Each of the lines should be a phrase or a statement and not just a single word. A list of words does not function as a stratal even if you argue that each word contains a whole paragraph.

A STRATAL ON CAR INSURANCE

... open to fraud by claimants and car repair shops

... rising cost of damage repairs because of labor and complexity

... state regulations and premium caps, etc.

... increasing legal and processing costs

... differing behavior of selected groups

From this come the following ideas:

1. Focus only on highly selected groups.
2. If it is not possible to focus on highly selected groups, get out of the business.
3. Offer to run and administer a state-run car insurance scheme.

The third of these ideas is the most original and probably has some merit. Insurance is coming to be regarded as a regulated right and therefore becomes increasingly difficult to run as a profitable enterprise. The profits can now come from administering a scheme.

A STRATAL ON "RECRUITMENT" OF SENIOR STAFF

... the best people are happy in their existing jobs

... difficulty of assessing future performance

... balance between personality and ability

... those who come easily may also leave easily

... what is the right price for talent

From this might come the following ideas:

1. It is cheaper to develop your own people than to buy proven talent.

185

2. Regard high-priced talent only as a temporary employment measure to achieve certain change objectives.
3. Use consultants rather than full-time employees.
4. Use consultants and then offer them employment if they are good.
5. Find a way of borrowing people and then returning them (with greater experience) back to their present jobs.

The borrowing idea is the most original.

A STRATAL ON "BEER"

... a predominantly male drink

... easy to buy, easy to drink

... difficult to show differences between brands

... often bought by women in supermarkets for the home

... market value of new drinkers or drinking occasions

From this comes the marketing idea of deliberately associating certain beers with certain types of food. For example, establish Heineken as the beer to drink when eating chicken. Establish Guinness as the beer to drink when eating fish or shellfish. Behind this is the concept of developing the beer-with-food market which also opens up the female market.

Using the stratals is a reflective process. You put together the stratal and then you read through it again and again and let some ideas start to form. Clearly there is no point to the method if you choose the stratal layers to fit an idea you already have and then use the stratal to circle back to the idea. If, however, the stratal is unconsciously formed by an unconscious idea, then the stratal may well serve to bring that idea into consciousness—and this is a legitimate value.

Putting together stratals requires practice. At first there is a strong tendency to try to be comprehensive and to connect up the layers. This should be resisted because a comprehensive description will not lead anywhere. It is the randomness and arbitrariness of the stratal that matters.

The more disconnected the layers of the stratal, the more widespread the sensitization. If all the layers are clustered in one area then there is little chance of a new line of thinking developing.

Think of stratals like wetting parts of the paper before painting a watercolor. When you come to the wet parts the paint will flow and form its own patterns.

This technique was actually created in a deliberate manner through the use of the random word technique. The random word used was "hair."

In the filament technique we take the creative focus and then put down some of the normal requirements when designing something for that focus. We then take each requirement separately and totally ignore the actual context of the focus area. We extend from the requirement a "filament" consisting of ways of satisfying the requirement. We then scan through the parallel filaments and pick out certain items along each strand. We then seek to put these together as a new idea. This picking out of items may be explicit or may be unconscious.

Consider a filament approach to advertising. (The normal requirements are in upper-case letters down the left-hand side. From each extends the filament.)

ADVERTISING

VISIBLE: large, brightly lit, in a dominant place, catches the eye, frequently handled.

ATTENTION CATCHING: noise, shouting, scandal, surprise, unexpected.

BENEFITS: promise, value, immediate reward, money.

GOOD IMAGE: warm feeling, associations, quality, good things, attractive.

CREDIBLE: believable, endorsement, authorized, official.

From this comes the concept of corporations running lotteries for charities: WWF, United Way, animal protection, Oxfam, and so on. The advertising for the lottery, the physical tickets, the winning ceremony (unless it is an instant rub-off lottery) would all be tied in with a particular brand image. The key words leading to this idea were probably "frequently handled"; "surprise"; "immediate reward"; and "authorized."

A creative thinking session is trying to find a new way of fastening shoes. The filament technique is being used.

SHOES FASTENING SYSTEM

ROBUST: hardwearing, rubber, glass, steel, ceramic, asphalt.

ADJUSTABLE: continuous, notches, elastic, springs.

STAY FASTENED: hooks, knots, screws, glue, bolts, nails.

STRONG: steel, Kevlar, plastic, metal, rope, chain.

SIMPLE: single action, open/close snap.

ATTRACTIVE: printing, color, design, sculpture.

From this comes the idea of a ceramic or enamelled metal buckle which has hooks at the side that hook into eyes on the shoes. The buckle can be changed easily according to the clothes that are being worn. The buckle becomes a fashion and jewelry item because of its shape and appearance.

The key words here were probably "ceramic"; "hooks"; "plastic"; "design."

In a way, the filament technique produces a different sort of "stratal." The filaments for each requirement form a layer of the stratal and sensitize the mind. There is also an element of the random word process because we can take different items in each filament and then try to connect them up in a new idea. So we can either let an idea emerge or seek to force an idea from some juxtaposition of items.

A creative thinking session is setting out to improve "banking premises" (retail banking).

BANKING PREMISES

EASY TO REACH: around the corner, at every corner, in the middle of a store, at transport points, at sports centers.

SUFFICIENT SPACE: large, uncluttered, waiting space, extra space when required.

WELL LAID OUT: moving spaces, waiting spaces, operating spaces, clear indication of places to go, no bottleneck, ease of entry and exit.

SUFFICIENT STAFF: no peak load problems, flexible operations, reserve staff if needed, operations not requiring staff.

In this particular case we shall take some items and put them together deliberately in an effort to force an idea.

We take: at transport points, extra space when required, clear indication of places to go, flexible operations.

From this comes the idea of mobile banking vans that can be temporarily located at need areas. Reserve vans can be called

up if necessary. The functions can be chosen to meet the needs.
Such vans might operate in car parks.

So the filament technique can be used in two ways:

1. Emerging ideas are formed when you look through the filaments and allow ideas to emerge.
2. Forced ideas are formed when you put some items together and then try to get an idea from them.

We have now come to the end of the specific lateral thinking techniques. But there is still a great deal to be done in order to complete the creative process.

Application of the Lateral Thinking Techniques

A number of formal lateral thinking techniques have been put forward. Most of these tools have been shown to work systematically and effectively through years of use with different people in different cultures. There is no question that these tools do work. If you find that a certain tool does not work for you, consider three possibilities:

1. That the tool has not worked for you on this particular occasion. This is to be expected, because every tool does not work in every instance it is used.
2. That you need further practice and confidence in the tool. This comes from experience.
3. That there is some "sticking point" in your use of the tool and this tool may not work well for you.

In essence, the tools are so fundamental and so basic to the creative process that anyone who cannot make the tools work is unlikely to be able to be creative. It is important, however, that students of creative thinking should make an effort to get the tools to work for them. It would be a pity if they gave up after the first try and decided that they are never going to be able to be creative. As with riding a bicycle, the first stages are awkward until you get the "hang" of it.

If someone at a seminar tells me that he or she finds that the techniques do not work, I reply:

> Maybe the techniques do not work for you, at this moment, but there are a lot of people who have found that the techniques do work for them.

That is the great advantage of years of experience in the field. You get to know when things work and this is no longer a matter of opinion.

Do the different techniques have different uses? Do the different techniques have different areas of application? Which techniques are best in which situations?

APPLICA-
TION
OF THE
LATERAL
THINKING
TECH-
NIQUES

GENERAL USE OF THE TECHNIQUES

In general, each of the lateral thinking techniques can be used on any occasion that demands lateral thinking. It may, however, be necessary to formulate the creative task in a suitable way. For example, the provocative "escape" technique works best when there is something from which to escape. So how could this be used in a "greenfield" situation where your difficulty is that you do not know where to start? So you need to formulate the task in the following way:

What would be the "normal" or standard thinking approach to this situation? Now let me escape from that.

For the opposite example we can look at problem solving. Here there is a definite point to be reached—removal of the problem. So how could the "random word" technique work here? By definition, the random word technique is not directed to a purpose and works best with a "general-area" type of focus. So we keep the problem needs in mind and carry out the random word technique. We then look to see if any of the ideas generated are directly of use for the problem. Even if this is not so then we try to shape or bend an idea to see if that idea could be of value in helping to solve the problem. There may be a principle that is usable even if the idea itself is not usable.

It is quite true that some people are happier with some of the techniques. Creative thinkers come to have their favorite technique because they find that a technique is easy to use or it works well for them. For example, many people favor the random word technique because it is so very easy. Others prefer the escape technique in order to escape from the usual thinking on the subject. The bolder people like the stepping-stone because it permits more extreme provocations. The concept fan is a favorite with more systematic people who like to proceed step by step.

191

Even if you do have a favorite technique it is important to practice the others from time to time. As a golfer you may have a favorite club but you need to retain some skill in the use of every club in your bag.

SPECIFIC USE OF THE TECHNIQUES

Some of the techniques are of direct use on any occasion when there is a need for new ideas.

Focus

The ability to focus precisely and to refocus and to create new subfocuses is of creative value on any occasion. Even if you are provided with a fixed task, there is benefit in clarifying the focus and also creating new focuses within the set task. Repeating the focus from time to time and giving alternative definitions of the focus (which might be a problem) are also basic creative habits suitable for all occasions.

Challenge

The creative challenge can be applied to something that exists or to the thinking that takes place during the creative effort. Why do we have to look at it this way? Why do we have to keep within these boundaries? Even when there is a formed solution or idea, that itself can also be challenged (or some aspect of it).

Alternatives

The simple search for alternatives is the very essence of creativity. Are there alternative definitions of the focus? What are the alternative approaches? What alternative techniques might we use? Whenever we extract a "concept" during the creative thinking we immediately look around for alternative ways of carrying through the concept. Even when we have a final idea we can ask: Is there a better way of doing this?

Random Input

The random input technique (as in the random word) has a very wide applicability. If you are stuck and have run out of ideas during the creative thinking process, you can try an instant "random word" to open up new lines of thinking. When you do not know where to begin, the random word will provide starting points. The random word works best when the focus can be rephrased as a "general-area" type of focus.

Stratal

The stratal is also a general-purpose technique. At the beginning of the thinking exercise you put together a stratal that refers to the whole situation about which you are thinking. This can apply to any situation. In the course of your thinking you can try another stratal, which this time refers to your thinking about the subject. What sort of things have come up in your thinking? In its general application the stratal is similar to the random word but is less provocative. It is more useful for dealing with complex situations.

The Filament Technique

Wherever the requirements of the situation can be spelled out, the filament technique can be used. The requirements are listed one under the other. From each requirement there comes the "filament" which steps outside the context of the present situation. Since broad requirements can be put down for most thinking situations, the filament technique is applicable to most situations.

BASIC TYPES OF THINKING

There are some very basic types of thinking that can be considered along with the most appropriate tools to use for each type. These basic types are an oversimplification of thinking but help to provide some guidelines for use of the different lateral thinking techniques.

Achievement Thinking (Reach)

How do we reach this point? How do we solve this problem? How do we carry out this task? We have a clear idea of where we want to be. In the case of problems we want to remove the problem or be without it. This type of thinking covers problems, tasks, projects, negotiation, conflicts, and so on. While many of

193

the techniques of lateral thinking are suitable in "achievement thinking" the most appropriate are as follows:

CHALLENGE.   The boundaries, the dominating concepts, the essential factors and even the definition of the problem can all be challenged. Why do we have to look at it this way? Why do we have took at it as a problem?

CONCEPT FAN.   This is the key technique for achievement thinking because it is concerned with "how do we get there?" What are the needed concepts? The concept fan may itself turn up new focus points, which will also need creative attention. Proceeding systematically through the concept fan should turn up many alternative approaches and routes of achievement. Obviously, the concept fan is an elaborated form of the search for alternatives. When it is not possible to go through the concept fan process then a simple search for alternatives is appropriate.

STEPPING-STONE.   This strongly provocative technique is useful in trying to get really new approaches by turning the problem inside out and putting things in a way that demands new thinking. While the concept fan will flush out a variety of possible approaches, the stepping-stone provocation will create some entirely different ones. If the problem has been around a long time it is important to try at least one provocative technique; otherwise the same ground will be covered again.

Improvement Thinking (Change)

Improvement thinking can often be phrased as achievement thinking (how can we get a faster process?) but is worth considering separately because there are certain special characteristics of improvement. The first characteristic is that there is already something in operation which works. The second characteristic is that the direction of improvement (speed up, less time, less energy, less mistakes) is phrased in a general and open-ended way. Again, many techniques can be used but the most useful might be as follows:

CHALLENGE.   This is the key technique. How did we come to do it this way? Why does it have to be done this way? Why do we work within these boundaries? We can challenge both what is and also our thinking about the process. Continuity analysis is particularly relevant.

ALTERNATIVES. We seek alternatives at every point. We define fixed points and then look for alternative ways of reaching those fixed points. This does not only apply to the overall process but to every part of it.

ESCAPE. This is the most appropriate provocative technique. We spell out the things that we "take for granted" in the normal process and then we escape from them. With improvement there are always things to escape from because we are seeking to improve an ongoing process. Even the most fundamental matters can be subjected to the escape provocation.

Greenfield Thinking (Start)

Where do we start? How do we get going? Greenfield thinking is the opposite of improvement thinking: with improvement thinking we have the existing process to work upon, but with greenfield thinking we have nothing to work upon except a general brief. Invention and design are obvious examples of greenfield thinking. So is the development of new opportunities or new concepts. Sometimes greenfield thinking is falsely treated as "achievement" thinking (I need a new invention here).

RANDOM INPUT. This is the key technique. The random input technique will immediately provide some new starting points whatever the situation might be. The random input leads thinking out in different directions. Once these directions are there they can be modified or changed. Further directions may be suggested. That is why rock groups and others use this technique.

THE FILAMENT TECHNIQUE. The general requirements of the task (the "brief") can be put down and then the filament technique can be used to develop lines of thought. You can let ideas emerge from this or you can use the "forcing" aspect of the technique in which certain things are held together in order to force a new idea.

WISHFUL THINKING. This is one of the methods for setting up the stepping-stone provocation. In the greenfield situation you can set up this "wishful thinking" fantasy and that can open up lines of thought. This is best combined with a strong effort to pick out and to formulate new concepts as ideas develop. What is the concept behind this idea? How else might this concept be used?

Organizing Thinking (Arrange)

All the elements are to hand. How do we organize things in the best possible way? This applies to plans, strategies, some types of design, and organizing in general. While much of this thinking can be analytical optimization there may also be a need for some new approaches.

ALTERNATIVES.   The key thing is to try out different possibilities. These should not only be "reasonable" alternatives but also provocative ones. What would happen if we put things this way?

CHALLENGE.   Much of "arranging" thinking will be guided by the traditional ways of doing things and also by assumptions, boundaries, and restraints. So challenge is very important to "challenge" the usual approaches and to attempt fresh approaches.

DISTORTION.   This is one of the ways of setting up a stepping-stone-type of provocation. It is particularly appropriate to the arranging type of thinking because the usual arrangements are "distorted" in order to force some new approaches. This type of provocation can lead to sudden insights and changes in the way things are done.

SPECIFIC SITUATIONS

I shall now go through some specific situations one by one. Much of what is written for each situation will repeat the comments given in the basic types of thinking. It would be impossible to leave this out. The lateral thinking techniques most applicable to each situation will be given. This does not exclude other techniques because there are occasions during any creative thinking when each of the techniques might be used. For example, if you are getting nowhere in solving a problem, you might want to use a random word then and there. So the techniques are not fixed recipes but suggestions to help you if you have no better strategy of your own. In time, you may set up your own preferred strategies and sets of techniques for dealing with each situation.

There are also times when one type of situation may include another. For example, in conflict resolution specific "problems" might occur. Or in a design situation there might be a need for "improvement." At other times you may not be very clear as to how to classify the situation in the first place. There is no harm in treating a situation in any number of different ways, so long as you make progress and develop the needed ideas. Be careful to not classify everything as a "problem" just because you need to get an output.

APPLICA-
TION
OF THE
LATERAL
THINKING
TECH-
NIQUES

In all cases, the relationship to information, analysis, and logic is assumed to be on the following lines:

1. You have tried hard with information, analysis, and logic and you have not gotten anywhere. Creativity is your only hope.
2. You have produced some alternatives through information, analysis, and logic but you are willing to try creativity to see if there might be a fresh approach.
3. These are old problems (situations) that have been around a long time and upon which a lot of logical effort has been expended. It is worth using creative thinking right away.
4. In the course of your analytical and logical thinking you have defined certain focus points where you know you need new ideas. The creative effort is focused on these points.
5. There is a constant switching from the analytical/logical mode to the creative mode as you go along.

Improvement

As I have mentioned many times, this is potentially the biggest volume use of creativity, because everything might be improved. The difficulty is getting anyone to make the improving effort because we are so used to thinking only about "problems."

Focus is important because we need to be clear about the focus. We also need to be able to focus on anything we choose. There is no need for it to be a problem. If we succeed in focusing on something that other people have not looked at then even a little creative effort can make a big difference.

Challenge is important because we have to assume that the current way of doing things may not be the best, but it is there for reasons of continuity. We also need to challenge boundaries, assumptions, essential factors, and so on, in order to obtain the necessary freedom to suggest changes. It is important to remember that challenge is not a critical attack but an exploration: might there be other ways?

197

The search for alternatives is of key importance because that is how we are going to make the improvement (unless we drop something altogether). The search for alternatives needs to be at different levels: the overall purpose, the concepts, the detail level. Defining fixed points will help keep the search for alternatives on track.

The concept fan is a way of examining how improvements can be made. What are the general "directions" of improvement and how might we proceed in these directions? The concept fan may also be applied to the overall "purpose" of the operation. Forget what we are doing right now. The purpose of this operation is this. Now let us set up a concept fan to see how we might achieve this purpose.

An examination of the "concepts" involved in the current process may lead towards a change in the concepts or the development of better ways to put the concepts into action.

The escape method of provocation allows us to "escape" from any aspect of what we are now doing. This forces us to rethink the process.

The stepping-stone type of provocation when applied to current systems can radically change the nature of the whole system. This method is less useful when applied to detail than when applied to whole systems.

Problems

Focus is important for defining the problem and trying out alternative definitions of the problem. Focus is important for creating subproblems within the overall problem. Focus can shift attention to aspects of the problem.

Challenge is important for challenging the presentation of the problem and for challenging the way the situation is being looked at. Perhaps it is as much opportunity as problem. Do we need to tackle the problem? Might it just go away? Challenge is also important for challenging assumptions, boundaries, polarizations, and all those things that limit the range of possible approaches or solutions.

Alternatives are important at every point. With small problems the search for alternatives out of our experience may be sufficient to solve the problem. The definition of the fixed point helps this search.

The concept fan is the major technique for problem solving. What are the "directions" or approaches? What concepts will work in each direction? What ideas can be used for putting the concepts into action? It must be remembered that the concept fan will turn up some sound ideas but is unlikely to provoke any really new ideas. In the course of doing the concept fan, however, several new focus points may emerge (how do we park cars above street level?)

APPLICA-
TION
OF THE
LATERAL
THINKING
TECH-
NIQUES

The escape type of provocation is used on the standard or current approach to this problem or to problems of this type. How do we usually approach this problem? Can we escape from this? The escape technique can also be used at any stage in the creative thinking. When it seems that something is being taken for granted then there can be an attempt to escape from this.

Stepping-stone provocations of any type can be used to alter the whole picture in such a way that new ideas may emerge. This is particularly so when the problem involves the behavior of some system. The stepping-stone may be the best way of getting radically new approaches.

The filament technique is useful when it is a "design"-type problem with many requirements that have to be met.

The random word technique is used when there is the feeling that there are no new ideas and the same ground is being covered again and again. This technique is unlikely to provide an immediate solution but can open up new lines of thought.

Tasks

If a problem is something that you have to do, then a "task" is something you want to do. The task may be given you by yourself or by someone else. We are concerned here with "creative tasks" that demand new ideas and not just competence.

Focus is important in order to be very clear as to what we are trying to do. Remember the bad habit of creative people of always wanting to have ideas about everything except the assigned task.

The concept fan is useful mainly to look at what the usual approaches to the task might be. The fan might indicate an important concept and then the focus shifts to ways of carrying out that concept (how do we make cars disappear once they have reached the city center?).

Concepts are extremely important. There is a need to generate concepts and to play around with concepts. Indeed, any idea that suggests itself is mainly of use in suggesting another concept. There should be no rush to get down to the practical idea level. There will be plenty of time for that later. Remaining at the concept level is more likely to provide a fresh approach.

The random word is central here. The random word is used to open up new lines of thinking that should be very different from the concept fan approaches.

Wishful thinking is probably the most useful of the stepping-stone provocations because it allows an open-ended step forward. There is no limit to the fantasies that can be put up as provocations.

The filament technique is used when the requirements of the task seem clear. Quite often the objective of the task is actually defined by a set of specifications or requirements.

Opportunity

There is some change in circumstance and the hope that this might somehow provide an opportunity. There is a new product of material; what opportunities does this provide? Surveys shows changes in attitudes and behavior; do these offer opportunities?

Wishful thinking is important here. This type of stepping-stone provocation can open up a range of concepts. The thinker is not fettered by reasonableness.

The stratal is useful because, by laying out aspects of the situation, it allows the mind to make new connections. The stratal can be used in the passive or active way (forcing ideas).

The random word might work to open up some line of thinking and to provide at least a starting point from which to move on to concepts.

Somewhere in the course of the thinking, but not necessarily at the beginning, it is useful to try to extract and to formulate different concepts. These may arise from the creative work that has already been done. Occasionally concepts suggest themselves right at the beginning.

The escape technique can be used from time to time in order to escape from the things which seem to be "taken for granted" in the opportunity thinking itself. Opportunity thinking can easily get bogged down in certain directions. Thinkers need to be forced out of these new assumptions.

Challenge can also be used on the thinking process itself. The reasons are the same as for the escape technique: why are we concerned only with the low price of this material?

Invention

There are many different starting points for invention. Some of these might be open-ended "general-area"-type focuses (I want to invent something for gardening). At other time there may be a specific focus (I want an infinitely adjustable nozzle for the water hose). Quite often the invention process is almost exactly the same as the "task" process.

APPLICA-
TION
OF THE
LATERAL
THINKING
TECH-
NIQUES

Focus is important because focus can change in the course of the thinking and it is important to note the new focus. An inventor may set out to invent something and end up inventing something else. With invention this is perfectly permissible.

The concept fan can give some approaches. If the focus has been an unusual one, then the concept fan may be sufficient to complete the invention because there may well be available methods of fulfilling the task.

The filament technique is most useful here by allowing the requirements themselves to be used to stimulate new ideas. Inventors usually have in mind a very specific set of requirements.

Wishful thinking (and other types of stepping-stone provocation) can provide a different approach if the focus for the invention is not an unusual one. The requirements of the task can be subjected to this type of provocation (Po, the water itself adjusts the nozzle of the hose).

The random input technique (using objects as well as words) can provide fresh starting points when the other starting points have not led anywhere interesting.

Challenge can be used in the course of the thinking to challenge why certain assumptions are being made and why certain boundaries are being accepted. Quite often the breakthrough in an invention comes precisely as a result of this challenge (why does a lawnmower have to have wheels?).

Design

An invention is a creative effort that may not have an outcome. Design is required to have an outcome. It is always possible to fall back to traditional and standard ways of doing something if nothing better can be found.

Challenge is important at the beginning to challenge the usual approach, assumptions, and received wisdom. Challenge is also useful in the course of the thinking to challenge the way things are going.

Escape provocation is important for the same reason as challenge. There is an escape from the traditional design assumptions. There is an attempt to escape from the initial thinking of the designer who is faced with the design task (what is my thinking here?). By itself escape can set off a whole new thinking direction. This direction can then be developed quite logically.

Alternatives can be used at all levels. There are alternatives in the broad sense of alternative approaches to the whole design. There are also alternatives of implementation (what materials can I use here?). Then there are alternatives of detail within the overall direction of the design. A very clear definition of the fixed point is needed when alternatives are being sought; otherwise, a change at one point can upset things elsewhere.

Concepts are also used in two ways. There may be a playing around with concepts right at the start of the design process. During the thinking process itself it is also useful to crystallize the concepts that emerge because there is a need to explore ways of carrying out the concepts. Without this conceptualization a design may have a momentum of detail and end up as a mess.

Stepping-stone provocation can be tried right at the beginning in order to provoke a totally new design concept. It is worth trying.

The random word is useful in design in order to overcome complacency. Often a design concept emerges early and then serves to trap all further thinking on the matter. It is difficult to get away from this. A random word can suddenly open up a whole new concept, which serves to show that the existing concept is not inevitable.

Stagnant Situations

A stagnant situation is one where creativity seems to have died. There are no new ideas. The same ground is being covered again and again. It seems impossible to find a new approach. This situation may occur in the course of thinking about something or it may occur over a longer term during which any attempt to think about the matter comes back to the same ideas. Stagnant situations can apply to any of the specific situations listed here.

The random word is by far the simplest and most effective way of getting ideas moving again. The random words just starts up new lines of thought. Even if these are unrealistic, the "log-jam" is shifted.

The escape provocation technique can also be used. This is not used on the subject matter of the thinking but on the thinking itself. For example, there can be an escape from something that is taken for granted in the solutions that keep turning up (Po, we do not have to keep people happy).

The filament technique used in the "forced" mode can also be useful because it operates in a similar manner to the random word.

APPLICA-
TION
OF THE
LATERAL
THINKING
TECH-
NIQUES

Greenfield Situations

These are "blank sheet of paper" situations. You do not know where to start. This is very different from the stagnant situation where you keep coming back to the same ideas.

The stratal can be useful in providing a setting from which ideas can start to emerge.

Where general requirements are available then the filament technique in both passive and active modes can also provide some starting points.

As might be expected, the random input technique is powerful in greenfield situations since it does not have to work on anything at all. The technique does not have to be limited to random words. There can be random objects, random reading, random visits to exhibitions, and so on.

Projects

A task requires a creative effort and a project requires a competence effort. There may, however, be a willingness to see if creativity can make any contribution to the competence of the project. There may just be a better approach.

Both the overall focus and chosen subfocuses are important. These are "thinking" focuses, not action objectives.

There can be challenges to the normal thinking, to one's own current thinking, to assumptions, to boundaries, and so on.

The concept fan is the classic achievement approach. The fan may itself turn up some new focuses, which are then subjected to further creative thinking (how can we transport it by water?).

The escape provocation may be used on the standard approaches to projects such as these. What do we normally take for granted? What happens if we escape from such things?

The filament technique lays down the project requirements and may then find a different approach. The passive mode of use is more appropriate here (let the ideas emerge).

Attention to the basic concepts involved in the project can lead to improvements in the concepts, changes in the concepts, or just better ways of putting the concepts into action.

The creative effort may apply to the whole project or just to various subsections of the project. That is why the focus process is so important.

Many of the points made about "design" or "task" situations also apply to projects.

Conflict

Bargaining, negotiating, and fighting are all aspects of the conflict situation in which opposing interests seek to have their own way. The usual methods involve power, pressure, fear, and pain. There is much more scope for creative thinking than most people (especially those involved in conflict resolution) suppose.

The search for alternatives is the basic process. These include alternative perceptions, not just of the overall scene but of every move or development. How is this being perceived? How could it be perceived? There are alternative ways of presenting suggestions. There are alternative values and interests. There are alternative packages. Being clear about the "fixed points" makes it easier to be precise about alternatives.

The creative pause is very important. Instead of instant knee-jerk reactions to what is proposed, there is need for a pause in which the proposal is seen as much as an opportunity as a threat.

The process of "challenge" is not directed at the opposing party but at one's own thinking. Why does the situation have to be looked at this way? Are these things really important? How much is continuity? Are we locked into certain positions? What are the polarizations? What are the "essential factors"? Are they really essential?

The escape process, which so often goes along with the challenge process, can also be applied to one's own thinking. If the conditions of discussion are suitable, then the escape provocation can be attempted on a joint basis (Po, there was no need to have fixed working hours).

There needs to be attention to concepts of value. The ability to perceive different concepts of value is the basis of successful conflict resolution. Once concepts of value have been perceived then there can be attempts to design ways of providing this value. Concepts of action and pressure also need to be extracted and redesigned (or blocked). It is a mistake to believe that all the pieces are already on the board as in a chess game and that it is only a matter of moving the pieces around.

The stratal can be useful both at the beginning of, and also after, a lot of thinking has taken place. The stratal allows the thinker to pause and stand back so that new ideas can emerge.

As always, the random word can be useful in one's own thinking in order to turn up some new lines of thinking when an impasse is reached. If conditions are very favorable then the random word can be tried on a joint basis with both parties taking part in the creative exercise.

APPLICA-
TION
OF THE
LATERAL
THINKING
TECH-
NIQUES

Futures

We normally get our picture of the future by extending present trends and anticipating convergences where different things come together to produce a new effect. There are times when we need to get a richer view of the future and to seek possible discontinuities. For that we need creativity.

The stratal is a very useful way of allowing separate factors to come together in the mind to create possibilities. There can be several different stratals around the same focus or around different focuses. It is important that the stratal be done honestly and not just "designed" to reflect our existing thinking. One way to prevent this is to put a number of stratal "lines" into a bag and just to draw forth five of them, randomly, to form the stratal.

All the ways of setting up stepping-stone provocations (exaggeration, reversal, distortion, wishful thinking) are useful in generating possible discontinuities. These provocations serve to move us away from continuities.

A combination of the escape type of provocation and concept analysis can be useful. We look at existing and possible future concepts and then we escape from them or from some aspect of them (Po, we did not have to work to earn money).

Even if some of the basic concepts stay the same there might be alternative ways of carrying them out (for example, alternative work styles). So the definition of fixed points and the search for alternatives is important.

Finally the random word can offer some new possibilities that might not have come up in any other way. These possibilities should be explored in their own right and also examined to see how they fit in with the other possibilities that have been generated.

The challenge process can be used at any stage to challenge our thinking about the future even as we are doing that thinking.

Strategy

Setting a strategy is a complex process that involves problems, opportunities, tasks, futures, and conflict, all of which are put together in a design process. Setting a strategy involves a considerable input from information and the analysis of trends, possibilities, and competitive responses. Creativity is needed for the introduction of new concepts and for the design of flexibility and fall-back positions.

Focus is, of course, very important. It is necessary to be clear about the overall focus and the various subfocuses that are needed. What is the purpose of the strategy? What is it going to achieve? How is it going to be treated?

Challenge is very important in order to challenge conventional and traditional wisdom and also to challenge thinking within the organization. Assumptions about the future and about competitive responses can be challenged. Boundaries set by regulations, values, and technology can also be challenged. Often there are polarizations (low-cost or premium operations) that can be challenged. There is always a cycle of concepts cohering into a strategy and then being pulled apart again through challenge. Eventually things settle down to the final strategy.

There are alternative strategies, alternative concepts, and alternative ways of carrying through a particular strategy. There are alternative views of the future. Here, even more than elsewhere, it is vital to define the fixed points before generating alternatives.

A great deal of attention needs to be paid to concepts, which in this case are more important than ideas. If a concept is wrong, then no idea will put it right. All ideas are treated as ways of getting concepts through "pulling back."

When there is a rich assortment of concepts, these can be organized as a concept fan. Such an organization will then give the broad directions in which it is possible to move. Ways of carrying through the concepts can also be attended to.

The escape type of provocation can be applied to existing thinking within the organization and also within the industry. Escape-type provocation can also be applied to the existing formulations of the strategy.

Radical new ideas will require the stepping-stone type of provocation and the distortion version in particular.

Planning

Much of what has been written about futures, design, projects, and strategy is also relevant to the planning process. It has to be assumed that the normal logical process of planning has been attended to and there is still a willingness to seek better ideas.

Alternatives can be sought out at every step. There may be different routes to be taken or different ways of taking the same route. There may be alternative places to put the monitoring points. Provocative alternatives can be used (what would happen if we did this?).

There can be challenges to the plan itself or to the conditions that the plan has to meet. Do we have to accept these boundaries? Are these really essential factors?

The escape type of provocation can be used both to generate new concepts and also to test the flexibility of the plan (Po, interest rates do not fall).

Any attempt to radically restructure the plan would need the stepping-stone type of provocation, which might serve to change perceptions about the situation. If the perception of the situation changes then the plan would have to change, too.

At this stage there should be a good general feeling about how the different techniques can be applied. We can summarize the basic uses of the techniques as follows:

Focus: to define the focus and changing focuses. To seek alternative definitions of the focus. To choose subfocuses.

Challenge: to challenge traditional thinking, existing thinking, and the thinking taking place during a creative session. Also to challenge the surroundings of the thinking: assumptions, boundaries, and so on.

Alternatives: to find different ways of doing things and of satisfying a defined fixed point. Can be operated at different levels ranging from the broad to the detailed.

Concept Fan: an elaborated method for finding different ways of doing things by going through concepts. Useful in achievement thinking.

Concepts: deliberate attention to concepts. Seeking to extract and crystallize concepts. Pulling back from ideas to concepts. Modifying and changing concepts. Finding ways of putting the concepts into action. Useful in all areas that are driven by concepts.

Escape Provocation: useful in all areas where challenge is useful. Escape provocation turns the challenge into a provocation. Useful for looking at existing methods and also for looking at existing thinking. Can be applied to the creative thinking that is taking place at the time.

Stepping-stone Provocation: generally used to try to get radical changes in the whole system or approach. The most provocative of the techniques. The wishful thinking method also has a special use in generating ideas from a greenfield situation. Stepping-stones generally work best when applied to the whole system.

Random Input: used to provide fresh ideas on any occasion. Used to get going in greenfield situations. Used to get going again when ideas have run out. Used to seek additional and different ideas when there are already some ideas on the table.

Stratal: Used at the beginning of the thinking to allow ideas to emerge. Used later on in the thinking to see what might emerge from the thinking that has already been done.

The Filament Technique: useful whenever there is a known set of requirements. Can be used in a passive way to let ideas emerge and can also be used in an active or "forced" way where it behaves in a similar manner to the random word.

THE SIX THINKING HATS

The Six Thinking Hats method has not been included in the techniques discussed in this section because it is a framework process that applies to thinking in general within an organization. The green hat is a specific request for a creative effort but does not indicate how that effort is to be made. This may be a simple pause in order to consider other possibilities or an attempt to suggest alternatives. Other lateral thinking techniques can also be used at this point. The main value of the green hat is the space it makes for creative effort.

The yellow hat has a high value in directing thinking towards searching for feasibility and values. So an emerging idea can be given constructive attention at the outset. Someone who opposes the idea might be asked directly to make an effort to discover value in the idea and to suggest how the idea could be carried out.

A very important aspect of the Six Hats method is the possibility of restricting black hat thinking to certain specific times instead of it being applied at every moment. Black hat thinking would be applied in the treatment of ideas in order to point out the defects that needed to be overcome. Black hat thinking would be applied in the assessment of the ideas.

It is in such ways that the framework of Six Hats facilitates creative effort.

There are times when a simple sequence of hats might be used almost directly as a creative procedure. In such cases the sequence might be:

White Hat: the information base. What do we know?
Green Hat: alternatives, suggestions, and ideas.
Yellow Hat: feasibility, benefits, and values of the ideas.
Black Hat: difficulties, dangers, problems, and points for caution.
Red Hat: intuition and feelings about the ideas.
Blue Hat: conclusion.

Harvesting

A farmer sows a whole field of grain but when harvest comes he is content to harvest only one-quarter of the field. The rest is wasted. That is what most people do when using creative thinking.

Harvesting, like focusing, is one of the weakest parts of creative thinking. The reason is that both seem simple and straightforward. There is nothing exotic or exciting about the procedures, so not much attention is paid to them. In fact, both processes are every bit as important as the more "glamorous" aspects of creative thinking.

When we set out to be creative we are only interested in coming up with an idea that is new, practical, and saleable to others. We search for that magic idea. We note such magic ideas when they arise and ignore everything else that is happening in the creative thinking session.

If you are not a bird-watcher, you look through binoculars at what the birds are doing and cannot really understand why anyone should be interested in this sort of behavior. But over time you start to notice aspects of behavior. You start to pick out patterns. You notice differences. Then it starts to become fascinating.

A person stands before a work of art and decides that he or she likes the work or does not like it. After some art appreciation classes, that same person starts to notice much more: the composition, the brushwork, the use of light and shade, the color choices, and so on.

It is necessary to be trained to notice things. Without such training we simply do not see what is in front of us. There is a need for just such training in order to harvest the outcome of a creative thinking session. It is not enough just to put down the "magic" ideas and to ignore the rest. That is a huge waste of what has been going on.

In any creative thinking session there are at least three purposes:

1. To find the magic idea.
2. To produce new ideas that can be shaped into usable ideas.
3. To stock the mind with a repertoire of concepts and ideas that may not be useful at the moment but that will enrich any future thinking on the same or related matters (and even on other matters).

With poor harvesting, the second and third of these purposes are ignored.

Careful harvesting may mean making notes during the session or listening carefully to a tape recording afterwards. It may mean thinking back over the session to pick out certain points. In this way the full value of the session can be extracted and recorded.

To help in this very important harvesting process it is useful to have a sort of checklist. Items on this checklist do overlap and there may, at times, be difficulty in deciding where to put something. This does not matter so much; the purpose of the checklist is to make us notice things—no matter in which box they might then be placed.

As I go through the points on the checklist I will give as examples the harvesting from a discussion on the design of a children's playground.

Specific Ideas

These are concrete ideas which can be put into action. Specific ideas include the "magic" ideas which everyone at once recognizes as marvelous but also includes other usable and workable ideas. This is the traditional output from a creative thinking session.

In the playground discussion some specific ideas that emerged were:

a cafe for parents

markings on the surface for "new games"

tight segmentation by age groups

"For-Instance" Ideas

These are ideas which are acknowledged to be unworkable but the ideas carry some concept or process that is seen to be valuable. The "for-instance" idea is merely an illustration or example.

211

In the playground discussion "for-instance" ideas included:

boxes for building things

a game in which teams pulled a heavy block across the playground

an inventors' corner

Seedling Ideas

A seedling idea is just the beginning of an idea. There is potential in the idea but the idea has to be grown and formed into something useful. Such ideas are going to need a lot of work done on them. But there is the sense of value and potential. A seedling idea is different from a "for-instance" idea because there is no intention of working on the latter.

In the playground discussion, "seedling ideas" included:

different private enterprise companies to sponsor the playground one day a week each

contracting groups to design playground games

playground colored uniforms

Direct Concepts

These are concepts that emerged during the discussion. Such concepts may then have gone forward to ideas or remained as concepts. In both cases the concepts are recorded as concepts. It is particularly important to record "value concepts." Concepts are not easy to record because they may only exist as concepts for a moment and because everyone assumes that the purpose of a concept is to lead only to an idea. A firm harvesting effort must be made to note and record concepts.

In the playground discussion the following concepts emerged:

the playground should involve children

a chance to meet other children

working together with others as a team

flexible use of the same space

"Pull-back" Concepts

These are concepts that never emerged directly as concepts during the discussion. They are concepts which were consciously "pulled back" during the discussion from ideas or "for-instance" ideas. This pulling back to concept level may have taken place during the session but should always take place at the time of harvesting. So it becomes important to go through all the different types of ideas and to make a conscious effort to "pull back" from the idea to a concept level. The concept may be implicit in the idea but there is great value in making it explicit as a concept in its own right.

During the playground discussion the following concepts were "pulled back":

commercial sponsorship

children to be allowed to innovate

team forming

structures for new games

Directions

The difference between "concepts" and "directions" was explained in the section on the concept fan. Directions are no more than very broad concepts or approaches to a situation. For this reason there may be overlap between the concept category and the direction category. This does not matter. The effort is to capture the broad directions, whether these were spelled out or remained implicit.

The directions in the playground discussion were:

involvement

playing with others

flexibility

Needs

In the course of the creative effort some clear needs might have emerged. For example, the need to find some way of turning a concept into a practical idea. There might also be defined directions that need concepts.

"We need to find a way of doing this."

The definition of need areas that become visible during a creative thinking session is an important part of the creative process.

213

To recognize a hole or gap is the start of doing something about it.

The following needs arose during the playground discussion:

the need for nonintrusive guidance

the need for ways to form teams

the need for ways to segment age access to the playground

the need for ways of involving commercial interests

New Focuses

New creative focuses can arise directly from the needs that have been noted. Even so it is worth putting down a new focus specifically as a "new creative focus." This means that the focus can later be tackled directly by the group or by individuals who have been assigned certain creative tasks.

In the playground discussion the following new creative focuses were defined:

playground team games (general area focus)

ways to organize teams (purpose focus)

involvement of commercial organizations (general area focus)

Changes

During any creative session there may be a change of thinking. New lines of thinking may open up. There may be a change of direction. The discussion may start off in one direction and then come to develop in a new direction. Such changes should be noted on a "from/to" basis.

We seemed to change from this direction . . . to this direction.
We started off looking at it in this way . . . and then changed to this way . . .

In the playground discussion the following changes were noted:

a change from looking at the playground as a place for individual play to a place for team effort.

a change from providing fixed and traditional amusements to devising new playground games

214

a change from avoiding commercial interests to trying to find a way to involve them

Flavor

The final point on the checklist is "flavor." This refers to the overall flavor of the entire session. The value of picking out this flavor is that in future sessions you may try to develop some different ideas. For example, if a thinking session was devoted to finding who was to blame for something, then a future session might try to be more constructive. There should only be one "flavor" that can be seen to cover much of the session even if there are elements that do not fit under that flavor.

The overall flavor of the playground discussion was "new children-centered approaches."

In the magazine world it is said that getting a new subscriber is four times as expensive as retaining an old one. Something like this applies to harvesting. To pick out an idea or concept that has been brought forward is very much easier than having to generate it all over again. So harvesting is important, even though it may seem tedious and time-consuming. It can also happen that during the process of harvesting, new ideas and concepts may emerge even as the existing ones are being noted.

Once you get used to harvesting with the checklist, you become more able to notice things during the session itself. You can now write down what you notice. This allows you to get more out of the session even as you go through it. For example, the ability to notice concept changes may lead to an effort to find ideas to put a concept into action.

The explicit noting of a new direction may lead to an effort to explore further directions (as in a concept fan). A concept "pulled back" from a "for-instance" idea may open up a whole new line of thinking. The deliberate noting of a new focus point may lead to an attempt, there and then, to find some ideas around that focus point.

So the harvesting procedure is not just a hindsight recording of the session but can become an integral part of the session. As with the bird-watching you get to see and to notice what is happening as it is happening.

The Treatment of Ideas

The deliberate use of the techniques and tools of lateral thinking has produced some ideas. What do we do with them?

There may be a few new ideas that are seen to be immediately usable or at least testable. These can proceed straight to evaluation where they will be evaluated alongside other ideas produced in any other way (copying, logical analysis, and so on). What happens with the remaining ideas?

This section is concerned with the treatment of ideas produced by creative thinking and not yet ready to proceed to evaluation. There is further work to be done on them. At this point I am not concerned with new concepts but with new ideas. An effort is made to convert concepts into usable ideas. How can this concept be put into action? If this effort succeeds, there are some further ideas. If not, the concept is subjected to further creative effort at a later date.

QUICK REJECTION OF IDEAS

The first thing to be avoided is the quick rejection of ideas. This is usually the result of the immediate application of real-world constraints. If the idea cannot meet these constraints it tends to be rejected. This premature use of black hat thinking needs to be countered with a request for yellow hat thinking and some more green hat thinking. The time for evaluation will come later. At the moment, the effort is still towards improving and building up the idea.

One of the most common and the most powerful ways of rejecting an idea is the simple phrase "the same as."

This idea is the same as we are already doing.

This is the same idea as the one we used to use.

This is the same as the idea we tried and it did not work.

The phrase "the same as" seems harmless but it is a powerful killer of ideas; it means that there is no need to pay any attention to the idea or to give the idea any thinking time because it is not a new idea at all. There is no attempt to attack the feasibility or value of the idea. In fact, the idea may be acknowledged as a good one—but it is the same as an existing idea. I have seen the devastating effect of this simple remark when used in a meeting to kill some very good ideas. It is very difficult to defend an idea against this comment.

Sometimes the phrase is used honestly in the sense that the person saying "the same as" is genuinely unable to see the difference between the proposed idea and an existing idea. Most often the phrase is used dishonestly because many people have learned that the simplest way to get rid of a new idea is to say that it is not new at all.

If we choose to go to a sufficiently broad concept level then it is possible to say that many ideas are similar to other ideas. For example, a horse is the same as an airplane because both are methods of getting from A to B. A credit card is the same as a bank card and both are the same as a check because all of them are ways of paying bills without using cash. Many important ideas and new values will be lost if we permit the use of this dangerous phrase.

So when you are seeking new ideas, never permit the phrase "the same as." If an idea does seem similar to an existing idea, "focus on the difference" (one of the methods of getting movement). Even if the difference is only one percent, focus on that one percent.

SHAPING IDEAS

In the normal design process we lay out the requirements and the constraints and then seek an idea to fit this "mold." So the constraints are present from the beginning.

In the normal judgment process we use the constraints as a sort of judgment screen. Only ideas that pass through this screen are acceptable.

In the creative process, however, we use the constraints to "shape" the idea into a more suitable form. This is an active and a creative process. The image is that of a potter using his hands to shape the clay on the potter's wheel. The shaping produces a better form.

217

This idea is too expensive. Can we do it in a cheaper way?

In its present form the idea is illegal. Is there a way of making it legal?

As it is the idea would not be acceptable. How can we make the idea acceptable?

Right now the idea is good but could be abused. Can we modify it to make abuse more difficult?

There is a conscious and active shaping effort to try and get the new idea to fit the real-world constraints. It is also permissible to challenge the constraints themselves from time to time.

If an idea cannot be shaped to meet the constraints then the idea stays on file or on the "back burner." We may return later to the idea with a renewed shaping effort.

TAILORING IDEAS

The operation of tailoring is not so much concerned with real-world constraints as with the resources available. A suit has to be cut to fit the available cloth. Can the idea be tailored to fit the available resources? A large company may be able to carry out an idea in one way but a smaller company may have to use a different way.

During the generation of ideas at one point should there be a consciousness of the actual resources available? It can be argued that to bring in such considerations at too early a stage may stop valuable lines of thinking. On the other hand, a certain background consciousness of the resources available may ensure that at every stage ideas are modified to be practical. This may require the development of further alternatives during the creative process itself. In my experience a background consciousness of the available resources is useful from the beginning of the creative process. But this must never be used to reject ideas or to close lines of thinking. Instead this consciousness is used to guide thinking in a certain direction.

STRENGTHENING IDEAS

Every idea has a certain power or muscle. This may be the benefits it offers, or the attractiveness of the idea, or the ease with which the idea can be implemented. Part of the treatment of an idea is to identify that power and to seek to strengthen the power. This is not an all-around process of improving the idea. It is an attempt to enhance the central power of the idea. For example, the power of the idea of a restaurant as an indoor picnic place is the low overhead through the elimination of chef, kitchen, food wastage, and so on. Because of this low overhead more money can be spent on other things, such as transport for the patrons or decor.

The power of an idea may benefit the supplier of the goods or services or it may benefit the consumer. If the benefit is with the supplier then some of this needs to be passed on to the consumer; otherwise, the strength of the idea may be too one-sided to be successful.

The process of strengthening the idea deals only with the power or strong points of the idea, which are made even stronger. No matter how wonderful an idea may seem, it can possibly be made more powerful. This may seem like gilding the lily, but it is more a matter of exploring the full potential of an idea.

The power of the idea of the advertising telephone could probably be enhanced by providing an option button so that the phone could be used in the normal way if the caller wished.

REINFORCING IDEAS

If a building has a weakness at a certain point, you seek to reinforce that point. So it is with ideas. We now focus on the weaknesses in an idea and seek to reinforce these points. A weakness is not so much a fault or a defect as a possible point of failure or trouble.

The weakness of an idea might be its complexity or the possibility of abuse. Difficulty with acceptability at first view may also be a weakness in an idea which would eventually be successful. In such cases some cosmetic attention would be justified.

The weakness of the stand-alone computer examination system in which a student could take tests at any time would be the need to provide a huge range of questions so that the answers could not be learned by heart. This might be overcome by using a combinatorial system so that the number of combinations could be huge. It might also be argued that a student who learned a

219

lot of answers by heart would probably have learned the subject anyway.

It is always useful to consider new ideas under conditions of poor motivation. Creative people often make the assumption that the users of a new idea are going to be as enthusiastic as the creators of the idea. This is never the case. To people other than the creators of the idea, a new idea means hassle, bother, and risk. So the users of a new idea need to know "what is in it for them."

Conflict with existing ideas and the difficulties of a transition period are other common sources of weakness in an idea. Can the idea be eased in, or does it have to happen all at once?

TAKE-UP OF IDEAS

Who is going to have to decide on the idea? Who is going to have to implement the idea? Whose cooperation is necessary?

A wonderful idea may get nowhere if there has been a failure to pay attention to the "take-up" steps. It may just be a matter of putting the idea in the right form or presenting it in the right context. It may also be a matter of building in, or at least emphasizing, the immediate benefits to those who are supposed to take up the idea. Ideas do not exist as perfect forms in isolation. There are people involved and these people have their own needs and agendas. A great cook knows that presentation of the food is almost as important as the quality.

As I mentioned early in the book, there are some ideas that in hindsight are logically obvious and immediately attractive. There are others that involve some risk and investment before the value comes through. How can the risk be reduced? Is there a way of piloting the idea and then using the results to increase the take-up of the idea? Is there a way of motivating people to feel some ownership in the idea? Is there to be some prestige in being the first to try the new idea?

COMPARISON

As I mentioned earlier, the Western tradition is to attack what is and then devise an alternative to overcome the current inadequacies. The non-Western (and Japanese) method is to leave the current method alone but to generate possible alternatives. When these are available then they are compared to the current method to see if the new methods offer any advantages. Comparison is very central to the process. Comparison is also very central to any process of evaluation. There is comparison between the new idea and the established idea. There is comparison between the different new ideas.

Comparison can quickly show up benefits, savings, and difficulties. Comparison may show that the new idea is a good one but does not offer any significant benefits over the old idea.

What are the points of difference? What are the points of similarity? Are the concepts different or is there just a different way of carrying through the same concept? Are the points of difference fundamental or cosmetic? Do the values provided by the different ideas come about through different mechanisms or through a different use of the same mechanism?

An idea which seems strong on its own very often seems much weaker when compared to other ideas. The advantages of the new idea may turn out to be based only on hopes, guesses, or ideal conditions. Any good new idea must pass the comparison test and must show that the promised benefits are soundly based. One strong point is if the new idea offers to obtain benefits where none were obtained before.

Very often someone who is seeking to show the benefits of a new idea will offer an instant comparison with the established idea. This is a useful way of showing benefits but it is not sufficient. To have a machine that is indeed less noisy than before is not as good as having a quiet machine.

FAULTS AND DEFECTS

At this point the specific faults and defects of the new idea can be considered directly. The reason for keeping this important procedure until late in the treatment process is that by this time many defects might have emerged. On the other hand some defects might already have been overcome in the reinforcing process and in considerations of the "take-up" of the idea. In any case a clear picture of the defects, faults, and problems should now be available.

Can these defined defects be overcome in a standard way or by some simple thinking attention? Or do the defects become new creative focuses that require a deliberate creative effort?

A serious defect only becomes a reason for throwing out an idea if an effort to overcome the defect is not successful. It must be expected that any remaining defect will be fastened on immediately in the evaluation of any new idea. People may be prepared to forego great benefits by refusing to take up an idea that promises such benefits. But people are not prepared to accept even a slight risk from a known defect in an idea. The balance between benefits and defects is much more easily improved by removing the defect than by increasing the benefit. People are risk averse and mistake averse. No one gets blamed for failing to take an opportunity. Everyone gets blamed for accepting an idea with a known defect.

At this point black hat thinking is very much in order. The new idea is scrutinized to pick out defects, problems, and potential problems. What difficulties might arise under different circumstances? What might go wrong? What unexpected events might interfere with the expected benefits of the idea?

Now is the time for negative caution. The positive and creative efforts are almost over. The defects must be identified and faced. The final creative effort is to overcome these defects by modifying the idea to "avoid" the problems or through direct creative problem solving.

CONSEQUENCES

The final step in the treatment of a new idea is to look forward to the consequences of the implementation of the idea. What will happen when the idea comes to be used?

This is a sort of moment-to-moment analysis and also a broader look at consequences.

What will happen immediately?

What will happen in the short term?

What will happen in the medium term?

What will happen in the long term?

The actual time scale of these different consequences will vary with the subject matter. For a fashion item, the long term may be anything over 6 months. For a new electricity generating plant the long term may be 30 years.

Examination of the consequences may show up new weaknesses, new defects, and new difficulties. All these have to be attended to as part of the treatment of the idea. There may be gaps and unknowns. Possible alternative scenarios may have to be suggested. The response of competitors is unknown but some possibilities should be spelled out. Different conditions under which the new idea will have to work also need to be considered. There should be fall-back positions and ways of modifying the idea.

TESTABILITY

The testability of a new idea is not directly part of the treatment of the new idea but ideas on testability will enhance the value of the idea so that when the idea moves on to the evaluation stage there is a suggested way of testing the idea. In some cases the idea itself may be modified in order to improve its testability.

Suggestions regarding the testability of an idea will need to be taken up again at the evaluation stage.

Some ideas cannot be properly pretested. In this case there should be a lot of flexibility built into the idea so that modifications can be made depending on the response to the idea. In this way the idea can be improved even as it is being used.

EVALUATION

When the 'treatment' of the new idea is complete, the idea can go forward to the evaluation stage. At the end of the treatment stage, positive and constructive thinking have done their best for the idea. The idea must now compete with all other claims on attention, time, and resources. The key elements of evaluation will be feasibility, benefits, resources, and fit.

Formal Output

There are those who find that discipline, structure, and formality do not go with creativity. This is because they have become accustomed to thinking of creativity as freeing oneself from restrictions and a general messing around in the hope that some inspiration will arrive sooner or later. This was indeed a useful stage in the development of creative thinking. But now we can go beyond that to systematic procedures that can be used in a deliberate way.

A fish has a very definite backbone to which are attached definite muscles, each with its nerve supply. The fish swims very freely in the sea. The better the structure, as in a dolphin or shark, the more free and wide ranging is the fish. Even a jellyfish has some sort of structure. In an earlier part of the book I wrote about the difference between restricting structures and liberating structures.

Without structure and discipline there is a general flailing about which may occasionally have a useful output. The effectiveness of the process can be enhanced by structure and discipline.

Discipline is characterized by the following aspects:

Time

You set a fixed time (for yourself or for others) to use a technique on a particular focus area. You stick to that time. If the time is short (two to four minutes) then the mind learns to work fast. What the time discipline does is to improve focus and concentration. When teaching thinking formally in schools we find that once children get used to the short time allowed, they produce huge outputs. If, however, they are given a long time, they just mess around. Time discipline also relieves the thinker of the need to reach a "wonderful" idea. You have done your best and when the time is up you can stop.

Focus

Focus discipline is extremely important. Creative people often earn themselves a bad name by refusing to focus on the task that has been set before them. They want to have brilliant ideas about some other focus. A creative person should show that he or she is perfectly capable of sticking to the required focus. It is quite easy to wander away from the focus during a creative thinking session because one idea leads to another and the thinker is inclined to pursue the more interesting direction. But it is essential to keep the real focus clearly in mind and to keep coming back to this. Focus discipline is probably the most important of all disciplines.

Technique

There are formal steps in each technique and these steps need to be taken in a disciplined way. You may use a provocative technique and therefore have to set up the provocation first. Then you proceed to movement. Then you shape and otherwise treat the idea. Although there may be overlap, each technique should be used in a deliberate and formal way. It is not enough to have the general attitude of provocation and to hope that something will happen. Again and again creative people have told me how much more effective they find their own creativity to be when they use the techniques in a systematic way. They find that they surprise themselves with fresh ideas.

Output

At the end of any creative effort there is an output. I have dealt with the need to "harvest" this output in a systematic way. There is a need to be formal and disciplined about the output. Those who have taken part in the creative session will know the ideas that have come up so only a hint is necessary to bring an idea to mind. But later on the session is no longer fresh in people's minds and the ideas are lost unless they have been formally laid out in a clear way. Although this may seem tedious and unnecessary at the time, there is a need for this discipline if some of the value of the creative thinking is not going to be wasted.

225

OUTPUT

The focus should always be repeated. The type of focus also needs to be stated. This may not seem so important with a "purpose" focus because the expression of the purpose automatically shows the type of focus. But it is essential with the "general-area focus"; otherwise there is no way of knowing what is going on.

The next step is to set down the concept in a formal way. During the creative thinking session the concept may have been spelled out as a concept in its own right. More often the idea has been arrived at directly. In the latter case an attempt is made to pull back from the idea to the concept that seems to lie behind it. This spelling out of the concept is important because later on someone may like the concept but not the idea.

The final step is to lay down the idea or ideas in a formal way. Each idea is spelled out separately, even if they seem similar and even if only one aspect differs. For example, if you are going to reward people with "money" or with "more leisure time" these two ideas should be spelled out separately.

It is useful to use the starting phrases: "The idea is ...," "The concept is. ..." This may seem redundant and unnecessary, but it is part of the dignity of the output. This formality gives increased value to the output.

Focus: The purpose-type focus is to do something to relieve traffic congestion in cities.

Concept: The concept is to reward people who could have driven into the city for not driving into the city.

Idea: The idea is to reward motorists who park in peripheral car parks with gasoline discount vouchers. Such parks might be owned by the oil companies.

In the example, note that the phrasing of the concept is very important. If I had written, "rewarding people for not driving into the city," this might suggest rewarding people who had cars at home but never did drive into the city. There is no need at all to be brief and succinct in the spelling out of concepts and ideas. It is better to be very clear. It is quite useless to put down a single word and hope that a later reader will see into your mind and know what you meant by that word. Be explicit rather than seek to sum things up or reduce them to a single word. Even if that is valid on the input side, it may be confusing on the output side.

Focus: General area type focus on restaurants.

Concept: The concept is that customers eat off their own plates in the restaurant.

Idea: The restaurant stores the customers' plates, which may carry corporate logos, so the customer can entertain his or her guests with these plates in the restaurant. This might encourage use of the same restaurant.

Here we see that a suggestion of value is added to the idea. Should this be done? Unless the value is explicit in the idea itself it is useful to spell out the value. This does not need to be done in detail but a later reader of the idea should not be expected to guess at the value. If necessary there can be a separate heading: "The value is. . . ."

Focus: The purpose focus is to increase the consumption of beer.

Concept: The concept is to increase the number of occasions when it is appropriate to drink beer.

Idea: The idea is to associate beer (or a specified brand) with certain defined foods like chicken or fish.

Value: The value is that women will buy more beer in supermarkets and women and youngsters may become beer drinkers. There are also the increased occasions for beer drinking.

In this case the main value of the idea may be implicit in the idea, but it is worth spelling out additional values. If this is done, then the main value must also be included again.

Focus: The purpose type focus is to deal with a shortage of police officers.

Concept: The concept is to get citizens to help the police in their work.

Idea: The idea is that citizens should keep a lookout for crime and suspicious behavior and should have a way of alerting the police.

Value: One value of the idea is that the surveillance role of the police is multiplied. Another value is that a notice that citizens are on watch would act as a deterrent to local crime.

Extra work put into writing down the creative output in this formal and disciplined way is well worth the effort. The ideas and concepts will be treated more seriously. The output of the creative thinking session will be firmly on record. The full value of the ideas and concepts will be more easily appreciated.

Should all ideas and concepts that arise in a creative thinking session be treated in this way? Here we need to distinguish between the private output of a session and the public output. The private output is the harvesting; this should be comprehensive. The public output only includes those ideas and concepts that are ready for public attention. The sort of idea put down in the public output will depend on the sort of "public" that is going to read the output. With some "publics" it is possible to put down unusual ideas and "for-instance" ideas, but with others it is best to restrict the output to ideas that show real value.

Putting down the output in a formal way also forces the creative thinker to be more definite in his or her own mind about the ideas and concepts.

Group or Individual

Should the lateral thinking techniques that have been de-scribed in this section be used by a group or by individu-als? I have considered this matter in the early part of the book but will do so again here.

Every one of the techniques can be used by an individual on his or her own without any group in sight. This is important to know because the brainstorming tradition has given the impres-sion that creativity is always a group process. This is definitely not so.

Traditionally, the purpose of the group was to bounce ideas off each other and to have someone else's remark stimulate your own thinking. With the systematic techniques of lateral thinking you can stimulate your own thinking. For example, the provocative techniques set up provocative situations to which your mind then responds. So the thinker can set up his or her own stimulants. That is one of the values of "po."

People do enjoy working in groups and usually feel they have achieved much more than they really have. It is lonely to work on your own and there is a need for discipline and a need for skill with the lateral thinking tools. But groups are very slow.

In a group someone talks and the others listen. A member of the group may feel obliged to repeat an idea or elaborate on it if he or she feels that the group has not fully appreciated the idea. There is often a tendency to be facetious in order to get a laugh from the group. In a group only one direction can be pursued at a time.

Individuals on their own can pursue many different direc-tions. There is no need to talk and no need to listen. An indi-vidual on his or her own can pursue an idea that seems "mad" at first and can stay with the idea until it makes sense. This is almost impossible to do in a group.

In practical terms, there may be an advantage with a group setting inasmuch as the whole group feels ownership of the ideas. This is important if the group must accept the ideas or act upon them.

On the other hand, an individual can set out to think creatively on any occasion—there is no need to call a group session or to wait until the next group session is scheduled. You can do individual creative thinking when and where you want.

In my experience individuals are much better at initiating ideas and opening up entirely new directions. Groups, however, may have an advantage once the idea has been initiated. The members of the group may be able to flesh out the new idea and also to develop it in directions that might not have been considered by the originator of the idea. The multiple experience of the groups can become an asset at this point.

Although all the techniques can be used by individuals they can also be used cooperatively by a group. For instance, a group may set out to construct a joint concept fan. A group may set up a random word provocation and then seek to move forward from this to new ideas. This can all be done in the usual discussion mode.

> The provocation is car park po sand. What ideas does that stimulate?
>
> Sand would slow cars down—maybe there is an idea in that.
>
> Sand suggests beaches. People sort of arrange themselves on beaches. Maybe we should let people organize themselves in the car park.
>
> To me, sand means a lot of small grains. That suggests a sort of "points" system for access to the car park. Need for the car, seniority, reward, and so on.
>
> Cars leave tracks in sand. What about some deep "ruts" so people have to drive the way they are supposed to and not take shortcuts in a car park?
>
> I like the idea of the points system. If you have not used the park for some time then you have more points. Everyone can start off with a number of points, which are deducted when you use the park. So you would only use it occasionally and when really necessary.
>
> That is not the way I meant the points system.
>
> I know. But it is another idea that was triggered by your idea.

Here we see how the group format allows ideas to interact. On their own, however, individuals would probably have pursued their initial ideas instead of just putting them forward and then forgetting about them.

There is value in combining individual and group creative thinking. This approach can get the best of both formats. Individuals can open up new lines of thinking and the group can develop the ideas. There are different ways of using the combination.

Interrupted Session

The session starts with a group discussion to define the focus and also to develop some ideas around it.

Then a specific lateral thinking technique is suggested. Individuals use this technique entirely on their own, working in parallel. The time allowed for such work is normally two to four minutes. With something like the concept fan, ten minutes would be allowed.

The individual working could take the whole technique from the beginning.

> Working on your own, set up an escape provocation and then use this provocation.

Alternatively, the initial setting-up work could be done as a group.

> The provocation is: Po we have a bathroom with no taps. Work on that on your own.

For example, the group might put forward a number of stepping-stone provocations. Then one of these is chosen and individuals work on this on their own.

The group may decide the fixed point for direct alternatives and the individuals would seek alternatives to satisfy this fixed point.

If individuals are not very skilled in the techniques, it is better to set up the process as a group and then ask individuals to work through the process. But with practiced lateral thinkers the individuals can be trusted to set up the process and to use it.

At the end of the individual thinking period, individuals give the output of their thinking. As a rough guide, about three minutes is allowed per individual. After this output the general discussion continues around the ideas that have been put forward. The group should not just receive and note the ideas but should try to develop them and to build upon them.

231

When the discussion seems to be flagging, a fresh technique can be introduced for further individual working.

In this way the process is repeated.

All individual work is directed to the use of a specified technique. Individuals work with this technique in a deliberate manner.

The group part of the session has three aspects:

1. Listening to the feedback from individuals
2. Discussing the ideas put forward and taking them further
3. Direct group use of the techniques

Sandwich Method

Here individuals are briefed with regard to the creative focus. This can be done with an initial group session or can be done by contacting the individuals (personally or by mail). The individuals then work entirely on their own for perhaps a week. The initial briefing may contain suggested provocations or it may be left entirely up to individuals (this depends on their degree of skill).

At the end of this individual thinking effort there is a group session to which the individuals bring their ideas. These should be expressed verbally, even if they are backed up by a formal written output. About ten minutes is allocated to each individual for this creative output. The rest of the group session is devoted to discussing the ideas and to developing new ideas around what has been suggested. Time should be allowed for this, in addition to the "report back" time.

At the end of the group session the individuals are sent away to do some further individual creative thinking. They can now consider any of the concepts or ideas to which they have been exposed. They can also improve their own ideas in the light of the comments of the group. At the end of a defined period, which may be another week, the individuals are required to turn in a full "harvesting" or report on their creative thinking. This is not a comprehensive report on the group session; it only extracts those points that an individual feels are of interest to him or her. These separate outputs are combined into one output. This output can then be circulated back to the group members. A final group session is optional. If the group is going to have to work on the ideas generated, then the final group session is necessary in order to further discuss and select ideas.

One of the advantages of combination methods (group and individual) is that people become more tolerant of the ideas of others. If a person knows that he or she is expected to put forward an idea then that person is going to be more constructive towards the ideas of others.

One of the weaknesses of straight group sessions is that some people may sit there without ever putting forward an idea and may be ready to disparage the ideas of others either through direct criticism or through being dismissive. With individual creativity everyone is required to "make an effort" and to show an output. This also leads to a greater motivation for creative training. With a group session some people feel that they are naturally creative and it is enough for them to sit in a group and wait for their natural creativity to work. But if they know that they will be required to use a specific technique and to turn up some ideas of their own, then they are more motivated to develop this skill.

PART 3

The Application of Creative Thinking

Application

The first part of the book was concerned with the nature, logic, and importance of creative thinking.

The second part of the book was specifically concerned with the deliberate and systematic tools of lateral thinking.

This third part of the book is concerned with the application of creative thinking.

There might be readers of the book who are mainly concerned with the central section because they want to "tune up" their own creative thinking. There may even be some readers who are most interested in the first section because they want to understand what creativity is all about even if they are not going to try to develop their own creative skill. Many readers will be interested in this third section because they are involved in introducing or using creativity within an organization.

The formal techniques of lateral thinking stand alone. They are ways of generating new ideas when we need them and when we want them. But there has to be a framework of application; otherwise, people are not going to find themselves in a position where they are expected to generate new ideas. No matter how good the techniques may be, if they are not used, they will not achieve much.

This application session will cover the difference between everyday creativity and specific creativity.

The introduction of creativity into an organization will be considered, as this has to be done carefully.

There is a need for someone within an organization to be "responsible" for the creative effort. Who should this be?

Then there are some specific structures for the application of creativity. These provide formal frameworks within which creativity takes place.

There is the matter of training in creative techniques. How is this going to be done?

There is a need to match the lateral thinking techniques to particular situations. Which tools should be used on which occasions?

Then there are suggested formats for individual creative sessions and also for group sessions.

237

Finally, there are some comments about the evaluation of the ideas that are produced by creativity.

The suggestions put forward in this section are based on years of experience in the field. Nevertheless different corporations have their own cultures and personalities. It can never be guaranteed that something that works with one corporation will work with another. Very much depends on who is involved in making things work.

One important point to remember is that the application of creativity is not as easy as it may seem to some people who believe that the occasional brainstorming session is enough or that it is enough to ask people for suggestions. Unless the application is handled effectively, creativity can become a sort of peripheral luxury that has little relevance to the operations of the organization.

Creativity is of serious importance and this importance can only grow in the future. There is a need for serious creativity. There is a need for the serious application of serious creativity.

Everyday Creativity/ Specific Creativity

There are two broad and distinguishable uses of creativity. One of these is "everyday" creativity in which creativity becomes part of normal thinking and can therefore be applied to any situations that require thinking. This should happen without any formal or deliberate effort. Then there is specific creativity where a definite need has been defined. In this case there is a formal and deliberate effort to use the systematic techniques of lateral thinking to generate new ideas.

EVERYDAY CREATIVITY

People who are naturally creative or motivated to be creative would claim to use creativity in this "everyday" fashion. Creativity becomes part of ordinary thinking. Creativity is as much present as any one of the gear shifts in a car or golf clubs in the golf bag. You use creativity automatically as appropriate. There is a creative and constructive attitude. There is a willingness to look for new ideas and to consider the new ideas that are turned up by others. Some of these basic attitudes of creativity can be related to the specific creative techniques.

Creative Pause

The willingness to pause and wonder from time to time. The willingness to interrupt the smooth flow of an operation or a line of thinking to ask questions: "Is there an alternative?"; "Do we have to do it this way?"; "What can we do with this?" The pause happens when you are thinking about something,

239

when you are reading about something, when you are listening to someone talking. The pause is just a pause. It is not as specific as a focus.

Challenge

This is a key part of everyday creativity. Do we have to do things this way? Is there a better way of doing this? Let's take a look at this.

It is very important to be clear that the challenge is not a criticism. As soon as a challenge becomes a criticism then it is no longer part of everyday creativity. Constant criticism is disruptive and unappreciated. The creative challenge is a willingness to consider that there might just be a different way of doing something and that this different way might just offer advantages. The creative challenge supposes that the current way of doing things may not necessarily be the best.

The challenge includes a pause to wonder why something is done in a certain way. This includes some consideration of continuity analysis. Is there a historic reason? Is the way of doing things locked in to the requirements of others?

The challenge is a gentle sort of dissatisfaction and a belief that there might be a possibility of a change for the better.

Green Hat

The attitudes involved in green hat thinking are very much a part of everyday creativity. You can "put on" your green hat without anyone knowing what you are doing. But you can also ask for green hat thinking in a conversation or in a meeting. This is a request to others to make a creative effort at some point. It is a request to look for different ideas and to try to come up with alternatives.

Simple Focus

The focus is more deliberate and more specific than the creative pause or the challenge. The focus is the definition of a creative need: "I would like to find some new ideas (here, or for this purpose)." The focus may be defined with the intention of following it up later. There need not even be this intention. The willingness to define a focus without any intention of follow-up thinking is a part of everyday creativity.

Consciousness that something has been defined as a "creative focus" will lead to a lot of casual creative thinking about the matter. This is part of everyday creativity.

Alternatives

Alternatives provide the most obvious occasion for the exercise of everyday creativity. There are times when it is obvious that alternatives are needed. Everyday creativity makes an effort to find more alternatives than the ones that immediately come to mind. Everyday creativity makes an effort to find unusual alternatives — this particularly applies to explanations. Everyday creativity encourages a search for as many alternatives as possible rather than an in-depth pursuit of each alternative in turn. What else may be happening? What other alternatives are there? Are there any more alternatives?

Less easy is the pause to look for alternatives when there is no problem, difficulty, or defined need to look for alternatives. This aspect ties in closely with the creative pause, the challenge, and the simple focus. It is part of the willingness to look at things that are not problems with a view to improving them.

Provocation

When the culture of creativity has been well-established in an organization, then provocation can become part of everyday creativity. In such cases people come to use "po" naturally and even to put forward strong provocations ("Po, this belt runs backwards"). Obviously this is not possible with people who are not aware of the methods of provocation. Nevertheless the "attitude" of provocation includes the willingness to consider strange ideas and even to encourage people to put forward ideas that are out of the ordinary.

There is also the willingness to take any idea and to choose to treat it as a provocation whether or not it was intended in this way.

The attitude of provocation is twofold:

1. That even from the most unlikely or incorrect ideas something useful may come if we make a "movement" effort.
2. That it is worth setting up "provocative ideas" in order to jerk our minds out of the usual grooves.

241

Listening

Listening in a constructive way is also part of everyday creativity. Even if you are never going to generate a new idea (or believe you are not) then you can still assist with the emergence and development of valuable ideas through listening and through encouragement.

It is important to remember that "tuned judgment" is also a source of creativity. As I explained earlier this is the creative contribution of a person who senses the potential of an idea and helps to develop that potential.

Encouraging creative attitudes and behavior in others and generally enhancing a corporate culture of creativity is also part of everyday creativity.

How is everyday creativity going to come about? It is easy to describe the attitudes and behavior of everyday creativity, but how does it get there in the first place? There are three possible routes to everyday creativity.

Sensitization

When people come to understand the nature, logic, and importance of creativity, they come to pay more attention to creativity. This sort of sensitization is best achieved with in-house seminars to senior management in the first place. Such seminars should be across the board and not restricted to certain groups. I once gave a seminar to KLM that involved the top 60 executives in the company; no one was absent. An in-house seminar at Du Pont drew some 1300 people. Video tapes are another, less effective method of sensitization.*

In my experience, if top management and the CEO take a direct and personal interest in creativity, then this spreads very rapidly throughout the corporation. This has been my experience with several major corporations. Unfortunately, attempts to spread creativity from a small focus within a corporation are not usually successful.

Training

I shall be addressing the matter of training in detail later in this part of the book. It is possible to encourage everyday creativity by

---

*For information on video tapes please contact International Center for Creative Thinking, Fax (914) 698-8619. For more information on seminars contact the McQuaig Group, Fax (416) 488-4544.

giving training in the formal techniques of lateral thinking. Once these techniques have been taught, then the attitudes attached to the techniques can be used even when the technique itself is not formally in use.

Effective training in creative thinking will always build up the attitudes of everyday creativity. The training does, however, have to be widespread.

At a minimum there should be training in the six hats method, since this provides a simple way of introducing creativity into an organization through the possibility of asking for "green hat thinking."

Programs and Structures

If creativity is fed into programs like "continuous improvement" or "Total Quality Management" then the attitudes of such programs can encourage everyday creativity. This can also apply to "customer satisfaction" programs. Because all such programs encourage rethinking and improvement, they can also help with the attitudes of everyday creativity.

Structures like quality circles and suggestion schemes can also help develop everyday creativity attitudes, though these may be limited to those who are involved in the structures.

Specific creativity structures like the "Creative Hit List" and the FAT/CAT™* system are other ways of developing the attitudes of creative thinking across the organization. These matters will be considered later.

People are very quick to sense the "game" that is in play. If they feel that creativity is appreciated, rewarded, and encouraged, then there will be an effort to be more creative. This general desire needs to be strengthened by training and by specific structures that provide a framework for creative behavior.

Ideally, everyday creativity should be spread right across an organization and should involve people at all levels and in all areas. Anyone who has to do any thinking needs some skill in everyday creativity.

SPECIFIC CREATIVITY

With specific creativity there is a defined focus or creative task. There is then a systematic and deliberate effort to generate new

---

*FAT/CAT is a trademark of McQuaig Group (Toronto). The acronym stands for Fixed Assigned Tasks/Creative Action Teams.

ideas and new concepts for that defined focus. Here creativity is used as a deliberate procedure for the production of new ideas. There are three aspects to specific creativity:

1. Defining the focus or creative task
2. Structure for the deliberate application of the systematic lateral thinking tools
3. Evaluation and implementation of the output of the creative thinking

Defining the Focus

There may be problems that arise and identify themselves. Individuals make definite creative focuses. There may be an obvious creative need. All these are ways in which creative focuses can emerge. There are also more formal ways, such as the "Creative Hit-List" and the FAT/CAT™ program, of setting up creative tasks. At the end of these different possibilities there will be defined creative focuses.

Structure for Creative Thinking

Once the creative focus has been defined, then that focus can be subjected to deliberate creative thinking. This can be done by groups or individuals or a combination of both, as mentioned. This thinking can take place within already existing structures such as quality circles or task-oriented teams or special creative teams can be set up (FAT/CAT™) for the purpose.

It often happens that the group that has the concern or problem will organize its own deliberate creative thinking session to tackle the problem. There may be a system of regular creative sessions into which the current focuses are fed.

Structures for the application of creative thinking will be considered in a later section.

Evaluation and Implementation

The group that has the creative focus may also be involved in evaluating the ideas that come out of the deliberate creative thinking. In such cases the process is continuous. If the "thinking" group is different from the "implementation" group, then attention has to be paid to the transfer of ideas so that those expected to act on the idea are brought in at an early enough stage to feel some ownership in the new ideas.

The important point about specific creativity is that new ideas should be considered in the same way as raw materials, technology, patents, designs, or energy. New ideas have a definite existence and importance. The fact that they are only products of the mind should not devalue new ideas. In the end all human progress is due to new ideas. Even when a new idea is not going to be used, the idea should still be treated formally. The idea continues to exist as an unused or unusable idea. It is not like trying to light a fire where the only value is when the fire is actually lit. Ideas continue to have value whether or not they are used.

With specific creativity it is important to be specific and definite at each stage. The definition of the creative task needs to be specific. The structure for applying lateral thinking needs to be specific. The output of the creative effort needs to be specific. Finally, the evaluation and implementation (if any) needs to be specific.

Specific creativity is not a matter of feeling creative, looking around for a focus and the hoping that inspiration will provide something useful as you go along. Serious creativity means being serious at each of the stages.

There are certain special groups (R&D, marketing, new products, new business groups, corporate strategy, and so on) that have a great need for everyday creativity. Such groups also have a need for specific creativity but are often reluctant to define creative focuses and to make deliberate creative efforts; they feel that because they spend the whole time being "creative," there is no need for a "specific" effort. This is a mistaken view. Even the most creative people can benefit from the deliberate nature of specific creativity.

The Creative Hit List

Consider two alternative approaches.

I want to be creative and I have developed my creative thinking skill. Now let me look around for something to be creative about.

I have this defined creative focus and I need some ways of getting some new ideas—what can I do?

In the first example the creative motivation and skill comes first and then there is a search for targets. In the second example there is a consciousness of a defined need and then the search for a way of generating ideas around that need.

It is not a matter of choosing which is preferable. The best way of developing creative motivation and skills is to show a definite need first. If the need is there and the expectation of action is there then learning creative thinking skills is no longer a peripheral luxury but a necessity. Even so, it is surprising how often people want to start the other way around.

Earlier in this book I discussed the importance of focus in creativity and I have mentioned this point again and again. Focus is important for two reasons:

1. By focusing upon things which no one else has focused we can develop valuable new ideas with little creative effort.
2. The systematic creative tools are most powerful when we are specific about the creative focus and stick to this.

I also mentioned that, in my experience, most executives were rather weak in setting creative focuses. Most executives believe that thinking is only for problem solving. There is no need to look for problems because they announce themselves. So the idea of looking for problems or seeking out creative focuses is not a normal executive thinking habit. There is a need to develop the habit of defining creative need areas. This is where the Creative Hit List comes in.

The Creative Hit List is a formal putting together of defined creative need areas. These are set down as creative focuses or creative tasks.

Compiling the Creative Hit List

1. As its creative exercise a group can meet to put together a Creative Hit List. The members of the group will have been briefed beforehand and bring to the meeting some suggestions. Further suggestions are put forward at the meeting. The final output should be a Creative Hit List with about 20 items on the list.
2. Individuals in a department can be asked to make their own Creative Hit Lists and to submit them to the head of the department, who will then compile the master Creative Hit List.
3. A team can be assigned the task of putting together the Creative Hit List. This team talks to people in the department and gradually puts together the Creative Hit List, which is then passed back for comment to the people who have been consulted.
4. An individual puts together a Creative Hit List, which is then sent out to others for suggestions, modifications, and additions.

There may be a Creative Hit List for an individual or a group or a team. There may be a Creative Hit List for a department, a division, or even the whole organization. There may be several Creative Hit Lists existing side by side and designated by some name or number.

Items on the Creative Hit List

There is a tendency to fill up the Creative Hit List with problems. This would then become another problem list. However, it would be unfair to exclude all problems from the Creative Hit List because problems also need creative attention. It is best to aim for a mix of four different item types.

PROBLEM: These would all be purpose-type focuses and would be of the classic difficulty or deviation type. How do we solve this problem and how do we get over this obstacle? There should be a mix of really tough problems that have been around

247

for a long time and other problems that might be easier to solve. There are two criteria in selecting problems:

1. Solving the problem would make a very significant and (preferably) measurable difference.
2. Creative effort might make a difference (for motivational purposes) in solving the problem.

The problems should not be so technical or require so much technical detail that people outside the area have no chance of working on the problem. Such problems are only appropriate for a Creative Hit List within a defined specialty area.

IMPROVEMENT TASK: The area is defined and the type of improvement is specified. So these are also purpose-type creative focuses. How can we speed this up? How can we reduce wastage? How can we improve the quality? The tasks may sometimes have a measured ambition. How can we reduce breakages by 50 percent in the next six months? The criteria for selection of the improvement tasks are similar to those for selection of problems. With improvement, however, there is even more emphasis on the measurability of results. It is important to show that creativity does work. So choosing tasks where the results produce a measurable result is important—at least at the beginning.

PROJECT: A project may be an officially assigned project that is taking place anyway or it may be a special project that is put in place as a result of a creative thinking session. The project may be self-imposed. The project may include invitations to invent or design something new. The project may occasionally include matters that are not directly work-related but may be related to the community. The project may also include as the task itself the design of new creative projects.

WHIM AND OPPORTUNITY: This final category is very much of the "general-area" type of focus. The "whim" simply chooses any area and invites thinkers to develop ideas in that area. Such areas may be the result of unusual focuses that have been invited. The areas may also be chosen quite arbitrarily. This category can also include "opportunities." If there has been any change or any new product then this can be seen as an opportunity area and creative ideas can be invited. If there is an area that is seen to have unused potential, this can also be put forward as an opportunity area.

The following example of a Creative Hit List shows the range of items.

PROBLEMS

Car park is too small

Absenteeism is increasing

Queues in the canteen

Competitor has better operating costs

Lack of communication between research and marketing

IMPROVEMENT TASKS

Reduce time taken up in meetings

Quicker response to customers' complaints

Better message taking

Faster cleaning of molds

Fewer scratches in finished surfaces

PROJECTS

Organize monthly outing for community elderly

Set up creative training system

Design a better product display case

Invent a PC stand

Memorize names of everyone in the department

WHIM/OPPORTUNITY

Light switches

The last five minutes of the day

Signatures on letters

Uses for a highly elastic fiber

Using the expertise of a hobby gardener

Use of the Creative Hit List

The Creative Hit List can be displayed on bulletin boards and kept on desks. A postcard version can be kept in the wallet. The Creative Hit List is published in house journals and suggestions regarding items on the list are published at the same time.

The Creative Hit List can provide items for creativity training and also for formal creative thinking sessions.

Individuals can set out to tackle items on the Creative Hit List. Groups can get together to focus on one item or another.

Items from the Creative Hit List can be assigned to Creative Action Teams in the FAT/CAT™ program.

There is nothing immutable about the Creative Hit List; items on it can be dropped or replaced by other items. The first appearance of the list may be very different from its form some weeks later when modifications have been made.

Creative Hit List and General Problem Solving

There are corporate problems that need to be solved by collecting information and further analysis. Some of these problems will already be under investigation by different departments or groups. The Creative Hit List is not meant to be a compendium of all the thinking that needs to take place within an organization. An item should only find its way onto the list if there seems to be a creative need; that is, if the problem or task is not yielding to other approaches and there seems to be a need for a new approach. The specific need for a new idea should be spelled out instead of the whole problem being presented.

In other cases there may already be some existing approaches and there is a request for a fresh approach.

The Creative Hit List will only give a brief indication of the focus area and creative need. There should be a much fuller description of the need available for those who choose to focus on the task.

It is always legitimate to ask the question, "Why is this particular item on the Creative Hit List?" The answer to that question should be a defined need for new concepts and new ideas. If the question is not answered in a satisfactory way then the item should come off the list.

Value of the Creative Hit List

The Creative Hit List has a number of different values.

1. There are matters that really need creative attention. The Creative Hit List invites people to think about such matters. There is the direct value of useful ideas that are produced by the creative attention.

2. In seeking to define items for the Creative Hit List, people have to look around and examine what they are doing. In time there develops the habit of picking out creative focuses. Even if these do not all make their way to the Creative Hit List, such creative focuses may be addressed in other ways.

3. The Creative Hit List is a reminder of the need for creativity and helps to foster a culture of creative effort.

4. The Creative Hit List provides immediate creative tasks for creativity training and the practice of the creative techniques. The list also provides creative tasks that can be assigned in the FAT/CAT™ program.

5. The Creative Hit List illustrates the need for creative thinking and so provides a reason for creative training.

6. Specialized Creative Hit Lists within special areas can serve to focus attention on real creative needs in those areas.

7. The Creative Hit List provides "official" targets for creative effort. Any item off the list is of value as a target.

8. The Creative Hit List provides a challenge to those who consider themselves to be creative. There is now some way in which they can show off this skill.

9. The Creative Hit List provides interest, involvement, and fun outside the confines of one's immediate work.

10. The Creative Hit List may provide a means for identifying both those who are really creative and those who are motivated to be creative.

Dangers

There are some dangers associated with the Creative Hit List. The first danger is that the list becomes filled with "general problems" that need information and analysis more than they need new creative ideas.

The second danger is that the Creative Hit List becomes filled with trivial items and so trivializes creativity itself.

Both dangers may be avoided by the custodian of the Creative Hit List carefully vetting and carefully phrasing the items that go onto the list. This extremely important function can be carried out by an individual or a small team.

Introduction of Creativity

> We are already doing all that needs to be done.
> We have other, higher priorities.
> Creativity is a matter of talent—there is nothing you can do about it except get creative people.
> We are pretty good at it.
> We have some pretty creative people.
> Let me tell you some of the creative things we are doing.

At my seminars I am often asked about the introduction of creativity to an organization. I have to respond that it is not at all easy.

Let me start at the easy end. The easy way is if there is a chief executive officer who is creative himself, or herself, or who clearly sees the need for creativity.

This was the case with the late Sam Koechlin, CEO of Ciba-Geigy. This was the case with the late Michael Pocok, CEO of Shell. This was the case when Phil Smith was CEO of General Foods (before the takeover). This was the case with Gunnar Wessman, who was CEO of Pharmacia in Sweden. This is the case with Ron Barbaro, who is CEO of Prudential. There are other examples. In such cases the interest of the CEO is followed by in-house seminars that serve to show the logic and nature of creativity. This is very important because there are so many misconceptions about creativity. It is simply not possible to get rid of those misconceptions in a conversation or in a paper presentation to a group. When Mano Kampourise, CEO of American Standard, became interested in creativity he set up a series of in-house seminars for his senior people in order to get everyone to understand what creativity is about. Although the lateral thinking tools are mentioned, these are not so much training sessions as sensitizing sessions. They are very important.

In other cases someone senior has attended one of my public seminars and has become interested in the subject. This is how

Du Pont's powerful interest in creativity came about. David Tanner attended a public seminar of mine in Toronto and became interested in the matter. This was followed by a number of seminars to senior executives at Du Pont. Once these people had seen that this was not "crazy" creativity but a serious and systematic approach to an important subject, it became possible to get support for a formal Center for Creativity, which now exists at Du Pont.

The serious introduction of creativity into an organization is a personal thing and there is a need for leadership. Everyone in a committee may nod and agree and accept that creativity is a valuable thing. But nothing ever gets done because there are crises and problems and cost-cutting exercises that take priority. Creativity is a luxury that no one is against but that no one is really pushing for. There is a need for a CEO or someone senior to be the "process champion" (to be discussed later).

Is it possible for a small motivated group in an organization to develop a high skill in creativity and then to use this as a base to spread creativity around the organization? I am sure it is possible but I have not come across this model. It needs a great deal of political skill to cross boundaries into other parallel areas. I suspect, however, that it does happen from time to time.

In theory it should be easy to introduce creativity as part of any ongoing program in quality management, continuous improvement, or cost-cutting since all such programs demand some degree of creative thinking in coming up with better ways of doing things. In practice, it is not so easy because the motivations and structures of such programs are often so rigid that there is no room for what is so obviously necessary.

So what are the ways of introducing creativity into an organization if there is not a forward-looking CEO?

Sensitization

This involves exposure of a sufficient number of senior executives, including the most senior, to a seminar on lateral thinking. This is the simplest and most effective way. It is possible to try and sensitize people using video tapes but this is less effective because there is not the mass effect.

Six Thinking Hats

This simple procedure has been rapidly taken up by many organizations because it is so powerful and so simple. The framework

253

is so effective in making meetings more productive and in get-ting more thinking out of people that it spreads itself. The Six Hats method is not solely concerned with creative thinking, but there are some direct points of relevance. The green hat makes time and space for creative thinking. The green hat is a request for creative thinking. When this request is made there is an increased consciousness that creativity may be needed and there may be a lack of skill in this area. The Six Hats method also lim-its the use of black hat thinking to certain specified periods. It now becomes possible to discuss new ideas more fully and more productively.

On a simple level, once executives see that the Six Hats method is both simple and powerful, they become more mo-tivated to try other aids to better thinking. So the introduction of the Six Hats method can be a useful first step.

Nominated Champion/Process Champion

If there is a senior executive who has ability and who makes "creativity" his or her "thing" then the introduction can take place. This will depend entirely on the energy and political ability of that person. The sooner creativity can show tangible results, the quicker will be the introduction.

This process champion need not be an especially creative per-son himself or herself. Political ability and organizing energy are more important.

Structures and Programs

Setting up a formal Creative Hit List system or some other struc-tures (to be mentioned in a later section) can help with the in-troduction of creativity, but who is to set up such structures in the first place?

Programs like the FAT/CAT™ program coupled with delib-erate creative training can provide a means for introducing cre-ativity, but the will has to be there first. Structures and programs can help when there is a will but no idea of how to proceed.

By far the most difficult thing to overcome is complacency. There are many organizations that genuinely believe they are do-ing enough about creativity. This is often no more than lip service or activity in some small sector. When such organizations even-tually run into trouble through lack of creative enterprise, they immediately set about a cost-cutting exercise because this is the most tangible and immediate way of getting some improvement.

Complacency is really its own best answer. No one who is really good at something feels complacent and feels that there is no need to get better.

Responsibility

> Who is responsible for looking after the creativity program?
> Whose business is it?
> Who is supposed to make things happen?

Creativity is a "good thing" and no one is really against creativity. Everyone needs creativity, so creativity is everyone's business. For precisely these reasons creativity ends up being no one's business and nothing happens. Nothing much will happen with creativity unless someone makes it happen.

THE PROCESS CHAMPION

With any new product there is a need for a "product champion." This is the person who puts energy into the product and gets it moving. This is the person who fights for the product and represents the product at any meeting when other people are fighting for resources for their projects. This is the person who puts energy into a flagging project and who supports it when things are not working out and everyone is demoralized. Without a product champion, at the first hint of difficulty the product would start to die.

In exactly the same way, there is a need for a "process champion" to make things happen with creativity. Creativity is as fragile as any product. Creativity needs energizing. Creativity needs a champion to fight for it. Because creativity seems such a good idea, people assume that it does not need pushing. But it does, because people are much more naturally inclined towards problem solving and information collecting.

Sir Colin Marshall, the chief executive of British Airways who was largely responsible for the turnaround in that airline, firmly believes in "nominated champions." He declares that without a nominated champion not much will happen. Many other people have come to this conclusion. There is a need for someone who

will be responsible for making things happen. There is a need
for someone to whom you can turn and ask:

What has been happening with creativity?

How far have we gotten?

Can you report back to me on this?

Although I fully agree with the need for a nominated champion, I do not think this goes far enough. Someone may be responsible but may not be in a position to put much energy into the matter. The way I see it, the "process champion" goes beyond the nominated champion. It is true that, in some cases, if the person involved is very energetic, then the two functions may be the same.

What are the needed characteristics for a process champion?

The process champion does not need to be especially creative. Very often there is within an organization someone who is motivated to be creative and has built up a reputation for creativity. This is the wrong person to be the process champion. Such a person has established a niche from which it is difficult to get out. Such a person may well have built up antagonisms (born of frustration) over the years. Such a person is not always taken seriously enough. Creative people are often competitive and judgmental about the ideas of others. For these reasons the process champion should have an interest and motivation for creativity, but he or she does not have to be especially good at it.

The process champion must have a lot of energy and a lot of organizing ability. Because creativity cuts across so many disciplines and because there will be a need to deal with so many different areas, there is no natural channel or momentum. Therefore the process champion cannot sit back and let things flow along an established channel. There is a need to set things up every step of the way.

The process champion should be someone at as senior a level as possible—compatible with having the available time and energy. Creativity needs to be represented at a senior level and at senior level meetings. The process champion must also be a very good "people person" with good contacts and the ability to use them. A great deal of liaison will be required. The process champion must be persuasive and a good salesman. It is easy to oversell creativity and to build up expectations that cannot possibly be fulfilled (solve all your problems in half an hour). On the

257

other hand, it is necessary to persuade people to take some action rather than to assume that nothing can be done about creativity.

The process champion needs to be able to build up a team and to motivate the team. Introducing creativity is not a one-man job. That is another reason why creative people, who tend to be loners, are not really suitable as process champions.

All these wonderful characteristics make it seem impossible to find such a paragon who is not already heavily overburdened doing far too many things. Such a person would not have the time and the energy. One possible source for the process champion is a person who has reached the top in a particular area and who is not interested in becoming the CEO. Such a person may be looking around for a fresh challenge. Continuing to do what he or she has been doing for years is no longer a sufficient challenge. Such a person would make an ideal process champion. There may be such people available in an organization. An alternative source may be a younger person who is earmarked for high things. This "project" can be given to that person to test that person's ability and also to give that person wide access across the corporation.

THE CONCEPT MANAGER

I believe that in the future, organizations will come to have a formal "concept manager." In a highly competitive world, where all organizations reach a base level of competence, the only thing that will make a difference is better concepts. We shall have to come to treat concepts as seriously as finance, labor, energy, and raw materials. It will not be enough just to hope that "somehow" better concepts will emerge. The need for formal "Concept R&D" is discussed in my book, *Sur/petition*.* The concept manager will be specifically responsible for collecting, generating, and developing new concepts. This role will be key to the success of any organization. The role will go far beyond corporate strategy.

In a small organization the role of creativity process champion and concept manager might be combined in one person. In a larger organization the process champion would work with and for the concept manager. The concept manager's role is to foster the development of concepts. The role of the creativity process champion is to be sure that all personnel develop and use a high degree of creative skill.

*HarperBusiness, New York, 1992.

David Tanner has been an excellent process champion for Du Pont. He set up a formal Center for Creativity with a full-time staff. His office was near the office of the chief executive. This is exactly the sort of seriousness with which creativity should be taken. Investment in creativity is just like investment in research—except that it is far cheaper.

Instead of the creativity element being supplied by a few individually creative people who do their best, there is now a formal effort to spread creativity to all personnel and also to set up structures for encouraging creativity as such.

The Creativity Center has trainers who are able to train in creativity. The Creativity Center has trained facilitators who act as "process managers" at a meeting. A facilitator would be invited to a meeting that needed to develop new ideas around some focus. The facilitator would guide the meeting in the use of the various creative techniques. In this way the participants at the meeting would be able to apply the techniques even if they had not been fully trained in them. They would also be learning the techniques even as they applied the techniques to their own problems.

The Creativity Center serves to organize seminars, meetings, and exhibitions, and generally serves to develop a corporate culture of creativity.

The Creativity Center has a very clear and defined responsibility for enhancing creativity within the corporation.

As a word of caution, it should be said that setting up a "Creativity Center" and leaving it at that would not be effective. The Creativity Center is no substitute for the process champion. The process champion is always necessary. Once there is a vigorous process champion then the Creativity Center acts to amplify and make concrete the efforts of that process champion. Once creativity is fully established as part of the corporate culture, the Creativity Center should be able to sustain the momentum.

It is important that Creativity Centers or Offices of Creativity should not trivialize themselves by seeking to justify their role with activities that are distractions from their main thrust.

There is sometimes a suggestion that if creativity is "institutionalized" with a Creativity Center or an Office of Creativity then everyone else loses interest. This is certainly a danger if that center presumes to do all the creative thinking that is needed. That would be a bad mistake. The purpose of the Creativity Center or Office of Creativity is precisely to make it easier and more productive for everyone else to be creative. There should be no question of setting up a creative enclave that excludes others. It is more like setting up an energy department in an organization. The purpose of that department is to supply energy to everyone else.

NETWORK

In addition to the Creativity Center there is a need for a distribution of people who are locally responsible and motivated to put energy into the creative process. In essence, there are two types of network.

1. A network of local "process champions" or energizers. Such people understand creativity, are able to run creative meetings, and even provide some creativity training. Such people may be in place in different departments, sites, factories, and so on. The setting up and sustaining of this network is a key part of the general distribution of creativity. It may not be enough to wait for people to volunteer. It may be better to select the right person and then to invite that person to become interested in creativity.

2. The second type of network brings together individuals who have always been interested in creativity and may indeed be very creative in their own right. Such people are examples to those around them and also provide a specific resource of creative talent. As I have indicated earlier these people are not necessarily the right people to become local process champions because their talent for creativity does not imply a talent for organizing or motivating others. There will in some instances be an overlap between the two networks but it is important to consider them as separate networks.

Within Du Pont both types of network are in place and growing.

HUMAN RESOURCE DEPARTMENT

As corporations have at last come to realize that people are their most important resource, so the importance and prestige of the human resource department (HRD) has been growing. This is as it should be. The role of the human resource department is comprehensive and ranges from training to assessment to problem solving and general care. People are what make organizations work, so looking after people must be a key role in any organization.

Should the responsibility for the introduction and running of creativity programs simply be handed to the human resource department? At first sight this would seem to make sense because the development of creative skills in all personnel is very much a matter of human resource development. Furthermore, the training aspect of creativity should come into the training that is already being organized by the human resource department. It can also be seen as a convenient way to handle the creativity "problem": "Give it to HRD and let them get on with it."

In practice, human resource departments are heavily overburdened with things that they are expected to do. Some of these are routine and some involve the introduction of new programs such as quality management and customer service. There is a danger that creativity could be seen as just another item on the catalogue of things to be done. Creativity would not get the focused energy and attention that is needed in the first place.

So handing "creativity" to the human resource department is not a good way to go unless there is someone in that department who has a high level of motivation and the available time and energy to become the process champion.

In any case, the process champion must maintain a very strong liaison with the human resource department because the development of personal creativity skills does fall within the activities of that department. In matters of specific creative training or the incorporation of some element of creativity into routine training, there is a need for the creativity process champion to work closely with the human resource people.

When the human resource department is involved in running programs on quality, cost-cutting, and the like, there should be close liaison with the creativity process champion in order to be able to introduce the creative techniques as a sort of "tool kit" for use in these other programs.

Where there is a specific program like the FAT/CAT™ program, the human resource department can take a lead in introducing creativity into the organization. There would still be a need for the process champion to work on the broad frame of the application of creative skills.

261

As I mentioned in an early part of the book, although creative skills are obviously needed in quality programs and continuous improvement programs, creativity needs to have an identity of its own. That is why the Du Pont strategy of keeping creativity and continuous improvement separate but cooperative makes sense.

TRAINERS

As a serious gesture towards creativity, organizations sometimes send people to be trained in the training of creative thinking techniques. The idea is that such people will go back and train others in the techniques.

This is certainly useful, but it only works if there is already in place a solid training scheme into which the trained trainers will now slot. This may indeed be part of some regular training schedule. In such cases the new skills of the trainers can be put to use.

But if the trainers are expected to take over responsibility for introducing creativity into the organization then it does not work. The trainers are simply not in a position to set up widespread training schemes or to otherwise develop creative structures. This is an unrealistic expectation.

Trained trainers can be an important part of the development of creative programs* but they are not in a position to provide the prime organizing energy.

The danger is that an organization that has sent trainers to be trained may then feel that there is nothing more that needs to be done about creativity. The trained trainers are a resource. But resources have to be used by entrepreneurs. The process champion is the creativity entrepreneur within an organization.

In the end, the serious introduction of creativity into an organization depends on the right person being in the right place.

*For training trainers contact Kathy Myers, APT/T, Fax (515) 278-2245.

Structures and Programs

I have often mentioned the fear that creativity is going to be killed by systematic techniques or stifled by institutionalizing structures and programs. Talented football or baseball players play on a formal field with formal rules and yet show their talent. The old idea that creativity simply meant freedom from any restrictions made sense only when there was nothing else we could say or do about creativity.

Structures and programs are frameworks for encouraging and rewarding creative behavior.

The most important thing about introducing creativity into an organization is to make creativity behavior an "expectation." The paradox is that at first we need to make creative behavior something special and something extra (because otherwise everyone would claim that they were being creative anyway) but then to make it an expectation. But how do you make something an "expectation"? One way is to put that person in a situation where this type of behavior is needed and has to be used to fulfill some task. That is what structures and programs are all about.

In this section I shall be going through a number of possible structures and programs. Some of these are traditional and some are new. There is no suggestion that an organization should attempt to use all of them or even many of them. I am simply setting out possibilities. In general, a structure is something that is more permanent than a program. A formal Creativity Center is a structure, whereas a quality program is a program that runs through existing structures. Nevertheless, programs such as continuous improvement and safety programs may be permanent.

Suggestion Schemes

Some organizations manage to get a lot out of their suggestion schemes, but in other organizations the scheme is barely in existence. The Japanese have a culture of suggestions for the reasons mentioned earlier in the book. One of the reasons the Japanese schemes work is that people are "expected" to make suggestions and the suggestions are usually considered at the level at which they are made. So shopfloor suggestions come through the quality circles and are considered at that level. In the West, suggestions are all fed into the scheme and then the suggestions are examined at some senior collecting point. This puts a huge load on the assessors, who are reluctant to find time for this work. As a result, "silly" suggestions are discouraged and the scheme is only used by the few who feel they are capable of really serious suggestions.

The reward system is often too remote. Usually a suggestion goes through various screening committees. If the suggestion is eventually put into effect, then a reward is given. Many people do not feel they are ever going to have this type of idea so they do not bother. Furthermore, certain fields, such as engineering, are open to money-making suggestions but in others, like customer service, it is difficult to put a value on a new idea.

It is better to give some "recognition" reward soon after the effort of making the suggestion. People should be rewarded, by acknowledgment, for putting in suggestions—no matter what the quality of the suggestion might be. In order to aid selection and also to indicate to the suggester why an idea has not been used, it is important to indicate that all suggestions must be accompanied by an explanation of why and how that suggestion is going to provide "value."

If suggestion schemes are kept ticking in the background, then many people cease to notice them. Since the scheme is always there, then there is no need to do anything about it today or tomorrow. Since it is possible to focus on everything, there is no need to focus on anything.

It is a good idea to have "short focus bursts." So for two weeks the emphasis could be on "safety" suggestions and this can be hyped with posters, signs, and so on. Then there is no special emphasis for a while. Later there might be another two-week burst directed towards "cost-saving" and this is also much publicized. Then there might be a focus on "energy saving" or "waste reduction" or "process improvement" and so on. Each focus is short and defined. Suggestions for the specified focus are asked for during the allotted time.

It is supposed that people putting in suggestions are using creativity, but there is no deliberate effort to improve creativity skills. It might be possible to make some basic creativity training available to those who asked for it.

QUALITY CIRCLES

Where quality circle systems are in place, creative training can be added in order to allow the circles to function more effectively.

It would not make sense to introduce creativity right at the beginning because the members of a quality circle might have a lot of useful suggestions to make using their experience and logical analysis. It is when the yield from these operating methods has started to fall off that creativity training will make sense. Before that such training might be seen as unnecessary and complicating.

The use of creative techniques within quality circles depends heavily on defined creative focuses. There should be a strong emphasis on finding such focuses either within each group or as a general exercise. The setting up of formal Creative Hit Lists could be useful here. The introduction of a creative focus that provides a "problem" that cannot be solved directly is the best setting for the use of the deliberate tools of creativity. Under such circumstances the value of the tools is seen.

It may also be useful to emphasize that while quality involves doing the same thing in a better way, creativity may involve doing something different. Creativity may also be involved in making improvements in the existing method.

QUALITY, CONTINUOUS IMPROVEMENT, AND COST-CUTTING

There are a variety of programs concerned with quality management, continuous improvement, cost cutting, and so on. Such programs have their own objectives, structures, and methods. There are times when there are problems to be solved. There are times when it is necessary to find a "better" way of doing something. There are times when it is necessary to generate further alternatives. Sometimes these needs can be supplied by experience, by analysis, or by further information. But there are times when there is a real need for creative thinking. There is therefore a real need to build creative skills into these programs.

265

When the need for creative thinking occurs, then a person can simply plug in a creative technique. Quite apart from the tool kit of techniques, the attitudes that arise from creative training are important in all such programs. For example, there is the habit of challenging what is being done. There is the willingness to stop at something which is not a problem in order to see if there might be a better way of doing things. There is the willingness to identify the "fixed point" and to search for alternatives.

There is an obvious synergy between creativity and such programs. Sometimes an element of creativity is built into the programs, but this is usually too weak. It is better to introduce a specific element of creative skill that is trained directly as "creativity" and is designed by people with experience in creativity.

CREATIVITY CENTER

A specific Creativity Center is a type of structure that has already been discussed. Such a center has its own activities and will also serve to coordinate many of the suggestions put forward in this section. For example, the Creativity Center could be responsible for the Creative Hit List and the Cloud "9" file.

The Creativity Center provides an energizing and a focusing structure. The Creativity Center provides a collecting and an organizing framework. The Creativity Center provides a way of doing things that need to be done but are no one else's business to do (in the field of creativity).

CONCEPT R&D

This is a major suggestion. The idea is that concepts should be treated as formally as technical R&D. Many organizations spend millions of dollars on technical R&D but nothing directly on concepts. Concepts are just supposed to emerge in an haphazard fashion. Yet as technology competence reaches a plateau, concepts are really going to make the difference. The Concept R&D idea is considered fully in another book.★ At this point it is enough to say that Concept R&D would be a heavy user of creativity and would seek to develop creative skills in all areas.

★*Sur/petition*, HarperBusiness, New York, 1992.

When organizations begin to set up Concept R&D departments then they will need to take creativity very seriously indeed.

STRUC-
TURES
AND
PROGRAMS

CREATIVE HIT LIST

The Creative Hit List has been considered in detail in a previous section. It is listed again here for the sake of completeness. The Creative Hit List (CHL) is a simple structure that can serve to introduce creativity and to keep it going.

The Creative Hit List should be organized in as formal and serious manner as possible. It is something that the process champion or the Creativity Center should supervise. There can be an overall Hit List for the whole company or major divisions. But there should also be "local" Creative Hit Lists, which can be much more specialized.

Suggestions regarding items on the Hit List can be put together and published (as they are or in summary form). Certainly the most interesting and successful suggestions should be highlighted.

Tasks can be assigned from the Creative Hit List for such programs as the FAT/CAT™ program.

CLOUD "9" FILE

This structure was developed by a construction company in West Canada. Cloud "9" signifies "dream." The file is a physical file which is circulated around a circulation pattern of executives (or others). There may be several such files circulating and also local files for special areas.

The file should reach a person once every month or every two months. Into this file go the following possibilities:

Novel Ideas. These are ideas that are not original and may be in use in another organization. But the idea is not yet in use in your organization. These are ideas which can be borrowed or imitated.

Original Ideas. These are ideas which are put forward as original. The creator of the idea can append his or her name

267

as wished. These ideas may be related to the focus items given in the field or may build on other material in the file.

Constructive Comments. These may be white hat comments that add experience or information to support an idea in the file. There may be yellow hat comments to indicate the value of ideas in the field. There may be green hat comments that suggest alternatives or modifications of the ideas in the file. There should be no black hat comments unless there is also shown a way of overcoming a possible problem.

New Creative Focuses. These can be suggestions for new creative focuses. These may be spelled out as problems, tasks, opportunities, and so on. A special place in the field can be allocated to creative focuses so that these can be seen at a glance.

The file is read, added to, and passed on. If the file becomes too bulky then there can be backup files and an index that indicates how further information can be obtained.

There are several values to the Cloud "9" file:

1. A periodic reminder to think creatively
2. The provision of creative focuses about which to think creatively
3. Ideas and concepts to react to
4. A simple channel into which ideas can be placed
5. The actual value of the ideas and suggestions

The "channel" value is very important. Many people do not like to have ideas because they do not want the "hassle" of trying to do something about a new idea. The idea actually becomes a burden. What do you do with it? Who do you have to convince? How can you show it works? The Cloud "9" file provides the simplest of channels. If you have a new idea, you just wait until the file reaches you and then you put your idea into the file. There is nothing more that you have to do.

CREATIVE TASK SHEET

The Cloud "9" file is an "opportunity." No one is asked to put anything into the file. You can read it and pass it on without adding anything. The Creative Task Sheet is, however, a specific creative request. The recipient is directly asked for his or her creative ideas on a defined focus.

Quite often people do have ideas on certain matters; when asked why they had not put forward these ideas, they reply:

It was not my business.

No one would have been interested in my idea.

No one asked me.

I did not want the hassle of putting up an idea.

The Creative Task Sheet is intended to overcome such reluctance and also to elicit new ideas.

At the top the Task Sheet sets out the creative "task" or focus. This should be defined adequately but excessive detail is not needed. The actual task is spelled out (a suggestion, a solution, further alternatives, a new concept, etc.).

There may be suggestions as to the techniques that might be used. A specific provocation (Po . . .) may be put forward in the Task Sheet but the recipient does not have to use this.

The Creative Task Sheet is sent out individually to named people who are being asked for their creative input. A deadline is given and the completed task sheet must be returned to the sender by that date.

The different ideas and concepts are then collected. If further information is needed then the creator of an idea can be contacted directly. If needed, those who have shown the most interest and ability in the subject may be brought together for a creative thinking session.

The Creative Task Sheet can be organized by the Creativity Center or the process champion. Any person in any area who needs creative input on a particular matter could send out a Creative Task Sheet. It is simpler, however, if this is coordinated through the Creativity Center or equivalent. Obviously, a "local" Task Sheet could be sent directly and this could become a habit whenever new ideas were needed.

OPPORTUNITY AUDIT

Executives are often blamed for making mistakes or not solving problems. But it is extremely rare for anyone to be blamed for missing an opportunity. The result is that very few people want to take the risk of trying something new. If they do try something new and it goes wrong, that is a negative mark on their record. If they never try anything new, they never risk making a mistake. So where is the innovation energy to come from? The late Sam Koechlin, CEO of Ciba-Geigy, once told me he would love to have his managers come to him each year to tell him all the mistakes they had made. If they were making mistakes then at least they were trying new things. He did not see it happening in Switzerland.

The Opportunity Audit* is a formal way of requesting executives to put forward the opportunities or new ideas that they have considered during the year. This now becomes an expectation and a task to be performed. Not putting anything in the Opportunity Audit is now a failing—doing nothing is no longer the safest play. So the Opportunity Audit is a structure that "demands" entrepreneurial thinking. The audit should spell out the considered opportunities, what was done about them, and why they were not taken up (or, if they were taken up, the progress that is being made).

The Opportunity Audit could be used as such or modified to give a Creativity Audit.

REGULAR CREATIVE SESSIONS

A schedule of regular creative sessions might be set up within a department or a local area. These sessions are scheduled on a regular basis; perhaps the first Wednesday in every month. A fixed time is set; this could be a breakfast meeting or an end-of-day meeting. The agenda is set for each meeting. Individuals can submit suggestions for the agenda. The agenda is circulated to individuals a week before the meeting and individuals are invited to do some creative thinking on their own in advance of the meeting. They might even bring to the meeting formal outputs of ideas and concepts.

The regular creative sessions would be organized by the "local" process champion. It is better not to call these meetings brainstorming sessions because that could give the wrong impression. The meetings would use "serious creativity" as described

*Suggested in my book *Opportunities*, published by Penguin Books, London, 1977.

in this book. The format of a creative session will be described in a later section.

The value of regular creative sessions is their regularity. This contrasts with setting up an ad hoc session as required. Once the regular sessions are known to be in place, creative focuses can be fed into the sessions. Each session can also seek to tackle one item from the Creative Hit List.

Because the creative session would be limited to a relatively few people it is possible to have several parallel sessions running at the same time or different times. In general, eight people is the maximum number for a creative session.

The organization of the creative sessions, like the organization of the Creative Hit List, Creative Task Sheets, Opportunity Audit, and the rest, is something that can be done by a Creativity Center.

TRAINERS AND TRAINING

Obviously, training is an important structure for developing creativity in an organization. Training will be considered in its own right in a later section.

In general, there is training which adds a "creativity" element to ongoing training as in induction training or in training for specific programs. Then there is specific training, the purpose of which is to impart creative thinking skills.

Training is an essential piece in the whole process of creativity within organizations. Without training, creative skills will remain rudimentary. To rely on natural talent or inspiration is very weak and wastes available potential. Training within a strong framework does have a high value, but to regard training as the sole way of introducing creativity to an organization is to expect too much.

FACILITATORS

The use of facilitators (part of the Du Pont culture) is an interesting concept which has already been considered before and is included here for the sake of completeness. Facilitators are not so much trainers as "process managers." They are invited to a meeting to run the creative process. So they become guides to the use of the specific creative techniques. In this way the participants get to use the techniques in a guided fashion and can build up some skill in the use of the techniques. At the same time the participants can see the processes being applied to matters of great concern to the participants at the meeting. So the motivation and utility are high.

Some words of caution are needed at this point. There is a danger that the participants come to rely so much on the facilitators that they never try to develop the skills for themselves. Ideally, the facilitators would try to do themselves out of the job.

Learning the creative techniques by applying them to your own immediate problems is not the best way to learn the techniques, because attention is largely on the content of the problem rather than on the thinking process itself. It usually makes better sense to learn the techniques on matters with which you are not directly involved and then to switch these skills to your own backyard problems.

Nevertheless, the "facilitator" system is a practical and powerful way of putting creativity to work in an organization.

THE FAT/CAT™ PROGRAM

This is a new program* designed specifically to introduce creativity in a formal way into organizations. As mentioned earlier, the acronym stands for:

Fixed

Assigned

Task

/

Creative

Action

Team

Tasks are fixed and assigned to small action teams. These teams have the responsibility to generate new ideas and concepts on the fixed task. Several teams may be assigned to the

*For information on the FAT/CAT™ program please contact Kathy Myers, APT/T, Fax (515) 278-2245.

same task. There is a specific structure to the program and also provision of the basic training required for the participating teams.

MESSING AROUND

In this section I have put forward a number of specific structures and programs for the formal introduction and application of creativity within an organization. The normal approach of having a few creative people messing around in the hope that they will inspire others is totally inadequate.

Training

It has been my contention throughout this book that people can be trained in creative thinking skills in a deliberate manner. This disagrees with two traditional principles of creativity:

1. That creativity is a natural talent that some people have and others do not have; that there is nothing you can do about creativity except to employ people who have this natural talent.
2. That creativity consists of being freed from fears and inhibitions and that once these are removed, it is enough to mess around and something useful will happen. To encourage this messing around, judgment must be suspended.

I do not intend to repeat here the reasons, both theoretical and practical, as to why those notions are out-of-date and inadequate. We can train in creative thinking just as we can train in mathematics, cooking, or playing tennis. It does not mean that everyone trained in creativity will become a genius. Everyone trained to play a good game of tennis does not become a Wimbledon champion. There is a huge amount of useful creativity to be done at all levels below the level of genius.

Training involves will, skill, and method.

Will. There has to be the will to train people in creative thinking skills. It is not just a matter of bringing out their own native creative talent. This is too weak. There has to be a determined attempt to teach certain techniques and procedures.

Skill. The teachers or trainers have to have the skill to train in creativity. This is not a complex subject, provided that the trainers have a clear idea of what they are doing. Just messing around and encouraging people to have "crazy" ideas is not good enough. The effect of that is very temporary. Learning the formal creative techniques is not unlike riding a bicycle for the first time. Everything seems very awkward and unnatural. You wonder how you are ever going to be able to master the skill. You wonder how other people could ever have learned. But after a while you get the "hang of it." Later, when you are a competent cyclist, you look back and wonder why it ever seemed difficult. Anything that requires us to do things which go against our usual habits and even our natural tendencies, must seem awkward at first. When learning to ski, it seems totally unnatural to lean outwards around a corner instead of inwards.

Overcoming the natural inhibitions through "fun" and "craziness" is not the only approach nor the most effective one. Understanding the logic of creativity is more powerful (and is the only way with technical people).

Method. There are formal programs for training in lateral thinking, which is a specific and deliberate approach to serious creativity. This book is not a "training book" as such. There are programs* for training trainers to be able to pass on the skills of lateral thinking to their students. Sometimes those responsible for creative training have the disastrous habit of picking a piece from this program and a piece from another program and believing that this must be better than any specific approach to the teaching of creativity. This is highly confusing to the students because some approaches contradict each other. Furthermore, there is not a uniform base to all programs. Some have no base at all. Then there is a tendency for a trainer to want to rewrite an existing program. Quite apart from the illegality of infringing copyright, this does no more than satisfy an ego. There is plenty of scope for amplifying existing programs and adding to them with local examples without seeking to rewrite the program. Where this is done to avoid the cost of the program, it is intellectual piracy and legally dangerous.

TRAINING NEEDS

The creative training needs can be separated into some well-defined areas. It is important for the trainer to have very clearly

*For information on training and training trainers please contact Kathy Myers, APT/T, Fax (515) 278-2245.

in mind the type of training that is being provided. This has nothing to do with the depth of training.

1. General Creative Skill

Any and every person who needs to think needs some creative skill. Anyone who has to deal with concepts, perceptions, and ideas needs some creative skill. Without creative skill you can only follow established routines or combinations of these.

Creative skill training of this sort should be part of education at all levels, from primary schools to universities. But it is not. So training in general creative skill needs to be provided within organizations that want to benefit from that skill.

This is the sort of creative skill that should be made available to every person within an organization—without exception. This does not mean that the same degree of creative skill is needed at all levels.

At the executive level there is a great need to understand the importance and logic of creativity. Creativity must be seen not as a peripheral luxury but as a central resource. The habits and techniques of lateral thinking should be made available. Some executives will proceed to use these methods thereafter, throughout their lives, and others will not. Techniques like the Six Hat technique and the Six Action Shoes technique should become established parts of thinking behavior.

At other levels, it may not be feasible to go into so much depth (but it would be beneficial if it were feasible). It can be enough to give a firm understanding of the value of creativity and to provide some basic techniques so that a person who wants to be creative will have specific tools to use. The exhortation to "think" has only a limited practical value.

2. Special Area Creativity

There are certain special areas where there is a constant high demand for new ideas. In a sense, "ideas" are the product of these areas. Most people believe that they are in these areas because they are already highly creative. To some extent this may be true. A natural talent (and motivation) for creativity can only be enhanced by learning systematic methods.

These special areas include research where creativity is not only needed to overcome problems but also to develop new lines of research and new concepts. Research should be driven more

by concepts than by the natural momentum of technology. It
should not be a matter of:

What can we do—now how can we use this?

but more a matter of:

It would be great if we could do that—now how can we
do it?

The training of scientists and technologists does not sufficiently develop creative thinking skills. The emphasis is placed
entirely on data collection and data analysis.

The research area also needs a lot of creativity to sense the
practical applications of new developments.

Whole new areas of research may depend on the ability to
develop new concepts.

New product departments may subsist on a diet of "me-too"
with improvements. It is possible to let others develop the market
and then to move in with an improved "me-to" product. Creative
thinking may be needed for those modifications or to get around
patents.

When there is the willingness to develop really new products,
there is a huge need for conceptual creativity. New products
are going to work only if they integrate fully into the complex
values of the buyer.* Being aware of these complex values and
finding ways to integrate with them is a creative exercise. Once
the concept is in place, there is the need to create ideas for
the carrying out of that concept. Finally, creativity is needed to
devise ways of pretesting the product.

Creativity is also needed to shorten production time and to
reduce the cost of product development.

Some organizations have New Business departments, which
are on the lookout for new growth areas. Sometimes this is a
matter of acquisitions and takeovers and sometimes of new ventures.

There is a need for creativity in looking at possible future scenarios. There is a need to conceive of discontinuities that may
provide problems or opportunities. There is a need to devise concepts that will be sufficiently adaptable to changing conditions
or imperfect forecasts.

Information analysis may show trends, but how are these
trends going to interact? The information analysis that shows
you the trends will also show the same trends to everyone else.

*See *Sur/petition*, HarperBusiness, New York, 1992.

What new concepts can you devise that will put you ahead? The building blocks may be the same but the building need not be the same.

Sometimes creativity is needed even in information analysis. The mind can only see what it is prepared to see. You may have to start an idea, hypothesis, speculation, or pattern in your mind in order to be able to spot this in the data before you.

The Concept R&D structure mentioned before is directly related to this area of new business.

Any competent organization has a powerful delivery capacity. That potential is wasted without good concepts.

Corporate strategy should be a heavy user of creativity because of the need to "design" concepts and alternatives. The many uncertainties (the future, competitive behavior, ecological pressures, government behavior) demand flexible designs and changes in direction. Some of these can be derived through logical analysis and the use of traditional concepts. Very often there is a need for a new concept. Can we be sure that traditional concepts give us the full value in any situation? How much should we invest in creative effort? If the rewards can be high—as they are at corporate strategy level—then it makes a lot of sense to invest heavily in creative possibilities. In the end all creative ideas will have to be subjected to black hat judgment so there is no danger in being trapped into an unworkable idea. Improve both the creative generating skills and the judgment/assessment skills. That is the best combination.

Any organization that prides itself on its assessment skills should be a heavy investor in creative effort.

Marketing is a mixture of analysis, tradition, me-too, and creative concepts. There is a huge scope for innovative concepts that have a powerful effect. As competitors catch up with your innovative concepts you have to keep moving forward. Established ways of doing things have to be used and challenged at the same time. New synergies need to be found and new routes to the consumer. Values are changing all the time and there is a need to keep up with value changes and to turn them to advantage. There is also a need to create new value changes. Traditional products need to be renewed and repositioned. Different market segments need to be discovered or created. Always there is the danger of being too clever and of overdoing things.

There is a special need for concept skills in marketing. There can never be too many new concepts. There can never be too many alternative ways of carrying through a concept. In some cases, like direct marketing, there is the possibility of testing

ideas quite easily. This puts a premium on the generation of
different ideas. There is always a temptation to do what others
are doing and to stay with ideas that are known to work. At the
same time, there is the fear that one day the old ideas will cease
to work or that a competitor will render them obsolete.

Negotiation and deal making are not traditional "special areas" for creativity but both involve the design of new concepts
and the suggestion of new values. With creative design it is possible for both parties to get things that make sense to them.
Negotiation does not just have to involve a trading of power,
pressure, and pain. There can be attempts to make the opposing
values fit together.

In the negotiations and conflicts of labor relationships there
is also scope for creativity. Again there is the need to create new
values and to find acceptable ways of implementing these new
values. The design of new alternatives goes beyond analysis and
is a truly creative process. Advertising, public relations, packag-
ing, design for manufacture, and process design are also special
areas with a direct demand for creativity.

I have spelled out some of the needs in these special areas to
indicate how central creativity is to them all. In each area there is
a danger that tradition and copying gradually edge out creativity
as there is a search for comfortable life and reduced risk. Why
stick your neck out if you can do a reasonable job without risk?

Creativity training in these special areas is not easy because
the people in these areas already consider themselves to be highly
creative and resent being "taught" creativity. Nevertheless, once
they have learned the techniques they are quite happy to use
them to achieve powerful results. There is a need to teach creativity in depth both as regards the "logic" of creativity and
also as regards the specific formal techniques. Repeated practice
must be provided. There is a need to emphasize the formality
of the techniques because this may contrast with the usual free-
wheeling approach in these special areas. Lateral thinking should
not be presented as being better than "natural creativity" but as
a way of getting additional ideas through a different approach.
In a sense, the formal techniques provide each person with a
"creative assistant" who is really the same person operating in a
different mode.

3. Operating Creative Skills

There are certain people who will be called upon to use creative
skills deliberately and formally to generate new ideas. For ex-

ample, the members of regular creative sessions will need the operating skills of lateral thinking because they will need to use them on a regular basis. The teams in the FAT/CAT™ program will need to be equipped with this sort of creative skill.

Facilitators will need to be able to demonstrate the creative techniques and also to lead others in their performance.

People involved in these special creative groups or teams are people who may not normally be involved in creative thinking. So the creative skills have to be added to their existing expertise in different fields. These groups are much easier to train than the special area people mentioned before. This is because there is not an existing style of creativity and there are less ego problems. The emphasis of the training must be on practicality. There is less need to understand the logic of creativity but a greater need to be able to carry out with precision and formality the different creative techniques.

It may not be practical to provide all team members with the full set of creative techniques. In such cases, the tool kit may be reduced but the tools that are taught must be taught to a high degree of readiness.

Operating creative skill is the most directly usable of all the types of creative skill. These are skills that are going to be constantly used. A person needs to be trained so that he or she can immediately apply the needed creative thinking technique. It is like training a surgeon not in the background medical knowledge that may be needed but directly in the "cutting" skills that are used in specified operations.

FORMS OF TRAINING

Training in creative thinking is skill training. This means the training of tools that are simple to use but powerful in their simplicity. There is a need to give plenty of examples to show how the tool works. There is a need to give plenty of practice. The practice should always be a mixture of "remote" items that are not the direct concern of those being trained. This is so that attention can remain on the thinking process itself and confidence can be built up in the use of the techniques. From time to time, directly relevant matters can be fed in to show that the tools are equally usable on such matters.

It is best to practice creativity on hardware subjects because with such subjects it is immediately possible to see the value of an idea. When soft subjects are chosen, the ensuing value may be a matter of opinion and so there is less sense of achievement and less consciousness of a "new idea." For example, if you suggest paying people on random dates instead of the usual date it is very difficult to be sure what would happen. If, however, you were to suggest a drinking glass with a rounded bottom then it is very easy to "see" what would happen.

Skill training is always training "from the center." This is in marked contrast to normal subject teaching, which is teaching "from the edge." In normal teaching there is emphasis on distinguishing one situation from another so that the designated action can be used. A lot of attention is paid to overlap areas and grey areas because decisions will still need to be made in such areas. The obvious cases are easy and obvious. A skilled judge spends all his or her time in these grey areas and seeks to clarify them. In "teaching from the center" you simply ignore the grey areas because they do not matter. Instead you use good and direct examples to make your point. You demonstrate with these examples. If something is confusing you just drop it and pass along. Your intention is to leave your students with a very clear idea of what they are supposed to be doing. Confusion is the great enemy of skill development.

ALLOCATION OF TIME

There are a number of training formats which I shall list here. These are merely suggestions.

One-Day Seminar ($6\frac{1}{2}$ hours)

Such seminars are useful for giving an understanding of creativity to large groups. They are very useful for sensitizing organizations to the importance of creativity. Some of the basic lateral thinking techniques are covered in this time but there is only a limited possibility of practicing the techniques. There is a great deal to cover in this time. This type of seminar is also suitable for top level management. There is no limit to the numbers that may attend such a seminar. It is possible to deal with audiences of 500 or more.

Two-Day Seminar (11½ hours)

The two-day seminar covers the same ground as the one-day seminar but includes some other material as well. The main difference is the much greater opportunity to practice the techniques and to get a feel for them. For this reason the number attending should be smaller (about 50). It is possible to run two-day seminars with larger numbers but there is less individual attention.

Train the Trainers (5 days or 40 hours)

This type of training is specifically designed to equip trainers with the tools and methods to pass on to their students. The style is quite different from the one- or two-day seminars, which are designed for the personal use of the participants. There is a great emphasis on practice so that the tools are clearly understood in a practical sense and misunderstandings that might turn up in later training can be cleared up.

Advanced Lateral Thinking (5 days or 40 hours)

This type of training is designed for individuals who have a high personal need for the use of creative skills. This is not a trainers' program but a users' program. Some of the more advanced techniques of lateral thinking (such as "flowscapes") are introduced. There is emphasis on individual practice and group work. There is personal attention in order to sort out individual problems. The number on these courses is limited to 20 persons.

There now follow different modules which are designed for use within an organization by that organization's trained trainers:

40-Hour Module

This is an in-depth course designed for special area people who are going to need to use a great deal of creative thinking in their work.

20-Hour (Executive) Module

This is intended for executives who do not have a special need for creativity but need creativity both in their own work and need to be able to encourage it in others.

This module would cover the basic lateral thinking techniques such as might be needed by creative operating groups. The emphasis is on the direct application of the techniques.

5-Hour (Minimum) Module

This module is the bare minimum and covers a selection of the tools. It is the sort of training that might be used with all personnel across an organization. If it is not feasible to provide fuller training, this module would suffice for the teams in the FAT/CAT™ program.

Each of these modules can be shortened by cutting down on the practice time allowed. This is not advisable, since with skill training there is a need to experience the use of the skill. You can take someone and show that person a game of tennis. Within twenty minutes that person may understand the game of tennis. But that hardly makes the person a tennis player. To become a tennis player you have to get out onto the court and practice. That is why guided practice is such an important part of creativity training.

The modules may be split into segments of different lengths depending on the training style of different organizations. For example, the 20-hour module might be split into five 4-hour segments. As a general principle, the more segments, the more effective the training will be because the intervening time allows both for practice and for a "sinking in" of the methods. Teaching creativity at one stretch runs the risk of tiring participants and resulting in some processes being favored at the expense of other (equally important) processes that get ignored.

For details on courses personally delivered by the author, contact Diane McQuaig, Toronto, Canada, Fax (410) 488-4544.

Formats

I have always preferred to treat the lateral thinking techniques as "tools." A carpenter has a number of tools (hammer, saw, plane, chisel, drill, and so on) and uses them as appropriate. There is no fixed sequence of steps that the carpenter has to follow. Once the carpenter builds up experience with the tools, he or she knows when to use them. I am always a bit suspicious of those training programs that lay out detailed steps for the student to follow. This looks impressive and is all very well in the setting of a classroom. But back at work, the student forgets the sequence and is lost. If, however, there is no fixed sequence, you use the tool as you feel appropriate. The sequence may not be the best possible one but it will still be effective.

The most important point in designing programs and in training is that what is taught should be simple and practical to use. This is too often forgotten by those who seek to put together a procedure that is impressive in its complexity but too complex to use. I am much more interested in "powerful simplicity." The Six Thinking Hats is a good example of powerful simplicity.

There is some value, however, in giving examples of practical formats in which the lateral thinking tools can be used.

INSTANT USE

It is possible to use a lateral thinking technique instantly and immediately. Consider the following scene.

> We have not gotten anywhere new. We keep coming back to the same ideas. Let's try a random word (technique). Purpose-type focus: too many people are late for work. The random word is "bridge" (obtained from a list of 60 words by consulting the second reading off a watch). Two minutes individual thinking.

What ideas have we got? Let's start with you.

Once you are on the bridge you have to cross to the other side. So the idea is to have people get onto our premises before they start work. We could offer morning papers to read, simple breakfast, and the like.

I reached the same idea from dental bridge, mouth, and eating.

Bridge is a way of getting people across something. Could we get people "across" town? Perhaps we could have our own bus picking people up at a central point. They might even be able to work on the bus. Perhaps meetings could be scheduled on this bus to make use of travel time.

I thought of a suspension bridge. That could mean suspending people who are late. But what about the opposite: giving a bonus to people who are five minutes early more than once in any one week.

Good. We have some ideas there. We can summarize them. . . .

The whole process might take six minutes. Further time could be taken exploring the ideas that were started by the random word, extracting the concepts and finding different ways of using the concepts (for example, the reward for early arrival).

We can look at another, even simpler, instant use of a technique.

We want some new ideas for covering tables in a restaurant. We'll try some direct alternatives. The fixed point is: attention to surface of tables for dining purposes. Let's have some instant ideas.

Tablecloths.

Diners to choose their own tablecloth.

Placemats.

Nothing at all. Just a clean table top.

Inlaid ceramic tiles.

Detachable table tops.

Some sort of moss or grass.

A glass surface with something interesting underneath such as an antique or even ants scurrying around in a sealed container.

Famous quotations printed on a formica surface.

Fine. We have some ideas there.

Such a process might take four minutes. It is interesting to see how the alternatives moved from the conventional to "new" ones as soon as the provocative "moss or grass" was suggested.

There could then have followed a whole lot of "interesting" table surfaces. At this point the concept of "something interesting to look at or talk about" might have been extracted and put forward as a new "fixed point."

It may be felt that these instant uses are so casual that there is no need to be formal. But formality adds value. For example, defining the fixed point when looking for alternatives is much more valuable than just saying "let's have some alternatives here."

INDIVIDUAL FORMATS

The place of individual and group use of lateral thinking is discussed elsewhere in the book. The great advantage of individual use is that it is very much faster because there is no group feedback and no need for discussion time. In general, the group use of a technique is between three and five times as time-consuming as the individual use of the same technique.

Another time-saving feature of individual use is that the ideas and concepts are written down as they are generated, which is not the case when ideas are generated in group discussion.

STAGE 1. FOCUS

Identifying and clarifying the focus

Information input, if required

Alternative phrasing and definition of the focus

Choosing subfocuses for later use

STAGE 2. TECHNIQUE

Choice of technique

Setting up the technique (that is, setting up a provocation)

Use of the technique

STAGE 3. OUTPUT

Extracting concepts

Working with concepts

Harvesting

Treatment of ideas

Formal output

It is difficult to give fixed timings because each stage can take a long or short time depending on the focus, the particular technique chosen, the flow of ideas, and the amount of work needed on the output. A general guide might be: 3 minutes on the focus stage; 3 minutes on the technique stage, and 6 minutes on the output stage. The length of time given to the output stage will vary according to the nature of the task. If the lateral thinking technique is being used to try to turn up some fresh ideas then there is not much to do in the output stage if none of the ideas generated are indeed fresh. If, however, the technique is being used to generate ideas as such, then the output stage has to be thorough.

Extracting concepts from the ideas and working with concepts to improve them and to produce fresh ideas is part of the output stage, because it follows the direct use of the technique.

More than one technique can be used at a time. It is not advisable, however, to use more than three techniques at the same session.

Focus

Technique 1

Technique 2

Technique 3

Output

With individual use, the concept work, harvesting, and treatment of ideas can be done together after the use of the final technique. With group work, it is best to do these things after each technique is used.

Example:

FOCUS

Improving traffic lights in any way

Purpose-type focus

Traffic lights to serve same function as at present

287

TECHNIQUE 1. CHALLENGE TECHNIQUE

Why are lights placed vertically

Why are lights placed at a height

Why is there one set of lights

Concept:

Multiple lights at multiple places

TECHNIQUE 2. ESCAPE TECHNIQUE

We take for granted that lights should be visible

Po, traffic lights are not visible

Idea:

A radio signal that lights up a red light in each car if the
lights are set at red.

OUTPUT:

Concept of multiple lights might suggest duplicate lights at
different places. Perhaps lights set into the road so a band
of road changes in color. Perhaps small lights arranged as
a special shape.

Concept pulled back from the radio-signal-triggered light
within the car is that each car would automatically respond
to the lights. This might be done by alterations in the road
surface to cause bumps or a physical barrier. A sound could
also be triggered in the car.

Harvesting:

Two broad directions: different shape and placement of lights
and something in the car which responds to the lights automatically.

For-instance ideas: light or sound in car triggered by a radio
signal; light band across road; alteration in road surface;
multiple lights arranged in shapes.

Change in thinking: from looking at the lights themselves to
looking at the response of the car. Also from looking at the
optional response of the car to a forced response, as with a
road barrier.

Shaping of ideas:

Possibly red light could be made much larger than the other
lights. There might also be two red lights.

The in-car response device would be in addition to ordinary lights so that if the device failed the ordinary system would still operate.

Further thinking required to develop the concept of a physical barrier that would impede progress of the car if the light was red.

Formal output:

Idea: the idea is a larger or double red light to make this more visible.

Value: it is more important to see the red light than any other.

Concept: an in-car response system to indicate the state of the lights

Value: early and powerful warning that the lights ahead are red.

In this example, the harvesting and treatment of ideas could have been done much more thoroughly. For example, the difficulty with a radio signal is to distinguish cars coming from one direction from cars coming from another direction (the signal might need to be before the junction). It is always useful to use the checklist for harvesting and also the different steps for the "treatment" of the emerging ideas.

GROUP FORMATS

The stages of the group format are similar to the stages for the individual format, but what happens within the stages is, obviously, different.

Focus stage

1. An individual who brings the creative request to the group may spell out the focus that the group is to work upon. The necessary data briefing is also given.
2. Suggestions for focuses are made by members of the group. Alternative focuses and definitions of the focus and subfocuses are discussed. A final form of the focus is decided upon. The type of focus is clearly spelled out.

289

Technique Stage

1. A facilitator or someone running the creative process may decide upon the technique and may even present the complete technique to the group for the members to work on.

"We are going to use the random word technique. Traffic light po cloud."

The group members then work on this either on their own for about three minutes or work openly as a group.

2. The facilitator can indicate the technique and then each individual sets up the technique and works on it entirely on his or her own just as would have been done with an individual format.

"I want you to use the escape technique. Set this up individually and use it."

3. The group can discuss what technique to use. If a provocative technique is to be used then suggestions can be made for the provocation. One of the suggested provocations is then chosen for everyone to work with. The work can then take place individually or as a group.

On the whole it is best if everyone works with the same provocation at any one time because discussion is then more fruitful. If everyone is working with a different provocation they might as well be working as individuals.

Output Stage

With group work there is always an output stage after each technique. This is not a full harvesting but a simplified form, which has the following elements.

1. Reporting back from individuals on their creative effort.
2. Noting of ideas and concepts
3. Pulling back to concepts from ideas
4. General discussion (building on the ideas)

Next Stage

The next stage may consist of continued group discussion or the introduction of a further technique. This is handled as indicated above.

The final output consists of full-scale harvesting of the whole session, the full treatment of ideas, and putting together the formal output.

The harvesting can be done by the group as a whole, or individuals can attempt their own harvesting and the different results brought together afterward.

The treatment of ideas and the formal outputs are done as a cooperative group effort.

Once again it is difficult to set fixed times, because time will depend on the number of people in the group, the nature of the subject, the techniques chosen (concept fan takes a long time) and the flow of ideas. The more ideas there are, the longer will be the harvesting period and the treatment of ideas.

Approximate timing for a 30-minute module would be:

Focus stage: 3 minutes

Technique stage: 3 minutes

Output stage: 10 minutes

Final output (harvesting, etc.): 10 minutes

Formal output: 4 minutes

As I mentioned before, the length of time spent on harvesting and the treatment of ideas will depend on the nature of the creative task. If there is only a search for fresh ideas then ideas that are not fresh need not be treated in depth. If there are no fresh ideas, fresh concepts, or even "for-instance" ideas, then the final output stage can be replaced by a further technique.

The 30-minute module can be repeated, but the final output stage only takes place at the end of the complete session, so the sequence would run as follows:

Focus

Technique 1

Output

Technique 2

RECORDING

Traditionally, group creative sessions are supposed to require a note-taker. In my experience I have found that note-takers slow down the process considerably and also much reduce the output of ideas. The reason is that the note-taker is overburdened; everyone looks to the note-taker to take down the idea. The note-taker puts down the idea in a simplified form or more often assumes that it could come under a previous heading. It is quite easy and logical to put a new idea under an existing heading because the idea does fit under that heading. But later on it is totally impossible to extract the special nature of the idea from that heading.

I have sat in on creative sessions that were very interesting as they were proceeding. Then I listened to the output, which was unbelievably dull. The essence of the individual ideas has been completely lost in the recording process.

My preference is for tape recordings, which can then be harvested at leisure. It is best to have several recorders, as intentions to make copies are rarely followed up. Such recordings also have the great advantage that even brief suggestions can be given full attention. It often happens that if many people are waiting to say something then a valuable remark is lost since the next speaker does not pick up on it but offers something that he or she has been waiting to say.

An alternative to the tape recorder is for each individual in the group to have the responsibility for putting down those ideas and concepts that seem valuable. Human nature being what it is, there is a likelihood that all ideas will be noted by someone or other. When individual work is done during a group session, the output can be given in written form even if it is given verbally at the same time.

Sticking up lots of pieces of paper on the walls around the room certainly gives a sense of achievement but may slow things down and may reduce the creative process since people try to work from ideas already noted. This is unnecessary when deliberate provocative processes can be used. With something like the concept fan there is a need for a flip chart or whiteboard when this is done as a group exercise.

GROUP STRUCTURES

A group is defined as a number of people brought together for a purpose. In this case, the purpose is creative thinking. In traditional brainstorming the group is an essential part of the process. In lateral thinking the group uses the formal lateral thinking techniques, both as a whole group and as individuals. The group can then add further value by allowing discussion and development of the ideas or concepts that have been generated. For example, an individual generates an idea, someone in the group then pulls back to the concept, and someone else suggests an even better way of putting that concept into action.

Number of People

Six people is the ideal number. Four creative and constructive people would do very well. Eight is about the maximum. Having eight people allows some members of the group to be quiet instead of everyone having to be active the whole time.

In the lateral thinking process, members of the group may, from time to time, work individually using the formal techniques of lateral thinking. When this happens, there is a need for these individuals to feed the results of their thinking back to the group. This takes time: about two to three minutes per person. If the group is large in size then too much time will be taken up with this feedback process.

Larger groups also allow some people to be lazy and to sit back and to let the others do the work. Large groups also encourage some people to take an "observer" or "critical" role and to comment on the ideas of others. In small groups everyone is expected to make an equal contribution. In large groups there is room for people to be there in an "official" capacity and this can inhibit the performance of the group.

Nature of the People

It is sometimes said that there is a need to have some complete outsiders to give a fresh approach. This does have a value but is not so necessary when provocations can be set up deliberately. In traditional creative thinking there was no formal way of setting up provocations, so there had to be more reliance on crazy ideas and innocence.

Part of the purpose of group creativity is the development of creative thinking skills. This purpose is best served by having the group made up of people who will be working together.

If, on specific occasions, the purpose of the group is seriously to create some needed new ideas then there can be merit

293

in having one or two outsiders or at least people from different departments.

When strategic issues are being examined, it is probably best to have the group members come from management levels that normally deal with such matters. But if the focus is on process or activity within a particular department then there is value in having a vertical cross-section, taking people from all levels.

Official Roles

There is only one official role; that is the "group organizer." The group organizer sets the time and place for the meeting and calls the group members together. The group organizer starts and stops the meeting. The group organizer sets the agenda (usually after consultation with others).

The group organizer acts as chairman during the meeting to be sure that not too many people speak at once. The group organizer can try to bring people back to the focus by repeating this at intervals or asking if there should be a formal change of focus.

In general, the group organizer wears the "blue hat" which controls the thinking. The group organizer suggests the techniques that are going to be used by individuals or by the group. The group organizer looks after the setting up of provocations, the provision of random words, and so on. The group organizer arranges the feedback from individuals. The group organizer makes arrangement for the recording or other output methods.

In some cases, the role of group organizer can be taken over by a trained facilitator who is the "process manager" for the meeting. The above listed functions then become the functions of the facilitator. In such cases the "chairman" of the meeting is not the same person as the facilitator. The facilitator is invited to the meeting by the meeting chairman, who is part of the group and who is responsible for setting up the group and for tackling the agenda. In these cases the facilitator is a "hired hand" who is brought in to help run the creative side of the meeting. The chairman of the meeting is responsible for content and focus.

There is no official note-taker for reasons that have been mentioned.

Time

Many factors affect timing. If the meetings are going to be held as regular creative sessions then each meeting can be short. If it is difficult to bring together the needed people who have to travel or cannot easily be spared from their own work, then maximum use must be made of the meeting. If there are important areas which badly need new ideas, then meetings can be longer in order to cover all the areas.

In general, however, I am in favor of shorter meetings of about 60 or 90 minutes. An extra half-hour can be added for additional harvesting or the treatment of ideas.

The first 15 minutes should always be spent practicing one or another of the formal lateral thinking techniques on some remote problems that are not the concern of the people in the room. This is a sort of warmup and also serves to develop skill in the use of that technique, since it is difficult to build up skill while the technique is being applied to some pressing local problem.

Formats

Formats within the meeting and the balance between group and individual work have already been considered.

Evaluation

There comes a time when the constructive indulgence towards a new idea must end. The idea must leave the nest and make its own way in the world. The new idea must compete with other possible ideas and must prove its own worth.

A preliminary evaluation can be part of the creative process because it can help the shaping of the idea into a better idea. This is part of the "treatment" of ideas. But when the treatment process is concluded the idea has to face proper evaluation.

The evaluation procedure is not part of creative thinking. It is part of the assessment, judgment, and decision capacity of an individual or an organization. This judgment capacity must be applied to all sorts of matters and ideas from any source. The assessment of creative ideas should never be different from the assessment of other ideas. That is why I always maintain that there are no "disasters" attributable to creative thinking. When disasters do occur, they are attributable to the poor assessment of creative possibilities. It is for precisely this reason that the judgment/decision system that is operating in the organization should be used in the final assessment of ideas produced by creativity.

The only exception to the above procedure is when an organization deliberately decides to allocate a fixed proportion of its resources to creative ideas that have both high potential and high risk. Creative ideas that seek to enter this category will clearly be assessed differently from other matters. The criteria for assessing a research project may not be the same as the criteria for assessing a change in the production schedule.

The notes on evaluation given here should be read in the light of what I have written so far in this section.

Compared to the few seconds it might take to start a new idea, the evaluation process takes a long time. This is as it should be, because it is the evaluation process that carries the risk.

I want to start with the "end categories" or the boxes into which the evaluated ideas could be placed at the end of the evaluation process. This will give a good indication of the nature of the evaluation. There is nothing special about these categories and there are many ways of doing the same thing.

Directly Usable Idea

These are ideas which are judged to have value and to be directly usable. This does not mean that the idea will be immediately used. An organization may have more directly usable ideas than it has resources.

Good Idea but Not for Us

The idea is judged to be valuable and workable but does not "fit" the needs or present status of the organization. This relates to the "best home" type of evaluation that will be considered later. The reasons why it does not fit should be given.

Good Idea but Not Now (Back Burner)

The idea is seen to be workable and to have value. There is the sense that in the future the idea could be revived and used. The idea, however, does not fit the needs or priorities of the moment. This is not at all the same as the previous category, which holds ideas that do not fit at all, now or ever. Putting an idea on the back burner means that it remains there to be considered from time to time.

Needs More Work

There are serious defects and insufficiencies in the idea. Nevertheless, there are no fundamental impossibilities and the idea does show potential. It is suggested that further work be done on the idea. This further work may be both logical and creative. A task force may even be assigned to do this further work on the idea.

Powerful but Not Usable

In this category go ideas that have great power but that, for a variety of reasons, cannot be used. Such reasons may include

297

regulations, environmental concerns, very high risk factors, cannibalizing existing products, and so on. There is a twin recognition that the idea is powerful but also that it cannot be used. Ideas in this category are put on file and looked at occasionally. Circumstances may change and the idea may become usable. Useful concepts may be taken from the idea and put into a more usable form.

Interesting but Unusable

These ideas are not "powerful" but they are "interesting" because they open up many possibilities. Interesting ideas suggest a change in the business and new perceptions. The effect of such interesting ideas on perception may be even more valuable than the actual use of the idea. These interesting ideas should be given attention and should be kept around to be looked at from time to time. Such ideas have a stimulating and creative value even if they can never be used.

Weak Value

The idea is workable and it does fit the organization. But the value of the idea and the suggested benefits are just too weak. There is no reason or motivation to use such ideas. It may be that the value of the idea is being underestimated, in which case it is the responsibility of the proposers of the idea to demonstrate a higher degree of value. Some ideas attract attention and interest because they have a high novelty value. But when such ideas are subjected to fuller evaluation it can be seen that "novelty" is about the only value. While this may be sufficient in the world of advertising, it is not usually sufficient elsewhere.

Unworkable

There are many ideas that are seen to be unworkable. This means there are fundamental impossibilities. It is not a matter of working harder on these ideas. They deserve to be rejected. They may surface later in a different form, but at the moment they deserve to be rejected. Creative indulgence should not seek to keep such ideas alive.

It may be seen that there are many categories between "directly usable" and "unworkable." Ideas put into these other categories can still play an important part in the thinking of an organization. But only ideas in the "directly usable" category go forward to the priority decision of implementation. Ideas in the directly usable category might still need to be subjected to testing or piloting, both in order to check out the idea and (more importantly) to build up a basis of support for putting the idea into action. The test results can be much more motivating than an idea on its own.

MAJOR CONSIDERATIONS

The major considerations that might be used in evaluating an idea are listed here. Each of them covers a very broad area and can be elaborated in much greater detail.

Benefits

This is the first and the most important consideration. If the idea offers no benefits, then it is not worth considering further. What is the relationship between "value" and "benefits"? Sometimes the two are used interchangeably and there is no great problem in that. Essentially the "value" resides in the idea and the "benefits" are enjoyed by those affected by the idea. Beauty may reside in a statue but the benefits of the beauty may be enjoyed by tourists, photographers, artists, and others who are affected by this beauty.

What are the benefits? How large are the benefits likely to be? How are the benefits derived? On what do the benefits depend? How durable are the benefits? These are all questions that need to be asked. For example, benefits that depend on current exchange rates may be large but may not last very long. Benefits of low-cost production in a certain country may or may not last. Benefits of a new financial concept may only last until competitors duplicate the concept.

Who would get the benefits? This is a key question. Would the benefits go directly to the producer in terms of lower costs and better profits? Would the benefits go to the buyer in terms of lower price, better quality, or extra functions? There are times when the benefits reach both buyer and producer. For example, a better design may have more appeal to the buyer and the increased sales would benefit the producer. What about the mid- dlemen or the channels through which the product or service has to pass? The concentrated detergent packs reduce handling costs in supermarkets by 45 percent and so are popular with retailers. Does the new idea make life easier or more difficult for retailers? Does the new idea make life easier or more difficult for agents and brokers? New items which require frequent maintenance or are difficult to demonstrate provide no benefit to retailers. Benefits to the environment may be real but are also good publicity.

The full range and extent of benefits need to be spelled out clearly with the logical and information reasons given for why these benefits are expected.

Feasibility

It may be argued that feasibility should come first. If an idea is not workable, then why bother about benefits? The reason benefits should come first is that if the benefits are perceived to be considerable then much more effort will be made to find a way of making the idea work.

Occasionally, ideas are not workable because they contravene some basic principle (like perpetual motion machines). There is no point in going further with these.

Sometimes ideas are not feasible because they contravene some regulations or are frankly illegal. Efforts can be made to keep the concept and to change the idea so that it is legal and does fit the regulations. Sometimes it may even be worth lobbying to get the regulations changed.

Ideas that are not feasible because they might upset certain people or cause environmental damage can be further worked upon to see if these dangers can be avoided.

Sometimes ideas are not feasible because there is no standard way of carrying them out or no available technology. There are many examples of very successful ideas where the first reaction was "This cannot be a good idea." It was only the insistence of the entrepreneur that eventually found a way in which it could be done. Many ideas may be rejected at this point because a feasible way of doing them does not exist. But if the benefits are strong enough then determined efforts can be made to find a way of carrying out the idea. When Ron Barbaro suggested the idea of "living benefits" for the life insurance industry he was met by a chorus of comments explaining why it could not be done.

The question is to see how much effort is going to be put into an idea to make it feasible.

If the idea seems immediately feasible, that makes things a lot easier.

Do we have the resources to make the idea work? Do we want to allocate the resources to this idea?

What is the cost in money? What is the cost in time? What is the cost in labor-hours and at what level? What is the cost in friction and disruptions of ongoing activities? What is the cost in hassle and complications? Who is going to have to work on the idea? Who is going to be responsible for the idea?

What about the diversion of resources and effort from other activities and projects?

It would be nice if it were possible to put into action all ideas that were valuable and workable, but there is always a matter of limited resources.

If the resources are simply not available, then the decision is easy. But if the resources are available then the decision is one of priorities and comparisons.

Clearly, a realistic assessment of the resources needed is very important. The resources needed to implement a new idea are almost always grossly underestimated.

Fit

Does the idea "fit" the organization?

"Fit" is a complex but very important issue. Does the idea "fit" the type of organization? One idea may be suitable for a newcomer trying to get into the market. Another idea might only be suitable for a large organization with enough market muscle to make the idea work.

Does the idea fit the policy, strategy, and objectives of the corporation? Does the idea fit the public image and expectations? Does the idea fit the stock analysts' hopes?

On an internal level, does the idea fit with the personality and ambitions of the chief executive and also those who have to decide on the idea? Does the idea fit with the motivations of those who are going to be immediately responsible for putting the idea into action? What is in it for me?

The difficulty with "fit" is that only traditional ideas will be seen to "fit" the usual behavior of the organization. By definition, any new idea will not "fit."

At the same time, it is very difficult to get a new idea to work if it does not fit the style and motivation of the organization. A very valuable and workable idea may fail because of this lack of "fit."

301

As with "feasibility" this may be an area for further effort. If the idea does not seem to fit, can it be made to fit? How much effort are we willing to put into making it fit?

The "best home" scrutiny is a way of assessing the most suitable home for an idea. It is not so much examining the idea itself but seeing where such an idea would fit. The ideal home for the idea is imagined and then this ideal is compared to the existing organization. What would be the best home for this idea? Can we provide this sort of home?

The perceived benefits of the idea will need to drive any effort to make the idea fit.

ESSENTIAL FACTORS

Although all "essential factors" can be challenged, this does not mean that they do not have a validity. When evaluating ideas and alternatives there is a need to be conscious of the "essential factors." These factors decide whether an idea is usable or not. If the essential factor is not present then the idea must be thrown out—or an effort made to include the essential factor.

There are two basic types of essential factors: vital and fatal.

Vital Factors

These factors are necessary for the "life" of the idea, which is why they are called "vital" factors. Without such vital factors the idea will not work. Such factors may include profitability, compliance with regulations, acceptance by unions, defined market, channel of distribution, allocation of resources, and so on. Some of these vital factors are inherent in the idea but others arise from the way the idea is treated. Adequate capitalization is a vital factor in the success of any new business. Adequate resource allocation is a vital factor in the success of any new idea.

Fatal Factors

Just as vital factors are necessary for the life of a new idea, so "fatal" factors lead to the death of the idea. If the idea contains these fatal factors then the idea cannot work. Today environmental damage is a fatal factor in many countries. Too high a price is another fatal factor. High legal costs and complications may be another fatal factor. Infringement of intellectual rights might

also be a fatal factor. Association with a failing corporation may EVALUATION
sometimes be a fatal factor. Perceived cruelty to animals or ex-
ploitation of minorities are further fatal factors.

As with feasibility and fit, the effort that might be made to
get rid of fatal factors (not just hide them) or to bring in vital
factors will always be driven by the perceived value of the idea.
Unless this is very high, ideas will be rejected on the basis of
vital factors and fatal factors—and this is as it should be.

Flexibility

Flexibility is being seen as an increasingly important characteristic of a new idea. Future conditions are uncertain. Future behavior of competitors is uncertain. Values are changing all the
time. Future costs are uncertain.

In the face of such uncertainty, it is difficult to predict that
a certain idea will work. Nevertheless, there is a need for new
ideas. It is not possible to sit back and to avoid all risk by doing
nothing at all. The answer is flexibility.

Can the idea be modified to adjust to changing conditions? Is
the idea sufficiently flexible? If competitors respond in one way,
can the idea be changed to meet the response? If there is a need
to change price, can this be done?

Rigid ideas are not good choices. It is an important part of
the design process to build flexibility into ideas.

If this idea does work, can it breed a whole number of additional ideas to take advantage of the momentum? Can we have
"son of Lassie" and "grandson of Lassie"? Can we turn a success
into a whole range of models? If we take the risk and it comes
off, how do we maximize that success?

FALL-BACK POSITION

If, for various reasons, the idea fails, what is the fall-back position? Can we minimize the losses? Can we gain anything from
the attempt (perhaps learning something about the market)? Will
failure of the new idea damage our existing products, image, or
distributor relations?

The usual fall-back position is to find a scapegoat or someone
to blame for the failure. Often this is set up in advance.

Although no one sets out with the expectation that an idea
will fail, it is prudent to design a fall-back position.

303

TESTABILITY

It should be part of the design process of any new idea to give some thought to the testability of that idea. Can this idea be tested in a pilot plant? Can this idea be tested in a consumer test market? Can this idea be tested by sampling? Can this idea be tested by consumer survey? Can the acceptance of this idea be tested in advance by "flying a kite" or by a press "leakage"?

Can this idea be tested by allowing someone else to try it first? Can this idea be tested through focus groups or in-store testing?

As I have already indicated, there are several values to testing:

1. To see if the idea works
2. To modify the idea in accordance with the feedback
3. To provide support for the idea

There may be a need for considerable creativity in designing practical and persuasive test procedures.

RISK

Underlying all judgments, decisions, and evaluations, there is the risk factor. The purpose of design and the purpose of assessment is to reduce the risk.

There is the risk that the idea may fail.

There is the risk that the idea may prove much more expensive than hoped.

There is the risk that the idea may cause damage (image, product liability, distributor relations, customer relations, and so on).

There is the risk that the idea may divert attention and resources from other matters.

There is the risk that an unforeseeable change in circumstances may wreck the idea.

There is the risk that a failure of technology will lead to failure of the idea.

There is the risk that the idea may trigger very effective competitive responses which more than negate the value of the idea.

This list of possible risks can be expanded almost infinitely, because everything to do with the future is uncertain.

Risks can be handled in a number of ways:

1. Being aware of possible risks
2. Designing fall-back positions and damage containment systems
3. Reducing the risk by testing
4. Reducing the risk by redesigning the idea
5. Early warning systems
6. Being as informed as possible
7. Insurance
8. Quick reactions and responses
9. Spreading the risk with partners and joint ventures
10. Assessing risk/reward ratios

When all sensible things have been done to reduce or contain risk, there is the final decision as to how much risk an organization is willing to take. If the cost of introducing a new product is reduced then there is less risk in such an introduction.

In the end, organizations need to make "venture" or "entrepreneurial" decisions. How much of the available resources are going to be allocated to new ventures where the potential reward is high but there is also a risk factor?

To refuse all such ventures and to stick to continuity and riskless activities is itself a high risk. Doing nothing is not the avoidance of all risk but the acceptance of a high risk through inertia.

Sometimes it is possible to catch up with a "me-too" product once someone else has developed the new market. But sometimes it is too late and the market is lost to a competitor.

THE FINAL DECISION

In the course of the examination of ideas, decisions will often just emerge. It becomes increasingly obvious that an idea does not offer sufficient benefits to take it further. It becomes obvious that there are many difficulties in the implementation of an idea. It becomes obvious that fatal factors cannot be excluded from an idea. Consensus opinions can gradually emerge; this is how the Japanese make decisions.

Discussions around the ideas will need Six Hat Thinking in order to bring to bear the different modes of thinking.

If the evaluation process does not make its own decisions, then more conscious decisions have to be made. Such decisions can be made in a number of ways.

Points System

The different evaluation factors (but not the essential factors) can be given a weighting and each idea given points against each factor. In the end, the favored ideas should emerge as the leading contenders. The difficulty with any points system is that they tend to produce bland and not very exciting ideas because these bland ideas score steadily in each area.

Direct Comparison

Direct comparisons can be made between the contending ideas or available alternatives. The points of similarity and difference can be noted, and the differing performances can be compared against the evaluation criteria. The advantage of direct comparison is that it allows consideration of factors other than those on any evaluation checklist. It is also easier to assess ideas as a "whole."

Usually comparison works best on a "rejection" basis. You focus on the risks and defects and this provides a reason for rejecting some of the contenders. Focusing on the good points makes it very difficult to reject any idea because there is a reluctance to put aside an idea with potential.

Hindsight Logic

You take each idea in turn and imagine that you have decided to choose (or use) that idea. You are now explaining to an audience why you chose that idea. You put together the logical reasons for the choice. Quite often an idea that seems very strong turns out to be weak when you try to put together the reasons for choosing that idea. It turns out that the appeal of the idea is more emotional than rational and more based on hope than on supportable expectations.

This is a useful exercise because it often helps to pull out the ideas which should be selected on grounds that can be explained. There is, however, the danger of rejecting more unusual ideas where the potential is high but the grounds for support are not strong.

Emotions

Though we do not like to admit it, in the end, all decisions are emotional. Information and logic only put us in a better position to exert our emotions. So we can seek out the emotional basis for our decision. We can look to see in the case of each alternative the basic emotion which would be driving that particular choice. If we were to choose that alternative, what would be the underlying emotion?

The three most relevant emotions are:

1. Fear
2. Greed
3. Laziness

The fear of risk and blame is the basis for rejecting ideas or feeling unenthusiastic about them. Sometimes fear can be a driving force. The fear of getting left behind, the fear of losing market share, or the fear of being attacked by a competitor can lead to positive action.

Although "greed" seems a derogatory word, in this context it covers the willingness to grow, to get bigger, to make things happen, to increase market share and price of the stock. It is a positive driving force.

Laziness drives many decisions. There is a disinclination to do anything different. There is a preference for the "quiet life" in which not much is happening. Any new project demands attention, extra work uncertainty, and even "thinking." All of these are best avoided. So reasons are found for turning down ideas when the basic reason is "laziness."

Why do I like that idea? Why do I not like that idea? How much do fear, greed, and laziness contribute in each case?

Circumstance

Under what circumstances would I choose this idea? Under what circumstances would I want to proceed with this idea?

Like the other frameworks, this "circumstance" framework can make choices easier. Perhaps the ideal circumstances can be provided. Perhaps the ideal circumstances could never be provided.

MAKING AN IDEA WORK

There is sometimes a belief that a marvelous idea will be so good and so powerful that everyone will be dragged along with it. This is almost never the case. It is always necessary to "make an idea work." There has to be someone or a group that decides that the idea is worth doing and is then determined to overcome obstacles and frictions to make the idea work. It is idealistic to search for an idea that will work without this work of effort. For the same reason, an idea that is not obviously a great idea can be made to work if someone sees the potential and determines to make that idea work.

Diamonds are not very beautiful in the raw state. It is the skill of the diamond cutter that reveals the beauty of the diamond. So the value of ideas is only revealed by those who set out to make the ideas work.

Summary

My purpose in writing this book has been to provide a comprehensive and up-to-date coverage of lateral thinking. The book is intended both as a reference book and as a user manual. Lateral thinking is specifically concerned with the changing of concepts and perceptions and the generation of new concepts and perceptions. The end products are usable ideas. Concepts, perceptions, and ideas come into all fields that require thinking. Unless what you are doing can be done with repeated automatic routines, there is a need for some skill in lateral thinking. It is my belief that every student in every university and every executive needs a copy of this book. The main points I make in the book can be summarized in the following way.

POINT 1

Creative thinking is rapidly growing in importance and will come to have as central a position as finance, raw materials, and people. As all organizations reach a plateau of competence, it is only better concepts that will provide the competitive advantage. Water is necessary for soup but soup is more than water. The water represents basic competence. As a business moves from competition to sur/petition the demand for powerful conceptual thinking must increase. New concepts will not come from the analysis of data because the mind can only see what it is prepared to see. There has to be the ability to create new concepts.

Competent organizations have a powerful potential, but that potential is wasted unless the organization machine is used to put powerful ideas into action.

Creative thinking is just as important for those organizations that are still climbing towards the plateau of competence. There is a real need for creative thinking to find better ways of achieving quality, cost-cutting, and continuous improvement.

309

The world faces a growing number of problems. Many of these will not yield to the simple analysis technique of searching for the cause and seeking to remove the cause. In many cases, the cause cannot be removed and there is a need to "design" a way forward with the creation of new concepts. From where are these new concepts going to come if not from creative thinking?

POINT 2

We now know, for the first time in history, that there is an absolute mathematical need for creativity in the human brain. Perception operates as a self-organizing information system in which incoming information arranges itself into patterns or sequences. These patterns are not symmetric and there is a need to be able to cut across patterns. This happens naturally in humor and in insight. It can be made to happen deliberately with the formal processes of lateral thinking. Because we can only recognize those creative ideas that are logical in hindsight we have mistakenly believed that logic is enough. This is totally incorrect in a patterning system.

It is the "time sequence" of our experience that sets up our concepts and perceptions. It is the time sequence of events that sets up our ways of doing things. It is the time sequence of history that sets up our structures and institutions. We may need to break free of this time sequence in order to make the full use of the potential of our experience that lies locked up by that time sequence.

POINT 3

Creativity is not a mystical talent that some people have and others can only envy. Lateral thinking is the type of creative thinking that can be learned, practiced, and used by everyone. Some people will be better at it than others, as with any skill. Learning lateral thinking will not make everyone a genius, but it will supplement existing thinking skills with a valuable ability to generate new ideas.

The traditional view that creative thinking is only a matter of releasing people from inhibitions and fears is old-fashioned and inadequate. The natural behavior of the brain is to form patterns and to stick to them—that is why the brain is so excellent an arrangement for making sense of the world. So release from fears and inhibitions will only result in a mild increase in creativity. To be effectively creative we have to learn to do some things which are not natural to the brain. For example, we have to learn how to set up provocations and how to use them with the new mental operation of "movement."

The "crazy" approach to creativity is very superficial and has held back the seriousness with which creative thinking should be treated. This "crazy" approach is based on insufficient understanding of what needs to happen in creative thinking. Creative thinking is not a scattergun approach in which we shoot out ideas in the hope that one will be useful. We can escape the restrictive effects of judgment in a much more powerful and deliberate manner using the formal and systematic techniques of lateral thinking. These can be used by individuals on their own or by groups. Groups are not essential, as they are in traditional brainstorming, which is part of the "crazy" tradition.

POINT 4

The systematic processes, tools, and techniques of lateral thinking are laid out in the book. Twenty-five years of experience have shown that these techniques can be learned and do work. Such basic processes as challenge, alternatives, and provocation can all be learned as deliberate techniques. It is not enough just to have a creative attitude and then to wait for something to happen. When you need a new idea it is possible to sit down and to use the systematic techniques to produce new ideas.

The ways in which the systematic techniques can be applied to such different situations as problem solving, improvement, opportunity design, and so on, are indicated in the book.

Creative thinking does not have to be a matter of waiting for inspiration.

POINT 5

In the book I have discussed the introduction of "serious creativity" into an organization. There is a need for someone senior to have responsibility as a "process champion"; otherwise, not

311

much will happen. Creative thinking should be established both in its own right and also to supercharge such ongoing programs as quality, cost-cutting, and continuous improvement. Practical points about training and structures for the ongoing use of creativity are discussed. Some leading organizations such as Du Pont and Prudential are already moving along this important road.

POINT 6

At the moment, most organizations pay lip service to the importance of creativity and make claims in the corporate advertising that are mainly cosmetic. Other organizations have an unwarranted complacency in the minor creative efforts that are being made. By and large, creativity is still regarded as something peripheral and as a luxury. The successful organizations of the future are those that have already begun to think differently. Creativity is essential to unlock the potential of your people and your organization. If there is a will to introduce and use serious creativity in a serious manner then there are available ways in which it can be done.* Unfortunately, there are many practitioners of creativity who have not advanced beyond the stage of believing that it is enough to encourage people to be a little bit crazy. That is no longer enough.

There is a real need for serious creativity. That explains the title of the book.

*For information on the introduction of serious creativity into an organization, please contact Diane McQuaig, Toronto, Canada, Fax (416) 488-4544.

APPENDIX 1:

The Lateral Thinking Techniques

SIX THINKING HATS

Each of the six fundamental modes of thinking behavior is given a hat of a different color. In this way thinking can be switched at will from one mode to another. A particular type of thinking can be requested at any moment. Critical thinking can be made more productive by restricting its use to the right moment. The six thinking hats provide a concrete framework for moving away from traditional argument and adversarial thinking to the cooperative exploration of a subject.

White hat: information thinking
Red hat: intuition and feeling
Black hat: caution and the logical negative
Yellow hat: the logical positive
Green hat: creative effort and creative thinking
Blue hat: control of the thinking process itself

THE CREATIVE PAUSE

This is a very brief pause, within the mind of the thinker, to consider whether there might be an alternative or another way of doing things. There is the willingness to give creative attention to any point. In the smooth flow of thinking or discussion many things are taken for granted. The creative pause allows the thinker to pause a little bit longer to look at something.

313

SIMPLE FOCUS

We normally think only about problems and difficulties that force our attention. Yet powerful creative results can be obtained by focusing on matters that everyone else has ignored. The simple focus is not an attempt to generate new ideas but a willingness to note a point as a potential focus for creative effort: "That would be a good creative focus." Noting down these focuses without any attempt to generate ideas is enough.

CHALLENGE

The creative challenge is one of the most fundamental processes of lateral thinking. The creative challenge is not an attack, a criticism, or an attempt to show why something is inadequate. It is a challenge to uniqueness: "Is this the only possible way?" The creative challenge assumes that something is done in a certain way for reasons that existed before and may or may not still exist. In all cases, there may be a better way of doing things.

The creative challenge can be directed at the matter itself but can also be directed at traditional thinking about the matter. The challenge can also be directed at the thinking that is taking place at any moment: "Why do we have to look at it this way?" The challenge can be directed at the factors that shape our thinking: dominating concepts, assumptions, boundaries, essential factors, avoidance factors, and either/or polarizations. With the challenge we take a direct look at these factors to see if they are really necessary.

The creative challenge also challenges "continuity" where something is done in a certain way because it was done that way yesterday. This process of "continuity analysis" looks at the following types of continuity:

The continuity of neglect: no one has bothered to think about it

The continuity of lock-in: having to fit in with other matters

The continuity of complacency: repeated success protects from rethinking

The continuity of time-sequence: trapped by the sequence of our experiences

ALTERNATIVES

THE
LATERAL
THINKING
TECH-
NIQUES

This is another of the fundamental processes of lateral thinking. The very essence of creativity is the search for alternatives.

It involves the willingness to stop to look for alternatives when there is no apparent need to do so, to stop to look for alternatives even when the next step is logical and available, the willingness to make an effort to find further alternatives instead of being satisfied with those that have been found (in practical matters there is a need for a cut-off point in this search), the willingness to "design" new alternatives through changing the situation instead of just being content to "analyze" the given situation, and the importance of defining the "fixed point" to which the alternatives will refer: "Alternatives with respect to what fixed point?" The fixed point may be purpose, group, resemblance, or concept. It is usually possible to define several fixed points in a situation and then to seek alternatives for each of these.

THE CONCEPT FAN

This is particularly useful for "achievement" thinking: "How do we get there?" Achievement thinking includes problem solving and task completion. The concept fan is an elaborated way of seeking alternatives by using concepts to "cascade" further alternatives.

We work backwards from the purpose of the thinking to the broad concepts or "directions" that we would have to take to get there.

Then we work backwards from the directions to the "concepts" which are the ways of moving in that direction. There may be several layers of concepts ranging from the broader to the more specific.

Then we work backwards from the concepts to the "ideas," which are practical and specific ways of putting the concepts into action.

When setting up a concept fan it is possible to start at any point and then to move forwards to the purpose of the thinking or backwards to the specific ideas.

CONCEPTS

It is important to be able to work with concepts and at the concept level. Concepts are general methods or general ways of

315

doing things. Concepts are expressed in broad, blurry, nonspecific ways. Every concept has to be put into action through a specific "idea." The purpose of working at concept level is to be able to "breed" further ideas.

Sometimes concepts are created directly. At other times it is useful to "pull back" from any idea to discover the concept behind the idea. Whenever anything is being done we should make an effort to extract the concept or concepts involved (whether they were designed or not). Once we can extract the concept, we can then strengthen the concept, change the concept, or find better ideas with which to put the concept into action.

There are "purpose" concepts, which relate to what we are trying to do. There are mechanism concepts, which describe how the effect is going to be produced.

There are value concepts, which indicate how something is going to provide value.

PROVOCATION AND MOVEMENT

There is an absolute need for provocation in any self-organizing information system (such as perception). Provocation and movement are needed in order to cut across patterns. Cutting across patterns is made necessary by the asymmetric nature of patterns: something that is obvious in hindsight may be invisible to foresight.

The new word "po" stands for Provocative Operation and signals that something is intended directly as a provocation.

With any provocation we need to use the active mental operation of "movement" in order to move forward to a new idea. Movement is an active operation and is not just a suspension of judgment.

ARISING PROVOCATIONS

A creative thinker may choose to treat as a provocation any statement, remark, or event that the thinker experiences. It does not matter whether or not this was intended as a provocation. The choice is entirely up to the thinker. An idea which is judged as being unsound or even ridiculous can nevertheless be used as a provocation to move forward to ideas that are useful. In this way provocations can be said to "arise" without being deliberately set up.

ESCAPE PROVOCATIONS

These are provocations that are deliberately set up by the creative thinker. The thinker takes any point that is "taken for granted" or normal in the situation and then proceeds to "escape" from this. The escape is carried out by negating the point, canceling the point, dropping the point, or simply doing without it.

The "taken-for-granted" point must never be a problem, complaint, or difficulty.

STEPPING-STONE PROVOCATIONS

These are also deliberate ways of setting up provocations. It is important that the provocations be set up boldly and without any thought whatsoever as to how the provocations might be used. There is no point in massaging an existing idea to form a provocation. The provocations should be set up mechanically. There are four methods for getting a stepping-stone provocation.

Reversal:

The normal "direction" of action is taken and then "reversed" to form the provocation. There must be action in the opposite direction.

Exaggeration:

The normal measurements or dimensions (number, size, weight) are exaggerated beyond normal either upwards or downwards. A downward exaggeration should never reach zero.

Distortion:

The normal relationship between involved parties or the normal sequence of events is altered in an arbitrary fashion to create a "distortion" of the situation. This forms the provocation.

317

Wishful Thinking:

Here a fantasy wish is put forward: "Wouldn't it be nice if . . . ." This must be a fantasy not just a desire or an objective. A fantasy is something that you do not realistically expect to happen.

THE RANDOM INPUT

The background principle is that if you start from a different point, then you increase the likelihood of opening up patterns different from those you would have used when starting from the "center."

The most convenient form of the random input is the random word, which can be obtained in a number of ways (including using the second reading of a watch to select a word from a list of 60 words). This random word is then used to open up new ideas around the chosen focus.

The random input process can also work with objects, pictures, reading, exhibition, and so on. The important point is that the input is random and is not chosen.

MOVEMENT

Movement is an active mental operation and is not just an absence of judgment. Movement can operate at the level of a general willingness to move forward from an idea to a new idea, but there are also systematic and formal ways of getting movement that can be used.

Extract a Principle:

We extract a principle, concept, feature, or aspect from the provocation and ignore the rest. We seek to work with that principle to build a new idea around it.

Focus on the Difference:

In what way is the provocation different from the usual way of doing things? Can we move forward from that difference to a useful new idea? Even if the difference is tiny, we still focus on that difference to seek a new idea. This method is also the best defense against the idea-killing phrase, "the same as. . . ."

THE
LATERAL
THINKING
TECH-
NIQUES

Moment to Moment:

We visualize the provocation being put into action—even if this is impossible in reality. We then watch to see what would happen "moment to moment." We try to pull out a useful new idea from this observation.

Positive Aspects:

Here we focus on those aspects that are directly positive in the provocation. We ignore the rest and seek to build an idea from these positive aspects.

Under What Circumstances:

We look around for special circumstances under which the provocation would offer, as it is, some direct value. We then seek to move forward to a useful idea, either for those circumstances or, more usefully, for other circumstances as well.

THE STRATAL

This is a "sensitizing" technique. We put together five unconnected statements about the situation and then see what new idea emerges. There should be no attempt to be descriptive or comprehensive with the statements, and no attempt should be made to cover all aspects. To make the stratal more random it can be useful to write statements on slips of paper, which are put into a bag from which five slips are drawn. The number five is for perceptual convenience.

THE FILAMENT TECHNIQUE

The basic requirements in any thinking situation are listed one under the other. Each of the requirements is then considered in a "filament" extending from this requirement. This consideration puts down ways in which that requirement is usually

319

met. The actual context of the problem or creative focus is totally ignored.

In the passive way of using the filament technique, the filaments are then considered until an idea "emerges" from this sensitizing process.

In the active or "forced" way of using the filament technique, items are picked out in each filament and then a determined effort is made to force these items together to give a new idea.

More complete details on these processes and techniques are given at the appropriate point in the book. In each case there is a fundamental creative process that is put into action in a particular way. For example, the fundamental process of provocation can be used in a systematic, step-by-step manner. Some of the processes, such as challenge or alternatives, are, of course, common to many approaches to creative thinking. The new word "po," the formal techniques of provocation and movement, and the random input technique were all developed by me many years ago as a systematic way of using provocation.

In using the techniques it is important to keep these clear and distinct. Mixing them up with other approaches to creative thinking much reduces the power of the techniques and risks creating confusion, which is the enemy of effective thinking.

Notes on the Use of the Lateral Thinking Techniques

It is extremely important that readers of these notes refer to the full section on the application of the lateral thinking techniques. The notes given here are brief points and do not cover the full use of the techniques.

Six Hats:

Used as a general framework for discussion. The green hat asks for a specific creative effort. The yellow hat asks for a positive and constructive view of the emergent idea. The black hat is used to put "caution" and logical negative thinking in its proper position as a later part of the treatment of the idea: "We do not need the black hat just yet."

Improvement:

Clear focus and choice of subfocuses. Challenge to existing methods, existing concepts, existing thinking. Fixed points for alternatives. Escape provocation to jump out of existing grooves of thinking. Stepping-stone provocation for radical change in whole system. The concept fan for major reconsideration of what is being done.

Problems:

Focus to define the problem. Alternative definitions of the problem. Subfocuses on parts of the problem. Challenge to definition and presentation of problem. Challenge to existing thinking. Challenge to the shaping factors of thinking (boundaries, etc.). Challenge to basic concepts. Fixed points and alternatives for simple problems and the concept fan for major creative efforts. Escape-type provocation to move away from standard approaches. Stepping-stone provocation for radical rethinking. The random word when blocked or to find a very different approach.

Tasks:

As for problems but the filament technique can be used at the beginning. There is less emphasis on challenge and more on desires. The wishful thinking type of stepping-stone is of great use.

Design:

Similar to tasks but with even more emphasis on requirements and the initial use of stratals and the filament technique. The random word can give fresh approaches. Challenge to existing concepts. Challenge to the thinking taking place during the creative effort. Escape provocations on requirements.

Greenfield:

Open-ended situations where there is no clear starting point and nothing to escape from. The use of the random word to give a starting point. The use of stratals to allow ideas to emerge. The filament technique if the requirements are known. Wishful thinking type of stepping-stone.

Opportunity:

Treat as a combination of greenfield, design, and task.

Invention:

This may take the form of "problem solving," task, greenfield, or opportunity, depending on the inventions brief.

Blocked or Stagnant:

When there seem to be no new ideas, then the random input is the most useful technique to get things going again. The escape provocation can be used on current thinking in order to get out of the existing cycle of thinking. Wishful thinking and stepping-stone may also open up new directions.

NOTES ON
THE USE
OF THE
LATERAL
THINKING
TECHNIQUES

Projects:

Use the concept fan on the project as a whole. Choose subfocuses and use challenge and alternatives on these. Problems and tasks may define themselves within the projects and these can then be treated as such. There is a strong need to define where the creative effort is really needed. Often projects can be treated as a combination of task and design.

Conflict:

The need to be very clear about the focus and creative needs. A combination of problem, greenfield, design, and task. There may be a need to design a way forward. There may be a need to try for a really fresh approach with the random word. Challenge and the escape provocation can be applied to current thinking and especially locked-in situations.

Futures:

Here stratals at the beginning to open up some ideas. The random word technique should provide discontinuities. The escape provocation forces new thinking about any matter. Concept analysis is also important here.

Strategy:

This is basically a design process that may include subproblems and a consideration of possible futures. The filament technique can be tried if the requirements are clear. The general procedure would be to put forward some strategy and then to make challenges at several points. There is a strong need for basic concept work: what are the concepts being used? Powerful changes are likely to come from the escape type of provocation. There is frequent need for fixed points and alternatives within the general strategy framework.

Planning:

This is best treated as a combination of design and task. Subproblems and emerging fresh focuses may need to be treated as such. Challenge is a powerful technique here, especially when applied to the planner's own thinking. Fixed points and alternatives are valuable at various points.

323

In time, the basic uses of the techniques will become familiar and the creative thinker will choose from the possible techniques the one that seems needed at the moment—just as a carpenter chooses his or her tools.

The basic functions of the tools can be summarized as follows:

Focus and subfocuses

Alternatives and elaborated alternatives (concept fan)

Challenge to the existing

Escape from the existing

Radical rethinking (stepping-stone)

Fresh ideas and new start (random word)

Sensitization (stratal and filament technique)

APPENDIX 3:

Harvesting Checklist

Harvesting is a deliberate attempt to harvest, gather up, or pull in all the creative value that has emerged during a creative thinking effort by an individual or by a group. It is useful to have a checklist to help this process instead of trying to remember everything.

There is considerable overlap between the items on the checklist given here. This does not matter. Put down an item under whichever heading seems most appropriate. Put the same item down under more than one heading if you like.

The full harvesting checklist is given here. This does not need to be used on every occasion. Often a simplified list will suffice. On occasions when there is a search for "fresh" ideas in addition to ones that have already been found, there is no need to put down every idea. It is enough to put down only those ideas that seem different from the existing ideas.

Specific Ideas:

Concrete ideas that can be put into action. There is satisfaction with the idea as it stands. The idea seems new and workable, and it appears to offer value. This is the desired output of creative effort.

"For-Instance" Ideas:

"Examples" of ideas; not intended as usable ideas. It is felt that the example idea incorporates some useful principle or concept and shows how this might be applied. Further work would be needed on these "for-instance" ideas to turn them into usable ideas.

325

Seedling Ideas:

The beginnings of an idea. There is a hint or a glimmer of an idea. The idea may be vague or poorly formed but there is the sense that this idea can be "grown" into a usable idea. The seedling idea differs from the "for-instance" idea, because there is no intention to develop the "for-instance" idea itself, but this is the intention with the seedling idea.

Direct Concepts:

Concepts that have been identified as concepts during the creative work. These concepts may or may not have led on to ideas. The concept may have been noted even if the thinking failed to find a practical way of putting that concept into action. It is not easy to record or to remember concepts because they are usually only seen as steps to ideas. But concepts do have an important existence in their own right.

"Pull-back" Concepts:

Concepts that are "pulled back" from ideas either during the creative session or during the discussion that follows or even during the harvesting process itself. It is always possible to pull back one or more concepts from every idea by looking for the "general method" behind the idea. With "for-instance" ideas there must always be a strong effort to pull back to the concept—in order to develop more practical ideas.

Directions:

The broadest concept that you can think of. A direction is the "approach" to a problem or situation. It should always be possible to pick out the major approaches that have been taken during the creative thinking. These may have been stated explicitly or may have to be extracted later. It is sometimes difficult to distinguish between concepts and directions.

Needs:

May be noted specifically during the creative work. There may be a need for a concept: "We need to find a way of doing this." There may be a need to develop further alternatives or more practical ideas. The needs expressed during the creative session are noted during the harvesting.

New Focuses:

Should have been noted explicitly during the creative work: "This is a new creative focus." It is possible but much less valuable to note possible new focuses during the harvesting stage. A new focus will require a deliberate creative effort of its own.

Changes:

The emphasis may change. The way of looking at something may change. The approach may change. The attention area may change. All the major changes that occur during the creative work should be noted in the following form: "There was a change from _____." Such changes may be easier to perceive in hindsight than during the session itself.

Flavor:

The overall "flavor" or taste of the whole creative session. This "flavor" may not include all points but gives a general indication of the sort of thinking that was taking place. For example, the "flavor" of a discussion on traffic congestion in cities might have been "condemning the selfishness of the motorist."

Any other points of interest that arise in the creative thinking session can be noted. The thinking itself can also be the subject of comment. It may be noted how certain approaches or techniques seemed to stimulate ideas whereas others did not. Harvesting is a "blue hat" process because we stand back to look at the output of the thinking.

APPENDIX 4:

Treatment of Ideas Checklist

A fter the harvesting process, it is necessary to take each individual idea and to work directly on that idea in an attempt to turn the idea into a usable idea. The ultimate purpose of any creative effort is the production of ideas that are feasible, valuable, and acceptable. Occasionally, such ideas are produced during the creative session itself, but much more often there is still work to be done on an idea before it becomes directly usable. Even when ideas seem perfect, they need to be subjected to the treatment process in order to see if they can be further improved.

A useful checklist of the treatment steps is given here. Fuller coverage of this important subject is given in the body of the book.

The treatment process can be a lengthy one and it may not be practical to apply it to every single idea that is put forward in the creative session. This is a matter of need, circumstance, and choice. It needs to be said, however, that even unpromising ideas can change dramatically as a result of effective "treatment."

Shaping Ideas:

The real-life constraints such as cost, legality, acceptability, and so on, are now brought in as shaping factors. Can the idea be shaped to fit these constraints? These constraints are not used as rejection criteria but in a constructive shaping way. Can this idea be carried out more cheaply? Is there a way of making this idea legal?

Tailoring Ideas:

While shaping factors refer more to external constraints, the tailoring refers more to the resources of the organization. Can the idea be tailored to fit our resources? Resources include people, time, motivation, money, and so on. Is there a way of making this idea usable by us?

Strengthening Ideas:

The effort is to increase the "power" of the idea. The "power" of an idea is the way the idea provides value. There is no reason to suppose that the first formulation of the idea is necessarily the most powerful. Even a good idea can be made better and a weak one can be made strong. The focus is on the value of the idea.

Reinforcing Ideas:

Ideas have their weak points even if these are not actual defects. Here we focus on reinforcing those weak points. Perhaps an idea is rather complex, can it be made simpler? Perhaps an idea would be more acceptable if it were made optional. What are the weak points? What can we do about them?

Take-up of Ideas:

Here the attention shifts from the idea itself to the "take-up" of the idea. Who is going to have to decide on the idea? Who is going to have to implement the idea? Whose cooperation and goodwill is necessary for the success of the idea? We focus on such matters and see how the idea can be changed to increase the likelihood of take-up.

Comparison:

There is a direct comparison between the proposed idea and the idea it is going to replace. There is a comparison between the new way of doing things and the current way of doing things. There may also be a comparison between alternative new ideas that have been proposed. The comparison focuses on points of difference, points of value, and points of difficulty.

Faults and Defects:

Here we use black hat thinking to find the faults and defects in the idea. This should be a thorough search. An effort is then made to correct these faults and defects. The purpose is to improve the idea and also to anticipate what will happen in the evaluation stage.

329

Consequences:

The consequences of putting each idea into action are followed forward into the future. What is likely to happen immediately, in the short term, in the medium term, and in the long term? This can only be reasonable expectation and guessing. The actual time frames depend on the nature of the idea itself. In the light of this examination of consequences, do we need to make any changes in the idea? If a new road will only increase the traffic load in the long term, what should we do?

Testability:

Can the idea be tested? Can we devise a way of testing the idea? Can the idea be modified to make it more testable? An idea that is testable stands a much better chance of being chosen. A successful testing provides power to the supporters of the idea. If nothing else, is there a possible "information test" in which collection of existing information might support the idea?

Pre-evaluation:

How is this idea likely to be evaluated by those who are going to do the evaluation? How can the idea be modified to meet these needs? How should the idea be presented? Knowledge of the evaluation process and the actual people involved is helpful here.

The treatment process completes the creative, constructive, and positive action on behalf of the new idea. The next stage is the evaluation process, and the creative idea should expect no better treatment than that given to any idea from any source. That is why the treatment stage is so important. If it is not done well, a good idea may be lost and the creative effort may be wasted. Ideas that seem wonderful because of their novelty need to be properly treated to get them to provide real value. The euphoria of novelty is only a value to the creators of the idea. The emphasis must be on use value, feasibility, resources, and fit.

Index

331